TESTIMONIO

TESTIMONIO

Canadian Mining in the Aftermath of Genocides in Guatemala

Edited by Catherine Nolin and Grahame Russell

Between the Lines
Toronto

First published in 2021 by
Between the Lines
401 Richmond Street West, Studio 281
Toronto, Ontario, M5V 3A8, Canada
1-800-718-7201 · www.btlbooks.com

Library and Archives Canada Cataloguing in Publication

Title: Testimonio : Canadian mining in the aftermath of genocides in Guatemala / edited by Catherine Nolin and Grahame Russell.
Other titles: Testimonio (2021)
Names: Nolin, Catherine, editor. | Russell, Grahame, editor.
Description: Includes bibliographical references and index.
Identifiers: Canadiana (print) 20210241748 | Canadiana (ebook) 2021024190X | ISBN 9781771135627 (softcover) | ISBN 9781771135634 (EPUB) | ISBN 9781771135641 (PDF)
Subjects: LCSH: Mineral industries—Social aspects—Guatemala. | LCSH: Mineral industries—Corrupt practices—Guatemala. | LCSH: Mineral industries—Government policy—Canada.
Classification: LCC HD9506.G912 T47 2021 | DDC 338.2097281—dc23

Cover photographs by James Rodríguez, MiMundo.org
Cover and text design by DEEVE
Front cover: Diodora Hernández. Back cover left to right: Carmelina Caal Ical, Amalia Cac Tiul, Lucia Caal Chun, Irma Yolanda Choc Cac, and Rosa Elbira Coc Ich, all five women plaintiffs in the Caal vs. HudBay legal case in Canada, stand on a log crossing a stream near their community of Lote 8.

Printed in Canada

We acknowledge for their financial support of our publishing activities: the Government of Canada; the Canada Council for the Arts; and the Government of Ontario through the Ontario Arts Council, the Ontario Book Publishers Tax Credit program, and Ontario Creates.

Contents

List of Figures

Foreword

W. George Lovell, FRSC

The United States has historically been the scourge of Latin America. From Mexico, which lost more than half of its territory in the nineteenth century to the juggernaut of US expansion, to Chile, a country whose government was undermined and eventually toppled on September 11, 1973 in large measure because of American meddling, the record is one of ignominious acts undertaken time and again by a self-righteous, would-be saviour. Unlawful deeds are perpetrated allegedly for the benefit of nations ideologically gone astray, but inevitably unfold to the detriment of their victimized citizens, especially the "Nobodies" only Eduardo Galeano seems to care about, deemed to know no better, and worthy of even less:

> Fleas dream of buying themselves a dog, and nobodies dream of escaping poverty: that one magical day good luck will suddenly rain down on them— will rain down in buckets. But good luck doesn't rain down yesterday, today, tomorrow, or ever. Good luck doesn't even fall in a fine drizzle, no matter how hard the nobodies summon it, even if their left hand is tickling, or if they begin the new day with their right foot, or start the new year with a change of brooms.
>
> The nobodies: nobody's children, owners of nothing. The nobodies: the no ones, the nobodies running like rabbits, dying through life, screwed every which way.
>
> Who are not, but could be.
> Who don't speak languages, but dialects.
> Who don't have religions, but superstitions.

Who don't create art, but handicrafts.

Who don't have culture, but folklore.

Who are not human beings, but human resources.

Who do not have faces, but arms.

Who do not have names, but numbers.

Who do not appear in the history of the world, but in the police blotter of the local paper.

The nobodies, who are not worth the bullet that kills them.[1]

Guatemala is full of nobodies and—ever since a coup d'état in June 1954, in which the CIA played a pivotal role in ousting the democratically elected Jacobo Arbenz Guzmán—has been a land ravaged by the legacy of that heinous intervention. After president Arbenz, the consequences of American actions linger and harm, but it is Canada that more recently has assumed the role in Guatemala of national bogeyman, as this book documents and attests.

The financial involvement of Canada in Guatemala, and its ties to US business interests there, dates back to the early twentieth century. In 1904, writes Peter McFarlane,[2] Sir William Cornelius Van Horne, "the lauded pioneer of Canadian railway construction," assisted the United Fruit Company (nemesis of Arbenz) in connecting Puerto Barrios on the Atlantic with Tecun Umán near the Pacific. This coast-to-coast feat was achieved by means of a narrow gauge rail line, its foundation creating a monopoly "able to charge Guatemalans freight rates that were among the highest in the world, and prevent local competitors from shipping bananas out of the country." Thereafter, Canadian complicity is exemplified by the operation in Guatemala of some of Canada's best-known mining companies, whose activities established a footing in the 1960s with the arrival on the scene of the International Nickel Company of Canada, Ltd., the iconic INCO.

Although INCO's investments, supported and subsidized by the Canadian government, over two decades amounted to a quarter-billion dollars, production at its EXMIBAL holdings in the Lake Izabal region was full-fledged only for one year, 1979, before the company mothballed its costly Guatemalan initiative in August 1980. INCO's activities, ominously but notably, coincided with the start of Guatemala's internal conflict, in which INCO's collusion with the national armed forces was nigh unavoidable, on account of EXMIBAL's location in the very region where guerrilla insurgency had sprung up. Soon after the signing of a peace accord in December 1996 between the rebel coalition, the Unidad Revolucionaria Nacional Guatemalteca, and the Guatemalan government, which formally ended a confrontation that had lasted some thirty-six years and taken an estimated 200,000 lives, Canadian mining companies returned and resumed operation, often in partnership with American associates but with the maple leaf emblematically prominent. Their schemes may pay handsome dividends to investors, but as this book's thirty contributors make clear, they do so at considerable expense, whether in terms of individual lives and livelihoods or, more broadly, in terms of community welfare and well-being.

Maya peoples, according to the country's latest census, constitute 43.5 percent of Guatemala's national population of 17.8 million, a figure that alternative sources suggest is closer to 60 percent.[*] Some time ago, I depicted Indigenous groups, since the arrival of Spaniards in the sixteenth century, as having survived three cycles of conquest.[3] These cycles of conquest I identified as (1) conquest by imperial Spain, (2) conquest by local and international capitalism, and (3) conquest by state terror. The editors of this incisive book, sadly but cogently, discern that a fourth cycle of conquest is underway—conquest by Canadian extraction, which they and their contributors lament. So too will anyone concerned with the slight to Canada's international reputation that its mining companies are responsible for provoking, and seem reticent to reverse.

---

[*] The last official government census, from which was derived an Indigenous tally of 43.5 percent, was conducted in 2018; see Instituto Nacional de Estadística Guatemala, *XXI Censo Nacional de Población y VII de Vivienda*, Guatemala City, 2019, censopoblacion.gt/cuantossomos. Other sources that indicate an Indigenous tally of closer to 60 percent include International Work Group for Indigenous Affairs (IWGIA), "Indigenous Peoples in Guatemala," Copenhagen, Denmark, 2019, iwgia.org/en/guatemala.html; and United Nations Human Rights Office of the High Commissioner (OHCHR), *Report of the Special Rapporteur on the Rights of Indigenous Peoples—Country Visit to Guatemala*, A/HRC/39/17/Add.3, 2018, ap.ohchr.org/documents/dpage_e.aspx?si=A/HRC/39/17/Add.3. For indications of government manipulations that consistently underestimate the Maya percentage, see W. George Lovell and Christopher H. Lutz, "'A Dark Obverse': Maya Survival in Guatemala, 1520-1994," *The Geographical Review* 86, no. 3 (1996): 398-407.

Preface

A Story that Cannot Be Buried

Grahame Russell and Catherine Nolin

We are so thankful to the Between the Lines (BTL) Editorial Committee for publishing this book, which has been years in the making. The path that led us to working with BTL was not direct and called on all to move forward carefully and with a bit of courage.

We have been working together since 2004, when Catherine initiated her University of Northern British Columbia (UNBC) field school course, Geographies of Culture, Rights & Power in Guatemala, and enlisted Grahame—who, through his work with Rights Action, had developed a trusting work relationship with community defence struggles in Guatemala—as in-country co-facilitator of the inaugural course. Together we organized education trips every two years (and on a number of occasions, twice a year), repeatedly visiting each of the community, human rights, environment, and land defence struggles highlighted in this book.

This work is, almost by definition, sad, angering, and inspiring at the same time. It is deeply sad to regularly visit mining-harmed communities, over the course of seventeen years, and find that nothing has been done about the violence and human rights violations suffered that we learned about on previous trips, and that more violence and human rights violations have occurred in between our visits. It is angering to know that the driving forces behind these harms, violations, and suffering that occur in remote rural regions of Guatemala are Canadian companies, international stock markets, and investors, all supported in many ways by the Canadian government, and a glaring lack of Canadian oversight, laws, and enforcement mechanisms.

At the same time, it is always inspiring to be in regular contact with the dignified, courageous women and men, elders and youth from the mining-harmed communities, who-despite the overwhelming wealth and power, corruption and impunity they confront—keep on resisting and fighting in defence of their lands, their families, and communities, their water sources and forests, and their rights.

Over the years, we have—through our own work, and in collaboration—published articles, reports, photo essays, and more about these community defence struggles, and about the roles and responsibilities of the Canadian mining companies and the governments of Canada and Guatemala.

Students who travelled to Guatemala as part of this course, as well as journalists, human rights accompaniers, staff of non-governmental organizations (NGOs), and filmmakers who sometimes joined the community visits, also produced their own articles, reports, and films on this subject.

In 2017, Catherine approached Springer Nature, an international academic publisher she had worked with before, with the idea of editing a collection of this writing. Springer Nature's editor for the CLAG-Springer Nature Latin American Studies book series responded positively to Catherine's suggestion and the idea to publish this book was hatched. Catherine approached Grahame and we decided to co-edit the book.

By the time we submitted our final manuscript to Springer Nature in 2020, we had published and facilitated the publication of a significant amount of information documenting these community defence struggles against mining-linked violence, corruption, human rights violations, and illegal land dispossession. We brought together some of our own writing to be included in the book along with contributions from others. Some of the material had already been published elsewhere; we solicited new pieces from experts to address certain issues; and we co-wrote our own new pieces. In 2018 and 2019, we carried out new community-based research in Guatemala to fill in some holes and gather testimonies from some of the courageous community defenders we had met with over the years, whom Rights Action has long supported.

In February 2020, after we had prepared all the contributions to Springer Nature's publishing specifications and standards, we submitted the final manuscript. Their initial feedback was completely positive. However, after months of increasing silence and obfuscation, in July 2020, Springer Nature abruptly sent us a contract termination agreement to be signed, stating that they would not publish the book, which they claimed contained "defamatory" materials and "unsubstantiated" information.

We asked Springer Nature to clarify which specific information in our manuscript was "unsubstantiated" and "defamatory." After several professional, though completely frustrating, attempts to communicate with Springer Nature concerning the abrupt about-face, their Latin American Studies book series editor Juliana Pitanguy wrote a final, short email message, stating simply and clearly: "there is a risk we [Springer Nature] could be sued for defamation if the third party files a case." Now, the months of silence, obfuscation, and forced contract termination made sense.*

It was tiring, but not surprising, when Springer abruptly cancelled the publishing contract, and we then learned of the threats by "the third party" to sue Springer Nature if they published the book. It was tiring because of how much heart, soul, and hard work we had put into conception and assembly of this book together, based on years of work in Guatemala; but it was much more tiring when we reflected on the realities of violence, displacement, and human rights violations that so many mining-impacted communities are suffering.

It did not, however, surprise us. This non-reporting and silencing of truthful information about the harms and violence that mining-impacted communities are suffering is a fundamental part of the problem. This non-reporting and silencing serves, in fact, to perpetuate the very serious problems our book denounces. Once Springer Nature unilaterally cancelled our publishing contract, we knew we had no choice but to proceed and seek other means to get this book published, and to add our voices to

---

* For more information about how this played out see: Catherine Nolin and Grahame Russell, "Public Letter," https://bit.ly/2S2oJJc; "CAUT Council Condemns Publisher's Reversal as Violation of Academic Freedom," Canadian Association of University Teachers (CAUT), December 1, 2020, caut.ca/latest/2020/12/caut-council-condemns-publishers-reversal-violation-academic-freedom; "CUFA BC Supports UNBC Professors, Condemns Publisher for Cancelling Book on Canadian Mining," Confederation of University Faculty Associations of British Columbia (CUFA BC), cufa.bc.ca/cufa-bc-supports-unbc-professors-condemns-publisher-for-cancelling-book-on-canadian-mining; Catherine Nolin and Grahame Russell, "Mining the Truth: Why a Publisher Buried a Book Exposing Human Rights Abuses by Canadian Mining Companies in Guatemala," interview by Dr. Bob Huish, *Global Development Primer* podcast, December 21, 2020, anchor.fm/robert-huish/episodes/Mining-the-Truth-Why-a-Publisher-Buried-a-Book-Exposing-Human-Rights-abuses-by-Canadian-Mining-Companies-in-Guatemala-endah6; and Andrew MacLeod, "Spiked. BC Profs Protest after Publisher Drops Book on Canadian Mining," *The Tyee*, November 25, 2020, thetyee.ca/News/2020/11/25/BC-Profs-Protest-Publisher-Dropping-Mining-Book.

increasingly widespread efforts to denounce these harms and abuses, this corruption and impunity, and the multiple "Canadian" participations in all this.

After Springer Nature made their decision to cancel their publication of the book, we received significant support from the Canadian Association of University Teachers (CAUT). In August 2020, David Robinson, CAUT's executive director, contacted Springer Nature with a formal letter requesting further information as to why, just as the book was to be published, they had terminated the contact. Springer Nature has yet to respond to his letter. CAUT also paid to put our manuscript—the exact version submitted to Springer in February 2020—through a full "libel review" by Canadian lawyer Peter Jacobsen, a lawyer with over forty years of experience who was named "Lawyer of the Year" by Best Lawyers for Defamation and Media Law in 2017. Jacobsen concluded that the manuscript did not contain a single instance of unsubstantiated, defamatory content that should prevent publication. Other than a few minor tweaks of sentences, made out of an abundance of caution, he did not recommend any changes.

Try as we could, we never found out who "the third party" was, nor how they obtained access to a copy of our manuscript. We can only speculate that Springer Nature was threatened with legal action by a corporation, or parties linked to corporations, quite possibly in the mining sector.

We are so appreciative that BTL chose to contact us and publish this book, in Canada, the so-called mining capital of the world and home to most of the companies addressed in this book. We also appreciate that BTL asked us to write this preface explaining the roadblocks we faced on the path to publishing.

We have told this story about how Springer Nature refused to publish the earlier (though almost identical) version of this book not to denounce the false allegations made against us of including "defamatory" and "unsubstantiated" content (though it is important to do so), but rather to expose what we believe was actually happening: the silencing of truthful information by a major international academic publisher, which, in turn, contributes directly to the underlying problems of the mining companies' abuse of power and wealth, corruption, and impunity that the book addresses.

We must denounce threats to academic freedom and support the dissemination of research free from political or corporate pressure, as part of the broader work and struggle to hold global corporations legally and politically accountable in their home countries where they operate, for crimes, human rights violations, and environmental harms that they directly and indirectly cause—and benefit from.

To truth, memory, and justice,
Grahame and Catherine

Acknowledgements

We dedicate this book to all land / environment / human rights defenders in Guatemala. The struggle continues and your dignified rage and actions, each and every day, are leading the work for human rights, justice, and defence of land and the environment, from the local to the global levels.

We also dedicate this book to those Canadians working to hold our government, companies, investors, and shareholders legally accountable, both in civil and criminal law, in Canada, for when our government policies and actions, and private sector business and investment activities, contribute directly or indirectly to crimes and/or human rights violations and environmental destruction in other countries, such as Guatemala.

This book is our collective witness to human dignity in the face of great cruelties and suffering. We thank all those who contributed to this book through their *testimonios*, writing contributions, receiving us for a visit or an interview, photography, everyday inspirational actions, and participation on one of our many delegations.

Several people and organizations assisted us through the challenges of 2020 including the University of Northern British Columbia Faculty Association (UNBCFA), the Canadian Association of University Teachers (CAUT), libel lawyer Peter Jacobsen, and Camila Rich for her eye for detail and superpowers to help us reach the finish line.

We thank the many individual and institutional donors to the work of Rights Action and, indeed, the work and struggle of many people and organizations profiled in this book. We thank the Office of Research at the University of Northern British Columbia for research funding provided over the years.

Acronyms

COCODES	Consejos Comunitarios de Desarrollo Urbano y Rural / Community Councils for Urban and Rural Development
COPAE	Comisión Pastoral Paz y Ecología / Pastoral Commission on Peace and Ecology
CORE	Canadian Ombudsperson for Responsible Enterprise
CPP	Canada Pension Plan
CREOMPAZ	Comando Regional de Entrenamiento de Operaciones de Paz / Regional Centre for Training in Peacekeeping
CSR	Corporate Social Responsibility
EITI	Extractive Industries Transparency Initiative
EMP	Estado Mayor Presidencial / Presidential Security Service
EXMIBAL	Exploraciones y Explotaciones Mineras Izabal, SA / Explorations and Exploitation Mining Izabal, SA
EXMINGUA	Exploraciones Mineras de Guatemala, SA / Exploration Mining of Guatemala, SA
FAFG	Fundación de Antropología Forense de Guatemala / Forensic Anthropology Foundation of Guatemala
FECI	Fiscalía Especial contra la Impunidad / Special Prosecutor's Office against Impunity
FEP	Fuerzas Especiales de Policía / Police Special Forces
FIPA	Foreign Investment Promotion and Protection Agreement
FPIC	Free, Prior, and Informed Consent
FREDEMI	Frente de Defensa San Miguelenese / San Miguel Ixtahuacán Defense Front
FRG	Frente de República Guatemalteca / Guatemalan Republican Front
GANA	Gran Alianza Nacional / Grand National Alliance
GHRC	Guatemala Human Rights Commission
GIZ	Deutsche Gesellschaft für Internationale Zusammenarbeit / German Society for International Cooperation
GREMIEXT	Gremial de Industrias Extractivas / Extractives Industry Association
IACHR	Inter-American Commission on Human Rights
ICEFI	Instituto Centroamericano de Estudios Fiscales / Central American Institute for Fiscal Studies
IDB	Inter-American Development Bank
ILO	International Labour Organization
IMF	International Monetary Fund

INCO	Canadian International Nickel Company
INDE	Instituto Nacional de Electrificación Guatemala / National Electrification Institute of Guatemala
KCA	Kappes, Cassiday & Associates
MEM	Ministerio de Energía y Minas / Ministry of Energy and Mines
MLN	Movimiento Liberación Nacional / National Liberation Movement
MSR	Minera San Rafael / Mining San Rafael
NGO	Non-Governmental Organization
OHCHR	Office of the High Commissioner for Human Rights (UN Human Rights)
PACs	Patrullas de Autodefensa Civil / Civil Defense Patrols
PAN	Partido de Avanzada Nacional / National Advancement Party
PBI	Peace Brigades International
PDH	Procurador de los Derechos Humanos / Human Rights Ombudsperson's Office
PNC	Policía Nacional Civil / Civilian National Police
PP	Partido Patriota / Patriotic Party
REMHI	Proyecto Interdiocesano de Recuperación de la Memoria Histórica / Recovery of Historical Memory Project
SAT	Superintendencia de Administración Tributaria / Superintendent of Tax Administration
SNDP	Sistema Nacional de Diálogo Permanente / National Permanent System of Dialogue
UDEFEGUA	Unidad de Protección a Defensoras y Defensores de Derechos Humanos de Guatemala / Unit for the Protection of Human Rights Defenders and Advocates of Guatemala
UN	United Nations
UNBC	University of Northern British Columbia
UNDP	United Nations Development Programme
UNE	Unidad Nacional de la Esperanza / National Unity of Hope

Timeline of Key Events

1970   Members of a committee of Guatemalan lawyers and aca-
       demics who wrote a 1969 report criticizing the 1965 agreement
       between INCO and the Guatemalan government are killed,
       injured, and forced into exile

1978   On May 29, 1978, the first large-scale massacre of the scorched
       earth / genocide era takes place in Panzós, thirty-five kilo-
       metres west of the mining company installations and plant,
       then owned by INCO/EXMIBAL. Hundreds of Q'eqchi' peo-
       ple from mining-affected communities and other land back
       struggles march to the central plaza of Panzós in a peaceful
       protest for land rights. The Guatemalan army opens fire on
       the crowd, killing dozens and, according to some witnesses,
       possibly more than one hundred people. According to some
       reports, Q'eqchi' people travelling on foot to Panzos are shot
       at by men in INCO/EXMIBAL trucks.

1982   Genocidal General Efrain Ríos Montt gains power following
       military coup

1996   Government of Guatemala signs and ratifies ILO Convention
       169 as part of Peace Accords (June 5)

1996   Álvaro Arzú elected president, signs firm and lasting Peace
       Accord with rebels, ending thirty-six years of armed conflict

1997   Mining Law is completed—Decree 48-97

1998   Establishment of Montana Exploradora de Guatemala, SA
       (Montana) by Montana Gold Corporation, a private Canadian
       company soon to be acquired by Glamis Gold and then
       Goldcorp Inc.

1998   Recuperación de la Memoria Histórica—Informe Proyecto
       Interdiocesano / Recovery of Historical Memory Project
       (REMHI) report presented to Guatemalan people, April 24

1998   Bishop Juan Gerardi, lead advocate of REMHI report and
       human rights campaigner, brutally murdered, April 26

1999   UN-backed Commission for Historical Clarification (CEH)
       documents that Guatemalan security forces were behind
       93 percent of all human rights atrocities committed during
       the armed conflict, which claimed more than 200,000 lives
       and forcibly disappeared 45,000 people, and that senior
       officials had overseen 626 massacres in Maya villages

1999   Ministry of Energy and Mines (MEM) grants Montana an
       exploration license for the Marlin project

2000 Canadian Junior Radius Gold Inc. discovers gold belt near San Pedro Ayampuc and receives concession

2003 Guatemalan government, via MEM, grants exploitation license for the Marlin project, now owned by Glamis Gold, acquired by Goldcorp Inc. in 2006

2004 Marlin Mine construction begin

2004 Skye Resources, a Vancouver, Canada-based mining company that was incorporated by former INCO company officers, announces it has purchased the El Estor mine from INCO by purchasing a majority stake in CGN (formerly EXMIBAL, INCO's subsidiary)

2005 Guatemalan government's Human Rights Ombudsperson's Office, PDH, issues report arguing that license for the Marlin mine should be revoked because, in violation of ILO Convention 169, the government failed to consult affected communities about the concession

2005 Sipakapa community consultation takes place, widely rejecting mining in their territory

2005 ILO investigates the complaint against Guatemalan government for violation of ILO 169 related to the Marlin project

2006 Goldcorp merges with Glamis to take over Marlin project

2007 Government declares mining of national interest and utility via Decree 499–2007

2007 Hundreds of police, military, and private security forces violently evict Maya Q'eqchi' farmers from various communities near El Estor on January 7, 8, 9, and 17

2008 Hudbay Minerals purchases Skye Resources; Skye Resources changes its name to HMI Nickel Inc.

2009 Adolfo Ich Chamán is shot and killed by security forces employed at Hudbay's Fénix mining project; German Chub Choc is shot and paralyzed by Fénix security personnel on the same day, September 27

2010 Angélica Choc announces that she is suing Hudbay Minerals and its subsidiaries in Canadian courts to seek reparations for the death of her husband

2011 German Chub announces he is suing Hudbay Minerals and its subsidiaries in Canadian courts to seek reparations for the wounds and paralysis he suffered as result of the shooting

2011 Rosa Elbira Choc Ich, Margarita Caal Caal, and nine other women from the Maya Q'eqchi' community of Lote Ocho, near El Estor, announce that they are suing Hudbay Minerals and its subsidiary HMI Nickel to seek reparations for gang rapes suffered by them at the hands of Fénix security personnel, military, and police during a forced eviction requested by HMI Nickel (at the time known as Skye Resources)

2011 Hudbay Minerals sells CGN, the Fénix Project, and all of its other Guatemalan assets to a Switzerland-based company, the Solway Investment Group

2011 Vancouver-based, Canadian-owned Tahoe Resources—incorporated by Kevin MacArthur, former CEO of Goldcorp Inc., who then became the first CEO of Tahoe Resources—hires International Security and Defense Management, LLC (a US security and defence contractor with experience working with corporations in war zones such as Iraq and Afghanistan) to develop a so-called "mine security" plan

2011 Exploitation license for the El Tambor mining project granted to Radius Gold by the Guatemalan government via MEM, November

2012 Radius Gold begins construction at the El Tambor mine site with partner Kappes, Cassiday & Associates (KCA), February

2012 Peaceful encampment of La Puya is formed at the entrance of the El Tambor mine site between San Pedro Ayampuc and San José del Golfo, March

2012 Attempted assassination of La Puya resistance participant Yolanda Oquelí, June

2012 Tahoe Resources sues the Guatemalan government, arguing the State was not doing enough to deal with protestors which hindered their operations, June; lawsuit later dismissed

2012 High-level meetings occur between former military general, then-President Pérez Molina, MEM's Erick Archila, GREMIEXT (Extractive Industry Association), and the CEOs of multiple mining companies, July

2012 Former military general, then-Guatemalan President Pérez Molina calls off proposed amendment to Article 125, August

2013 In San Rafael Las Flores, Guatemalan government commences a pilot initiative called the Inter-Institutional Group on Mining Affairs that frames opposition to mining as a threat to national security, March

2013 Guatemalan government grants Tahoe Resources' exploitation license, April

2013 Vancouver-based, Canadian-owned Tahoe Resources' private
security open fire on peaceful protesters outside their Escobal
silver mine, in municipality of San Rafael Las Flores, south-
east of Guatemala City, April

2013 Military siege imposed by Guatemalan government in municipalities where people overwhelmingly voted against mining
in San Rafael Las Flores region, May

2013 Former General Efraín Ríos Montt is found guilty of genocide
and crimes against humanity—and sentenced to 80 years in
prison—in a courageous, landmark ruling of the Guatemalan
Supreme Court on May 10, 2013. Ten days later, in a 3-2 ruling,
the Constitutional Court annuls the verdict on a technicality
and orders a new tribunal to hear the case. Though Ríos
Montt died on April 1, 2018, while facing retrial, genocide
and massacre survivors and the human rights community
continue to uphold the May 10, 2013 verdict as legitimate.

2013 In a precedent-setting judgment in Canada, Justice Carole
Brown of the Superior Court of Ontario rules that Hudbay
can potentially be held legally responsible in Canada for the
shootings, murder, and gang rape that occurred at Hudbay's
Fénix mining project in Guatemala; the claims of the thirteen
Maya Q'eqchi' plaintiffs can proceed to trial in Canadian
courts

2014 Riot police illegally and violently evict the La Puya Roadblock
at the entrance of the El Tambor mine site, May

2014 Another landmark lawsuit filed in British Columbia courts
against Tahoe Resources by the Canadian Centre for
International Justice (CCIJ) and CALAS, asking the Supreme
Court to declare Tahoe Resources responsible for injuries
caused by mine security to seven men shot outside the mine
site in April 2013, June

2015 Four hundred police arrive to evict the La Puya Roadblock at
the entrance of the El Tambor mine site; permanent police
encampment set up at the mine's entrance, May

2016 Guatemalan Supreme Court of Justice reaffirms suspension
of the El Tambor mine site due to lack of free, prior, and
informed consent (FPIC), August

2017   Guatemalan Supreme Court rules in favour of the Xinca Indigenous people for Tahoe and MEM's failure to obtain free, prior, and informed consent; two of Tahoe's mining licenses are suspended, July

2017   A Guatemalan criminal court acquits Mynor Padilla, previously head of mining security for Hudbay, on charges of murder in the death of Adolfo Ich Chamán and aggravated assault in the shooting of German Chub at the Fénix mine owned by Hudbay Minerals—the same incident that is at the heart of the Ontario, Canada litigation; an appeal completely overturns that ruling and Padilla faces a second prosecution regarding the murder and the shooting, April and September

2018   Guatemalan Constitutional Court issues a final resolution, after several appeals and lower court rulings, on the consultation issue, ordering Tahoe and MEM to complete a new consultation process, following principles of ILO 169 and also nullifying the Juan Bosco license, September

2019   Pan American Silver acquires Tahoe Resources, February

2019   Final resolution achieved in the *García v. Tahoe Resources* case and Pan American Silver, on behalf of Tahoe Resources, issues a formal apology to the victims and the community, July

2020   Hudbay Minerals loses attempt to block the Maya Q'eqchi' plaintiffs from amending their lawsuit to add new details about the assaults and rapes suffered by them in Guatemala, perpetrated not only by mine company private security forces, but also military and police; Ontario Superior Court of Justice finds for the plaintiffs on all points, January

Introduction

Canadian Mining in a Time of Violence, Corruption, and Impunity in the Aftermath of Genocides in Guatemala

Catherine Nolin and Grahame Russell

In Central America, contemporary and overlapping crises of resource extraction, export-driven crop production, gang violence, and survival migration are some of the devastating legacies of the region's internal social and armed conflicts that culminated, in Guatemala, in state-directed terror and genocide in the countryside. The physical erasure of Indigenous Maya communities—through death and displacement—and progressive, mostly urban Ladinos is central to these crises. This massive death and destruction—well documented in both the Proyecto Interdiocesano de Recuperación de la Memoria Histórica / Recovery of Historical Memory Project (REMHI) report *Guatemala: Nunca Más*[1] and in *Memoria del silencio*, the report of the United Nations–sanctioned Commission for Historical Clarification (CEH)[2]—is an almost forgotten component of contemporary studies of neoliberal development and escalating violence.

In Guatemala, Maya activists and their supporters describe the growing presence of Canadian mining interests and other foreign-financed megaproject developments as the "fourth conquest" or fourth invasion.[3] W. George Lovell writes of three cycles of conquest: the 1524 Spanish imperialist invasion, the nineteenth-century establishment of the plantation economy, and the 1960-1996 US-backed state repression and genocide.[4] The violent transformation of land to "property," through the dispossession and displacement of Indigenous people, as J. P. Laplante and others recount, is central to these "conquests."[5] Contemporary neoliberalized mining law and "development" strategies continue the trend through the granting of mineral and property rights without consultation with, or consent of, affected communities.

In this edited collection, based on long-term community-based relationships, field work, research and documentation, activism, and Rights Action's direct community support work in Guatemala between 2004 and 2021, we collaborated with a wide range of our colleagues to illuminate and examine what Peruvian José De Echave calls "predatory and uncontrolled mineral exploitation"[6] and the accompanying chaos that violence creates and exploits using several contemporary, illustrative cases and the lived reality of affected community members and leading human rights advocates through interviews and *testimonios*. We focus attention on four main mining-resistance struggles in different regions of the country: (1) Goldcorp Inc.'s Marlin mine; (2) Tahoe Resources' Escobal mine; (3) Hudbay Minerals' Fénix mining project; and (4) the struggle at La Puya against Radius Gold / Kappes, Cassiday & Associates' El Tambor mining site (Figure 1).

Figure 1. Map: Guatemala, Four Main Mining-Related Community Defence Struggles. Produced by Kyle Kusch, 2019.

2

Over the years, we have been able to collaborate with some amazing people within Guatemala and beyond and we want to bring some of those voices together in this edited collection. We work to document and share the very human experience of living with traumatic memories, seeking truth through exhumations of mass graves and military and police records and pursuing justice in a variety of ways; and to confront some of the same type of violence and repression in so-called "post-conflict" Guatemala related to four major mining struggles throughout the country, all related to Canadian- (and partially American-) owned mining operations.

Genocides

Guatemala is recovering from thirty-six years of US-backed state repression and genocides (1960 to 1996), supported by a range of international players, particularly the US, and carried out by the Guatemalan military regime as a devastating response to a small leftist insurgency. As a result, we know there are at least 250,000 civilian victims: 200,000 hunted down, tortured, starved, killed in rural communities and urban centres; children, women, men, the elderly. Then there are 45,000 others . . . the missing, the ones who people are still looking for, the disappeared / *los desaparecidos*, mainly snatched from the urban areas—but not only urban areas, as we now are learning.[7]

In both urban and rural terrorized spaces, Guatemalans witnessed state-sanctioned and state-perpetrated violence, the killings and disappearances of hundreds of thousands of people, and the massive displacement of more than a million Indigenous and non-Indigenous people within the country (of a population of ten million) and at least a million people beyond the borders.[8] Importantly, approximately 83 percent of the victims were Maya and approximately 93 percent of violations can be attributed to the Guatemalan state forces (government, military, police, death squads, and so forth).

The United Nations Commission for Historical Clarification determined that genocides were planned and carried out in four particular Maya-majority areas of the country, detailed by Elizabeth Oglesby and Amy Ross: (1) Maya-Q'anjob'al and Maya-Chuj territories, in the municipalities of Barillas, Nentón, and San Mateo Ixtatán, in the northern Huehuetenango department; (2) Maya-Ixil territories, in the municipalities of Nebaj, San Juan Cotzal, and San Gaspar Chajul, in the department of El Quiché; (3) Maya-K'iche' in the municipality of Zacualpa, department of El Quiché; and, (4) Maya-Achí territory, in the municipality of Rabinal, Baja Verapaz.[9]

Former President General Efraín Ríos Montt was convicted of genocide in 2013—a major achievement within the country—but his conviction was annulled due to legal manoeuvrings and he has since died. The point for survivors is that he was indeed convicted and the truth was made known in a court of law. Two more key points: that the surviving family members want the world to know that these crimes and violations happened; and that their killed or missing loved one was not a criminal, they did nothing wrong.[10] Though truth-telling and justice-seeking initiatives are inspirational and courageous, no serious challenge is evident to the impunity with which the ruling military / business elite / state power-players operate; rather they continue to enrich themselves at the expense of the majority, poor and Indigenous Guatemalans.

Violence of Mining in a Time of Impunity

Structural Violence

Structural violence, Paul Farmer explains, is evident when social forces are at work that structure the risk for most forms of extreme suffering such as hunger, rape, torture, disappearance, and displacement.[11] Who will suffer abuse and who will be shielded from harm? Who benefits from "development" and who suffers? Who gains from the suffering of others? Farmer documents that, of course, the poor and Indigenous are most likely to suffer and are the least likely to have their suffering noticed. The unequal distribution of wealth and power we witness in Guatemala—where a set of military and elite alliances with international support have, by all measures, ferociously targeted, repeatedly, a largely defenceless Indigenous and progressive Ladino majority population—generates brutality that is both obvious and yet largely censored on the world stage.

This brutality of structural violence, Kent State geographer James Tyner argues, is often shaped, reinforced, and driven by state policies and practices that work to institutionally legalize violence.[12] Therefore, over time, violence is seen as instrumental and rationalized by the state for the purposes of "development" and nation building and the maintenance of the status quo. James Tyner articulates how a geographical perspective on state violence must highlight the way this violence, in the imagination of the perpetrators, is viewed as an effective and legitimate form of state building.[13]

The most recent form of state-orchestrated structural violence, on a massive scale, involves the violent transformation of land to "property," through the dispossession of Indigenous and poor non-Indigenous rural people. Contemporary neoliberalized development strategies involve, for example, the granting of mineral and property rights without consultation with, or consent of, affected communities.[14] Simon Granovsky-Larsen writes that "land fits within neoliberal economic and political discourse as a purely economic resource independent and devoid of social relations" which encourages the acquisition of land for large-scale productive and extractive projects.[15] What is land? A resource to be exploited? A commodity to be traded? A home to cherish? A mother to love? The contested approach to land and life is central to contemporary mining projects in Guatemala, where mining companies are guided by global and national policies and profit-seeking interests, but the strongest impacts of mining practices are felt in the local communities and environments.

Mining in a Time of Impunity, Post-Genocides

For us, the connection between genocide and mining is that Guatemala is a country still reeling from the almost complete tearing apart of the social fabric, the destruction of communities and families. Both the Catholic church's REMHI and the UN-sponsored CEH (1999) documented in the late 1990s the experiences of state terror in Guatemala and stated that political violence and large-scale, widespread massacres, at their height between 1978 and 1982, became genocide of the Maya population.[16]

This atrocious violence and brutality was carried out with complete impunity for those who committed these atrocities (they actually still run the country). These people who planned and carried out the genocide of the Indigenous population and the murder of progressive Ladino supporters and fellow citizens working for change—these are the very people who are signing agreements to allow Canadian mining companies (and others) to operate on the land occupied by those who survived the political violence of the 1970s and 1980s.

These are the very people and elite sectors of society who facilitated Canadian mining executives to rewrite the Guatemalan mining law back in the 1960s, and again in 1997, to profit most handsomely. Our many meetings with Canadian ambassadors and their staff over the past many years only reinforce our understanding that the Canadian government's position is to encourage and facilitate Canadian mining operations in Central America at all costs, while turning a blind eye to, or even denying, the violence and harms.

Rethinking Development

Our research and work in Guatemala dates back to the late 1980s and early 1990s. Rights Action's work in Guatemala began in 1995 and our academic and support work connections with mining-harmed communities began in 2004. With the 1996 Peace Accords discussions and truth-telling and justice work, it was an empowering time for surviving communities to dream out loud again. And yet, those dreams and aspirations, for the most part, have been dashed by government and private sector repression (which continues today) that aims to keep in place an economic, racial, social, and political order favourable to the interests of Guatemala's economic elites and their global business partners.[17] These partnerships, from the 1990s onward, included the Canadian-dominated global mining industry.

While we focused our work on migration, community-driven truth-telling, and justice-seeking and society-rebuilding efforts, we, like many, missed the passing of the 1997 mining law reform and the way in which the Peace Accords ushered in international investment in other so-called development projects, detailed by Granovsky-Larsen, in the sectors of hydroelectric energy, African palm production, and oil and gas.[18] Guatemalans, mostly Indigenous people and progressive Ladinos, lived through a series of genocides, disappearances, fear, paralysis, and silence only to find out that the Guatemalan elite and their international backers (primarily the US) had gotten away with killing and disappearing more than 250,000 people and managed to keep in place an economic system that so many in civil society struggled to transform.

Change was underway in so-called post-conflict Guatemala, and Canadian mining companies started to emerge (again) on the scene in 2004. Their presence, cited in their own documents, in the words of Canadian Embassy staff, and by Canadian government officials in Canada, was an attempt to "bring development" to poor communities, to lift people from poverty and enhance their well-being. The mismatch between the reality and the discourse of "mining as development" couldn't have been greater while on the ground in mining-affected communities.

As a challenge of "rethinking development"—which in some ways means seeing development issues at different scales and in different parts of the world as interconnected—scholars and activists are urging a better understanding of "development" issues in both the Global South and the Global North.[19] In *Rethinking Development Geographies*, Marcus Power argues that "geographers interested in development must move to encompass issues and policies of development wherever they occur."[20] Therefore, explicit reference is made to the linkages between the Global South and the Global North, between Canada and Guatemala, the many ruptures created by Canadian mining interests.

We both work to situate our research, Rights Action's work, and the writing of this book on Canadian mining in Guatemala in a transnational understanding, and recognize the need to turn around and face the connections with Guatemala's genocidal past and violent present. Based on our now decades-long connection with Guatemala and Guatemalans, we argue that the contemporary predatory actions of Canadian, and other, mining companies are the children of genocide. American funding, training, support, and facilitation is now a well-documented reality of the genocide of the early 1980s. Here with this edited work, we are shining a light on the Canadians' willingness to cash in on the aftermath. This is our challenge to document and denounce.

Violence and Space

How do we begin to understand the global and local linkages of Canadian mining activity in Guatemala, the "predatory behaviour" of these mineral exploitation companies, and the spatial expressions of violence in the name of development?[21] Kay Warren helps us explore our geographical interests in violence and space in her work on death squads and the anthropology of violence. She argues, as do we, that:

> What becomes important is to wander off the paths of our specific examination of local expressions of violence to examine spaces of violence wherever they occur as aspects of interpenetrating social fields, many of which are increasingly transnational even as they are locally and intimately experienced.[22]

Additionally, we turn to Paul Farmer's work on anthropologies of structural violence and his work on "pathologies of power" to "embrace an historically deep and geographically wide approach" to human conditions of suffering. He states:

> Our inquiries often start with the current events and the ethnographically visible. When we study the social impacts of a hydroelectric dam, of terrorism, or of a new epidemic, we run a great eliding risk. Erasures, in those instances, prove expedient to the powerful, whose agency is usefully unfettered. Imbalance of power cannot be erased without distortion of meaning. Without a historically deep and geographically broad analysis, one that takes into account political economy, we risk seeing only the residue of meaning. We see the puddles, perhaps, but not the rainstorms and certainly not the gathering thunderclouds.[23]

Insurgent Research, *Testimonio*, and Activism

Our research and activism—and Rights Action's work in Guatemala since 1995—are grounded in an approach that empowers, transforms, and sheds light on those parts of the world, those issues, those people who are seen as peripheral but are central to a "rethinking" of development, violence, power, and place. We see our research and community-based work and activism as grounded in an insurgent research approach[24] which explicitly employs Indigenous world views and comes from a place of witnessing, reporting, and working to address and remedy the underlying causes. We see our responsibilities as researchers, teachers, and social justice / human rights advocates as directed almost exclusively towards the community and participants (rather than involving ourselves in the "extraction" of knowledge) and we work toward the exposing of and demise of (neo)colonial interference within all of our lives and communities and especially in the communities we know well in Guatemala. It is our responsibility to listen, witness, and speak and act out.

Since our first days in Guatemala in the late 1980s and early 1990s, we have attempted to understand power, violence, genocide, exile, impunity, and justice-seeking. To do this work, we value *testimonio* as a tool for individual and community recollection of traumatic events. Some twenty years ago, Catherine and Finola Shankar wrote about the need for geographers and others interested in understanding political violence to embrace *testimonio*, a method that honours the authority of men and women to speak for themselves. We wrote: "Testimonies recount personal experiences and communal struggles that are shared with the community of the narrator; thus, the subject of these memories speaks not only for him/herself, but on behalf of the whole community."[25] We saw *testimonio* as a flexible alternative to more structured interviewing when we are positioning ourselves as researchers in solidarity with the people with whom we work. Our collaborations in communities and with contributors to this book are part of our listening, witnessing, and work and struggle for a better world.

Transnational Plunder: Illustrative Cases—
Four Main Mining-Related Community Defence Struggles

In recent years, we led research and solidarity excursions to Guatemala to re-examine and update documentation on four major mining struggles throughout the country, all related to Canadian- (and partially American-) owned mining operations. Our investigation and reporting work is complementary to Grahame's work with Rights Action in direct support of community-led human rights, land, and environmental defence struggles such as the ones addressed in this book.

At various times, our collaborators have included documentary photographer James Rodríguez, filmmaker and academic Steven Schnoor, human rights advocates Rob Mercatante and Jackie McVicar, and independent journalist Sandra Cuffe, among others. Together, we worked to document, yet again, the environmental, human rights, and community defence struggles of Indigenous and non-Indigenous communities that have suffered repression and a wide range of harms caused directly and indirectly by Canadian- (and American-) owned mining operations.

Canada has come to dominate the global mining industry, and is home to approximately half of the world's publicly listed mining and exploration firms. According to the Government of Canada in 2019, "over 55% of the world's publicly listed exploration and mining companies were headquartered in Canada. These 1500+ companies had an interest in some 8000 properties in over 100 countries around the world."[26] Additionally, 70 percent of the equity capital raised globally by the mining industry was raised on the Toronto Stock (TSX) and Venture (TSXV) Exchanges.

We underscore here, again, the ugly point that the Canadian government and Canadian businesses are earning handsome profits while conducting business, since the 1990s, with Guatemala's genocidal generals, militaries, and corrupted politicians; transnational plunder. Some of these same military officials and politicians are facing criminal trials today over corruption and money laundering, as well as for their roles in the genocides and other war crimes of the 1970s and 1980s.

Our experience, revisiting the mine-harmed communities, reinforces our call to Canadians, to Parliament, and to the office of the Prime Minister to—at a bare minimum—bring about long overdue civil and criminal law reforms in Canada so as to be able to hold our companies fully accountable in Canada for repression, harms, and violations they are causing in other countries.

The underlying problem in all of these cases (let alone in other sectors of the economy) is that the Canadian government and our companies are choosing to do business in the racist, exploitative, repressive conditions of Guatemala wherein corruption, impunity, and a fundamental lack of democracy are the norm. In fact, the Canadian government and mining companies are contributing to and benefiting from racism, exploitation, repression, corruption, impunity, and the lack of democracy.

From this underlying reality, the first right that all mining companies are violating through lack of consultation is the right to free, prior, and informed consent (FPIC) of the communities, prior to mine development.[27] Most community members learned of the mine once the equipment arrived and the shovels hit the ground—usually accompanied by armed police, soldiers, and company security guards. All other harms and violations flow from this initial violation.

Throughout this collection, partial and incomplete as it is, we bring together the words and voices of colleagues we have worked with over the last seventeen years: academics, land and water defenders, human rights advocates, journalists, and lawyers, along with the photographic contributions of James Rodríguez. Many more people in Guatemala, Canada, and countries around the world struggle with these issues and we encourage their work to be sought out, as well.

No More Impunity for Mining-Related Repression, Violations, and Harms

In Guatemala's historic and ongoing context of corruption and impunity, and of staggering mining profits, the mining-related repression, violations, and harms—which have been documented since 2004—are both logical and predictable, with no end in sight. We must act to hold Canadian and

American mining companies accountable for their crimes, harms, and violations that take place abroad. This book is part of our effort to do just that.

> Wake up. Wake up, humanity. We are out of time.
> —Berta Cáceres[28]

Chapter 1

Genocide's Legacy on the Land and Dominant Economic Model

The US-backed repression and genocides of the 1970s and 1980s paved the way for the onslaught of mining in the 1990s and 2000s. In the film *Gold Fever*, documenting environmental harms, human rights violations, and repression caused by Goldcorp Inc.'s mining operation in the western highlands, Noam Chomsky says: "You can't say the mining companies are responsible for the Ríos Montt slaughter but they are benefiting from the structures that were left in place after those many years of savagery and violence and repression."[1]

In this chapter, both Cyril Mychalejko and Nathan Einbinder set out the direct relation between the repression and genocides of the 1970s and 1980s and the dominant, global "free market" economic system being operated by, and for, the Guatemalan economic elites and their "international community" partners, including other countries, notably the US and Canada, and companies, investors, and banks, notably the World Bank and Inter-American Development Bank (IDB). All of this set the stage for the mining-related harms, abuses, and repression of the 2000s and 2010s, in partnership with the corrupted repressive regimes of today.

Woven amongst their work are the voices of victim/survivor/protagonist Sebastian Iboy Osorio, who lived in his own flesh the genocidal rampage through his territory, as well as the Reverend Emilie Smith who, after many decades, continues to walk with and witness the bravery of survivors and the honourable work of organizations such as the Fundación de Antropología Forense de Guatemala / Guatemalan Forensic Anthropology Foundation (FAFG), who exhume the remains of those killed during the time of state-directed terror and search for those disappeared and dearly missed by their families.

Profiting from Genocide:
The World Bank and IDB's Bloody History in Guatemala
Cyril Mychalejko

The World Bank and the IDB supported genocide in Guatemala and ought to pay reparations, according to a recent report, *Generating Terror*, by Jubilee International.[2] The report examines lending investments by international financial institutions, such as the World Bank and the IDB, that helped empower and legitimize Guatemala's genocidal regimes of the 1970s and early 1980s, essentially subsidizing their terror campaigns.

"The lending of Western States and banks, and the multilateral banks they control (including the World Bank, IDB, and International Monetary Fund [IMF]) was an important element in sustaining the long period of military rule which followed the US-orchestrated military coup against President Jacobo Arbenz in 1954," the report states. "Particularly worrying, however, is the very dramatic increase in lending that coincided with the highest waves of terror, which reached genocidal proportions in the late 1970s and early 1980s."

Jubilee's report uses the Chixoy hydroelectric dam project as a case study.[3] The World Bank and IDB spearheaded and agreed to fund the project with the murderous military regime of General Fernando Romeo Lucas García in 1978. Between 1978 and 1989, the banks invested over $400 million in the project. Between March 1980 and September 1982, there was a series of massacres committed against the Maya Achí villagers of Río Negro, resulting in the murder of over 440 men, women, and children. These massacres "relocated" the village of Río Negro, to make way for the filling of the dam flood basin.

Moreover, these Chixoy dam massacres were part of a scorched-earth counterinsurgency campaign targeting the country's Indigenous population. According to the United Nations (UN)'s report, this amounted to a genocide resulting in more than two hundred thousand murders, more than forty-five thousand people "disappeared," and other war crimes such as torture and rape.[4]

"The institutions that finance and profit from international development are responsible for their actions. Organizations such as the World Bank, a UN-chartered institution, are obligated to act in ways that reflect international human rights law," said environmental anthropologist Barbara Rose Johnston, senior research fellow at the Center for Political

Ecology who authored the *Chixoy Dam Legacy Issues Study*.[5] "The major conclusion emerging from the *Chixoy Dam Legacy Issues Study* is that hydroelectric energy development occurred at the cost of land, lives, and livelihood in violation of national and international laws, and considerable profits were achieved."

The Jubilee report notes that thirty-three communities were adversely affected by the dam, and more than 3,500 Mayan community members were forcibly displaced.[6] As a result, many of the displaced and surviving families were sentenced to lives of extreme poverty.

"When even the US government came under pressure to reduce support for the regimes in Guatemala, these institutions were able to continue supporting these regimes without accountability to western parliaments, let alone the people of Guatemala," the *Generating Terror* report stated.[7]

Mayan People "in the Way of Development"

Socio-cultural anthropologist Kathleen Dill first traveled to Guatemala in 1994 to work with the FAFG and help with the exhumation of the remains of massacre victims. "The people of Río Negro had no way of knowing that they were standing in the way of the Guatemalan government's opportunity to reap great rewards from the World Bank and IDB. Although the electricity that the dam was supposed to generate was touted as critical to economic development, I believe the dam was just a step in a much bigger project," said Dill. "The dam was an invitation by the neoliberal managers of the global economy for Guatemala to get on the grid."

The international debt accrued as a result of the World Bank and IDB's investment in the Chixoy dam, which included over $100 million in interest, eventually had the desired economic outcome of getting Guatemala "on the grid." In 1992, the IMF lent Guatemala an additional $50 million to assist debt repayment to the World Bank. The World Bank itself lent Guatemala a further $120 million in bailout loans between 1992 and 1996, with the condition that the Guatemalans liberalize and deregulate the economy, leading to the mining law "reforms" of the 1990s and the eventual handing out of hundreds of mining concessions across the country.

From the Chixoy Dam to Mining: The World Bank and Goldcorp Inc.

The Jubilee report also found that even in the light of the Chixoy dam massacres and forced displacements, the World Bank refused to change its harmful investment practices. In 2004, the World Bank invested $45 million in Goldcorp Inc.'s Marlin mine, an open-pit gold mine project in the department of San Marcos, where, as in Río Negro, a majority of community members affected by the project are Indigenous.

The Genocidal Chixoy Dam Project
Nathan Einbinder

In the cool grey dawn at Río Negro, a small Guatemalan village, Sebastian Iboy Osorio and his companions walk the steep sandy paths to the water, and wait. Inside the homes, women dressed in their finest *huipiles* and skirts work the yellow corn dough in their hands, carefully stacking the tortillas into covered baskets. From the wooded ravines and open fields comes the sound of mourning doves and the laughter and whistles of children playing.

I wrote this on March 13, 2014, and was present as the residents of this isolated community received hundreds of guests: survivors and surviving family members, just like them, of a massacre that took place thirty-two years ago to the day. Today, all will hike some three kilometres up from the remains of the Río Negro village to a place on the mountain ridge above known as Pacoxom, to participate in an all-night Mayan and Christian ceremony in commemoration of the victims of the Chixoy dam / Río Negro massacres that killed 444 villagers, back in 1982.

One of over six hundred villages wiped off the map between 1978 and 1982 by the US-backed Guatemalan military regimes, Río Negro was once a community of almost eight hundred Maya Achí farmers, artisans, and fishermen. For generations the community existed along the edge of the Chixoy River (also known as the Río Negro), worked the land, and traded with a string of other nearby communities. Because of their independence and seclusion, they had—until the 1970s—escaped much of the discrimination, repression, and dispossession suffered by other Maya communities whose lands and labour were illegally and often violently usurped by governments and wealthy economic interests, over the course of centuries.

Their lifestyle of local trade and relative seclusion changed abruptly one day in 1976 when members of the Guatemalan government's INDE (Instituto Nacional de Electrificación Guatemala / National Electrification Institute) showed up in a helicopter to serve an eviction notice. "They told us we would have to leave, because of a dam they would build a few miles downriver," Sebastian told me. Sebastian was a teenager at the time.

In the years to follow many men would show up, from government and army officials, soldiers, and police to employees of the World Bank and IDB which invested hundreds of millions of dollars in the Chixoy hydro-electric dam, named after the river that winds its way through the narrow valley and eventually to the Bay of Campeche in Mexico.

There were many promises made by the World Bank, IDB, and military-controlled INDE regarding Río Negro's forced relocation: guarantees of free electricity, education, better homes, and sufficient land and water to grow their *milpa*—the age-old Maya trilogy of corn, beans, and squash, the foundation of their nutritional and cultural sustenance.

Yet as the time grew closer to Río Negro's imminent expulsion, as well as that of thirty other communities in the way of the dam and its thirty-mile-long flood basin, it became evident these promises would not be fulfilled.

In January 1980, project staff and soldiers led a handful of community leaders to the military-established "model village" of Pacux, a six-hour trek over the mountain from Río Negro, to catch a glimpse of what would be their new life in forced relocation. They walked through the rows of cinder-block and wooden homes and noticed the hard-packed earth and tight confines. In disbelief over the complete lack of access to arable land and water, the leaders returned to Río Negro and held community meetings to plan their response: either demand the fulfilment of original promises, or refuse to leave. In the end they would choose the latter—and pay dearly for it.

Repression came swiftly to Río Negro after the villagers refused to leave. According to Carlos Chen Osorio, a leader at the time (and a key negotiator in the Chixoy dam reparations campaign ongoing today), the first assault occurred after the militarized INDE accused two men from Río Negro of stealing beans at the dam site. When military police arrived in Río Negro "to investigate," an argument took place and the officers opened fire, killing seven villagers. One officer was chased into the river by residents and, as many people recount, it was there that he drowned.

Shortly following this incident, two community representatives delivering the community's *Libro de Actas*—documenting community decisions, land titles, and the Chixoy dam compensation promises—to yet another meeting with INDE, the World Bank, and IDB were found mutilated; the *Libro de Actas* was never found. "It was after this," Carlos told me in an interview, "that we were labelled guerrillas. And this is how the war and repression in Guatemala reached us here, in Río Negro."

* * *

The history of the Guatemalan social movements, the small armed uprising, and the US-backed state terrorism used to crush them is both complex and predictable. Like much of Central America, a firmly entrenched export-driven economy, historic racism and inequality between the landless majority and the elite minority, a fundamental lack of democracy and rule of law, and systemic government and private sector repression to maintain the status quo resulted in social movements and rebellions throughout the isthmus.

In Guatemala's long history of inequality, racism, and repression, it is impossible to pick one single incident or motivation that spurred the social movements, armed resistance, and attempted revolutionary changes of the 1960s, 1970s, and 1980s in Guatemala. In recent history, roots of the widespread opposition lie in the aborted agrarian reform under social democratic president Jacobo Arbenz Guzmán, who was deposed in 1954 in a CIA-orchestrated military coup for his attempt to tax, expropriate, and allocate to landless peasants a small portion of the vast lands unused by Boston-based giant United Fruit Company.

Following the coup, increased repression and a rollback—by Guatemala's economic and political elites supported by the army and police—of the many progressive reforms established under Arbenz sparked a failed rebellion by a group of junior officers in 1960, initiating the thirty-six-year-long armed insurgency. However, the armed revolutionary movement was not relegated to ex-military personnel. As University of California Santa Cruz professor Susanne Jonas explains: "The 'rebels' were not simply those who took up arms, but were the unseen hundreds of thousands among Guatemala's majority population who refused to accept a fate of poverty and discrimination."[8]

A combination of global economic crisis, a widening gap in wealth distribution, the lowering of wages (despite growth in GDP), and the earthquake of 1976, which left one million homeless and twenty-three thousand dead, all reinvigorated popular movements that originated in the 1960s. On top of this, an increase in tension between for-export plantation owners—experiencing a boom in commerce, while using repression and paying slave-like wages to a mainly Maya labour force—and the landless peasant workforce generated logical conditions for some people to join the guerrilla groups. As Jonas puts it, the racism, exclusion, and repression that facilitated capital's boundless growth in Guatemala had reached a "boiling point."[9]

The "Development" Model: From the Chixoy Dam to Mining and More

During the period of construction of the Chixoy dam (1978–1983), much of the nation experienced an unprecedented level of repression to crush all opposition to the military regime. The back-to-back regimes of Generals Fernando Romeo Lucas García (1978–1982) and Efrain Ríos Montt (1982–1983) propelled the disappearances and massacres into genocidal proportions, especially in certain rural areas. Under these military governments—which received extensive political, economic, and military support from successive US governments and certain US allies—a scorched-earth policy involving the razing of entire villages, always justified in the name of "fighting communist guerrillas," led to the annihilation of 626 primarily Maya communities.

The military also established PACs (Patrullas de Autodefensa Civil / Civil Defense Patrols) as a means of controlling the population throughout rural Guatemala. Up to one million men and boys (mostly Maya) were eventually forced into the PACs, intended to be an extension of the army's terrorization and repression campaign.

The four large-scale massacres of Río Negro villagers—and other repression and evictions linked to the Chixoy dam project—were emblematic of the era.

In a 2013 interview, Guatemalan economist Luís Solano points out that the Chixoy dam was not just a means to create cheap energy in a time of oil insecurity, but rather "a symbol of a model of development that propelled the government of Lucas García, destined to satisfy the interests of the industrial bourgeoisie. Those interests were encrypted in the development of certain sectors that required the granting of secure electricity: oil, mining, maquilas, non-traditional exports, and free-trade zones."

For the military government and their national and international business and investment partners—often one and the same, according to Solano—the farmers and fishermen of Río Negro represented an impediment to the progress of the nation. Their elimination would be the fastest, and cheapest, way to deal with the problem.

From "Impediments" to Survival

In total, the Río Negro massacres resulted in the death of 444 individuals—over half the Río Negro community. Soon after the final massacre in September 1982, the remains of the burnt-out village disappeared under the rising floodwaters of the dam.

Following the final massacre, survivors fled into the mountains where they lived for up to three years in hiding. "We lived off bark, raw fish, and insects," an orphan named María tells me, who travelled around with other young boys and girls that managed to escape the mass murder and rape at Pacoxom.

Despite the fact that INDE, the World Bank, and IDB were now free to complete the dam—and did—the military and PACs continued to pursue remaining inhabitants on foot and by helicopter, ambushing them in the abandoned village of Los Encuentros on May 14 (ninety-two killed, fifteen women disappeared) and Agua Fría on September 14 (thirty-five children killed).

Eventually, disease and starvation led the Río Negro survivors to come out of the mountains and "surrender" to the military. Survivors arrived at the entrance gates of Pacux, which, at that point, constituted an army garrison. "We were tortured in the base and forced to admit we were with the guerrillas," recalls Sebastian, who himself spent eleven days bound to a filthy latrine.

Over time the remaining families trickled into Pacux, where most still remain today in debilitating poverty and ongoing intergenerational trauma. Some left immediately after realizing that they would still be controlled and harassed by the military. They went to work as almost slave-labourers on the sugarcane plantations at the coast or the shanties outside Guatemala City to eke out a living, much like millions of other internal refugees.

From Survival to Return

Others, like Sebastian, would eventually reach their physical and mental limits in relocation, and in time decided to walk back over the mountain to see what was left of the land of their birth.

From the deck of the Centro Histórico Educativo, a fine wooden building perched high over the dark abyss of the Chixoy dam reservoir, Sebastian and other inhabitants of today's Río Negro relate to me their stories of suffering and loss, and recuperation and rebuilding. It was here in 1991—nine years after the final massacre and subsequent relocation (indeed, the massacres were the "relocation")—that he and two other survivors arrived and decided to stay, even if it meant death, to live once again as independent farmers, fishermen, and parents. "When we first got back, we wept for what had happened," he tells me. "And we were still scared. But little by little we rehabilitated. We figured out how to use the land again and brought our families."

Today over one hundred people live on the steep slopes above the original village (now under water, down below), farming corn and other crops and raising their families. "It's not like it used to be," Sebastian says, looking down to the reservoir. "The best land was at the river's edge. We had fruit trees—mango, peanut, citrus, jocote, papaya, among others—and we caught many species of fish. Now, it's much harder, but it's still better than life in Pacux. Here we have space for our *milpas*, and are free to develop our community as we wish."

In time the new residents were able to rebuild proper homes, a school, and a health clinic. Through the help of a German development group, they built the Centro Histórico in which they receive guests and teach them their history and way of life, while also bringing much-needed income into the community.

From Survival to Justice and Reparations

While many who still remain in Pacux wish to return to Río Negro and the *campesino* livelihood they grew up with, some find the demons too overwhelming. Others, like Carlos, have remained in Pacux to fight for justice and reparations from both the Guatemalan government and the World Bank and IDB that funded the project.

Over the past ten years, through remarkable persistence, local groups have succeeded in two landmark achievements: a winning case at the Inter-American Court of Human Rights in November 2012, which obliges the Guatemalan State to pay each survivor a given amount of money, offer a public apology, and fund community projects; and the signing of the 2014 Reparations Agreement, which would help rebuild every community impacted by the Chixoy dam.

Inter-American Court of Human Rights

Because only low-ranking PAC members were found guilty of the Chixoy dam crimes, and no soldier or officer in the military chain of command was even detained, let alone tried, the Río Negro survivors filed a petition with the Inter-American Commission on Human Rights, arguing corruption, impunity, and lack of justice.

After years of delays, manipulations, and threats to the Río Negro survivors leading this struggle, on October 20, 2012, the Inter-American Court of Human Rights found the Guatemalan government responsible for the Chixoy dam crimes and ordered the government to: investigate the Chixoy dam crimes; prosecute the perpetrators; search for the disappeared; carry out exhumations and identify the victims; publicly acknowledge its responsibility; build basic infrastructure and services for Río Negro survivors in Pacux; implement projects to rescue the culture of the Maya Achí people; provide medical and psychological treatment to the victims; and pay compensation to surviving families for material and non-material damages suffered.

While this ruling of the Inter-American Court is a hugely important achievement of partial justice, it is noteworthy that the Court did not individualize responsibility—the ruling had no impact on the material and intellectual authors of the Chixoy dam crimes.

Furthermore, the Inter-American Commission pointedly refused to investigate the roles and responsibilities of the IDB and World Bank, reinforcing their corruption and impunity.

Finally, as of the updating of this article, the government of Guatemala began in mid-2019—seven years after they were ordered to do so by the Inter-American Court of Human Rights—to make initial payments on the reparations funds they owe to surviving family members of the Río Negro massacre victims.

Chixoy Dam Reparations Campaign

While not a formal legal process, the Reparations Campaign is an extraordinary achievement. After years of mass grave exhumations, ceremonial reburials of loved ones, and other truth-telling struggles, the Río Negro survivors united with approximately thirty other Maya villages harmed by the Chixoy dam crimes to demand comprehensive reparations. (A clarification: The Inter-American Court sentence deals with the Río Negro massacres directly linked to the Chixoy dam project; the Reparations Campaign deals with all other losses and destructions caused by the project.)

As with the Inter-American Court case, it was only after years of delays, manipulations, and threats to the survivors leading this struggle that on November 8, 2014, then-president and former army general Otto Pérez Molina (now in jail on organized crime corruption charges) was pressured to apologize on behalf of the government for the human rights violations and sufferings caused by the Chixoy dam project, and signed into law Decree #378-2014, the *Public Policy of Reparations for Communities Affected by the Construction of the Chixoy Hydro-electric Dam Project*.

As of this writing, the government of Guatemala has paid out some of the $154 million they have been ordered to pay in family compensation and rebuilding projects for the communities harmed and destroyed in varying degrees by the project.

Notably, the World Bank and IDB easily resisted all pressures to be included in the Reparations Campaign investigation into their roles and responsibilities. As with the Inter-American Commission process, the corruption and impunity of global "development" banks has again been reinforced.

Many international supporters, including Grahame Russell, director of the Canadian/American organization Rights Action (that has long worked with and supported the Río Negro / Chixoy dam survivors), believe that these so-called "development banks" should also be held fully accountable for their part in spearheading and investing hundreds of millions of dollars in the Chixoy dam project. "Both the World Bank and IDB knew what was going on with their investment project in the 1970s and 80s and turned a blind eye," says Russell. "The banks actually profited from their investments in this murderous project and they, together with the Guatemalan State, should be held accountable and obliged to pay for the reparations."

* * *

Back at the annual commemoration at Pacoxom, high above the new and the old Río Negro, the sun had set and the first fires were lit. In the now-excavated mass grave site, family members lit candles and placed photos on the soft pine duff, in preparation for the night of ceremony and commemoration.

While it remains unclear whether this community will ever receive their much-deserved reparations—and whether justice will ever be served for those who ordered and those who committed the massacres, other killings, and forced evictions—there is little doubt that the people of Río Negro will continue to strive for a better life and make their story heard.

"Our only duty as survivors," Sebastian tells me, "is to teach our children and grandchildren about what happened. And it's our right to reclaim what was lost—our land, our culture, and our memory—through the courts, or by our own means."

Testimonio: **Sebastian Iboy Osorio**
with Catherine Nolin and Grahame Russell

My name is Sebastian Iboy Osorio and I am the president of the Río Negro COCODE [Consejos Comunitarios de Desarrollo Urbano y Rural / Community Councils for Urban and Rural Development] and coordinator of the Río Negro Centro Histórico Educativo / Historical Education Centre which is a work in progress. I'm here with you with my son Nelson. We are thirteen families living full-time in Río Negro.

I was sixteen years old in 1982 when it all went haywire. February, March, May, September 1982 were the months of the massacres, and there were selective killings before then. The first massacre of Río Negro people took place in the nearby community of Xococ. The Xococ PAC [Patrullas de Autodefensa Civil / Civil Defense Patrols] called some community members from Río Negro to come to Xococ. They were abused and accused of being guerrillas. The PAC kept their *cédulas* [identification cards], which we needed to move outside of our communities at the time, and ordered them to come back the next Saturday to present themselves to be accounted for by the military commissioner. I wanted to go with my dad that day but he told me that there might be violence, they may even be killed, so to please stay at home with the rest of the family. My dad returned to Xococ and he and about seventy-five people, mostly men, were killed by the PAC. One survivor, Teodora Chen, escaped from Xococ and returned to Río Negro and told us what happened.

Then into early March, the soldiers and Xoxoc PAC continued to harass us. They captured Patrocinio and tortured him, demanding that he tell them where to find where the rest of the men and boys were sleeping at night. He, too, escaped and told the community what was happening. At that time, leading up to mid-March, when the dogs barked, the men and boys would hide in the bush, in the mountains. Then, the Xococ PAC and soldiers entered Río Negro and my mom told me to run, that they might take us to Pacux [the military-established "model village" outside Rabinal] or they might even kill us. That was the day of the March 13 massacre of 177 women and children.

I ran and later came back in the afternoon and everything was the same, with tortillas on the table, but completely abandoned. I came across Carlos Chen and a few others and we walked up the mountain to Pacoxom, to the site of that massacre. Thirty people were killed here before the massacre in Río Negro, and 440 people were killed during that year. In total, seventy-five to eighty men and boys were killed in Xococ on February 12, 177 women and children killed at Pacoxom on March 13, about ninety people killed or others disappeared from Los Encuentros in September, and ninety killed at Aguas Frías—thirty-three were children of Río Negro and sixty-six people were from Aguas Frías.

Some days after the March 13 massacre, I snuck back into the community to get food and supplies and I took it all into the mountains. We dug holes and hid things. We lived for two and a half years in the mountains in small groups. Every two or three weeks, the soldiers and PAC members came patrolling, stole and burned down everything. We didn't eat much, maybe one or two tortillas a day, since we weren't able to cook—the smoke would give away our location. We lived two or three or six or seven living together, though quite scattered from each other. We slept in caves, sometimes in the open air. I remembered that my grandparents taught me that *bejuco* is edible, so we ate that—it's a root like yucca. We ate the fruit in the heart of palm leaves. We fished a little with rope and hooks.

My wife Magdalena is from a different community—Canchún—and we married up in the mountains; a catechist married us. After two or two and a half years of suffering with no shoes, our clothes worn out, no hats to shield the sun—we made hats from palm leaves—the children sick and malnourished, in August we started coming down to the river. We flagged someone down on a boat who worked for the [Chixoy] dam and he said "okay" and took twelve of us to Pacux. He took us to a government vehicle that brought us that same night, in 1984. We presented ourselves to the military commissioner of Pacux and the next day the whole group presented ourselves to the Army at the military base.

At 6 a.m., we were woken up, not given any food, and we had to give our names. Nine men and boys were separated off from the rest of the group and pushed outside. We were taken to a dirty latrine and put in different stalls. We were tied up to the latrines, feces and urine everywhere, with our arms chained to the pipes. The feces and urine, sometimes they made us eat it with ground up chili stirred in. I could hear others; each has their own stories. For me, kicking, grabbing my head; they put a knife to my neck, asking, "Are you supporting the guerrillas? How many soldiers did you kill?" Yes, we did collaborate by giving them things like sugar and some food, but that's it. I was held there in that terrible place for six days. My brother, José Iboy Osorio, after all the massacres, joined the guerrilla for a while but then rejoined us in the mountains. My brother was held in that place with me, too. We spoke together after about three days. My brother had cuts on his face. My brother told me that he was going to try to escape and thought that he might be shot or killed. He told me, "You're not of age. Stick with your story." After that, my brother did try to escape from that military base. I heard shooting. I didn't see it but was told that they got him.

Six days I was seated on the toilet with my hands chained behind me. I couldn't lay down. Later, I was thrown into another room, still tied up, and more and more people were thrown in there with us from various communities. Many complained of thirst and hunger. But I felt nothing like that. I felt nothing. I think I survived because I spoke with my murdered parents and siblings. I spoke with them the whole time. They gave me so

Figure 2. Río Negro Massacres and the Chixoy Dam. Massacre survivor Sebastian Iboy Osorio explains to a delegation the repressive events that took place on that spot known as the Conacaste Tree on March 13, 1982. Río Negro, Rabinal, Baja Verapaz, Guatemala. May 17, 2014. Photo: James Rodríguez.

much strength and courage to go on. I remembered what my parents taught me, that I had to look after them even after death. I knew I had to survive to fulfil that obligation. I was held at the military base for eleven days in total and then taken to Pacux. [Sebastian shows scars on his wrists].

I lasted three months in Pacux. I was forced to participate in the PAC but then got permission from the military commissioner to leave. I went to work cutting sugar cane in Escuintla for one and a half years. I went alone and my wife Magdalena remained in Pacux. Eventually, I sent for Magdalena and our first daughter, Gloria. I eventually went to look for work in the Petén with a friend for two years and later brought my wife. But the war caught up with me there, too. Guerrillas attacked the military base up near Sayaxché. The air force started bombing the little town and blew up the school. After that, I took the decision to move on and returned to Pacux. I had to go back in the PAC. There was no work and it was a hard life but I had a house from the World Bank project in my name.

But where to go? What to do? Don Cristóbal started talking about going back to Río Negro. But I had to get permission at the Salamá military base and could only get a license for fishing. The only way to get there was to walk, and I ended up getting caught by the Xococ PAC but was able to show the written permission from the military base to continue my walk back to Río Negro. Little by little, we fished in Río Negro and sold them in Rabinal. Eventually, we built huts near the river—this was in about 1992.

I sometimes think about why the military spared some of us taken to the military base and not others. I guess it was because we were not "of age"; we were under eighteen and they knew that. They had to let us go because we didn't have *cédulas* and this would be considered arbitrary detention.

Genocide's Legacy: Can These Bones Live?
Emilie Smith

> The spirit of the Lord set me down in the middle of a valley; it was full of
> bones. He led me all around them; there were very many lying in the valley,
> and they were very dry.
> —Ezekiel 37:1-2

It is a March morning in Guatemala City: sunny, cool, windy. I walk down a dry, dusty lane, out along a finger of land jutting perilously between ravine and ravine. To one side, vultures circle in lazy spirals on the updraft, watching everything down below—waiting. We are near the garbage dump and the slums that surround it. Here, on the road through La Verbena cemetery, hospital waste trucks rumble by; when they reach the end, they tip their pile down into the valley.

I am early, so I walk slowly, kicking stones through the rows of niche tombs, stacked five high, artificial flowers drooping down. I pass some of the nicer mausoleums, and then I am among the graves in the scrub grass, markers tilted over or gone. Some are simple piles of dirt; others are human-sized hollows, where the bodies have been removed and dumped into the bone pits.

I stand outside a cement block wall, papered with the faces of the disappeared. A few young staff members arrive and wait as well, under pine trees that are blowing wildly now, this way and that. They eye me, but we say nothing.

Some of the tens of thousands of Guatemala's "disappeared" also stare at me from the abyss of silence. Many are women, their hair and clothes out of style now. The men sport moustaches from the 1980s. I imagine each one grabbed by the murderers, thrown into a van, driven somewhere dark, filthy, disgusting, sticky with blood, urine, and feces. The women are raped, the men too, and all of them are mutilated, burned, or electrocuted, and finally killed. Some are then brought here and dumped into large gaping pits.

It's nine o'clock. Someone with keys arrives and we all file in. Jorge Mario Barrios shows me around. He's a forensic anthropologist with the FAFG in charge of the project. He's tall for a Guatemalan, nicely dressed in crisp black jeans, combat boots, and a button-busting black shirt. He explains: Many people were dumped here at La Verbena cemetery as "xx": unknowns, equivalent to John or Jane Doe. They are supposed to be buried in the ground for seven years and then gathered up and thrown into the ossuaries, the bone wells. But between the years 1978 and 1984—the peak years of US-backed state repression in Guatemala—there was a massive upswing in the numbers of bodies being brought and buried, many without being registered. Some, it seems, were dropped straight into the well. It doesn't take much imagination to see that La Verbena was a dumping ground for the murderers.

The FAFG, under its executive director Fredy Peccerelli, was created in the 1990s to investigate these crimes and uncover both bodies and hidden history. It is orchestrating these exhumations at La Verbena. This is one site out of hundreds they've investigated.

There's no building, just grey walls squaring in the huge work site, wooden pillars, and tin roofing, which sometimes keeps off the rain. The work tables are covered in thick black plastic; black sacks on the ground are for loose bones pulled out of the pit. Then there's the pit itself. Huge metal crossbeams, dangling with ropes and harnesses, stand over Well #3. The first well gave up 2,114 bodies. The second, massive well, twenty-five metres deep, held 12,168 bodies. Well #3 is a perfectly round sinkhole, eight metres deep. In the end, investigators exhumed 15,557 skeletal remains from five bone wells at La Verbena.[10]

The UN commission that investigated the thirty-six-year war and genocide in Guatemala estimates that two hundred thousand people were killed during the years of state repression.[11] FAFG and other human rights organizations have figured that in addition to the people killed, forty-four thousand people were detained and "disappeared." Jorge Mario tells me that they hope to identify one hundred remains from the pits as some of these disappeared people—a slim percentage.

I have been walking with and accompanying the people of Guatemala since 1984, when these wells were in full operation, gaping open, swallowing the dead. Out of the horror of my Guatemalan experience I became a priest and theologian. My focus of study has been what the genocide that took place in Guatemala means. Death. Crucifixion. So here I find myself, in Golgotha, *Xilbalba*, the underworld, the very place of the skulls. If we stay here long enough, and resist the too-quick, cheap, or artificial resolution, we may see that the place of death is in fact the place of life. That God works in the universe by pulling life out of the grisly tomb. Those who work here, then, are God's hands of reconstruction.

> Thus says the Lord God: Come from the four winds, O breath, and breathe
> upon these slain, that they may live.
> —Ezekiel 37:9

But before new life comes the way of the cross, the crucifixion. Candi, an anthropology student and full-time FAFG employee, finds me a smock and takes me to her table. Slowly we untangle a pile of bones. They look like a right mess to me, but Candi knows how to read them. These bones speak to her. She is unravelling the language of the dead and preparing to speak these things to the world of the living. No longer secret, no longer forgotten.

Slowly I begin to see. I'm back in high school biology. This is a radius. This is an ulna. This is a tibia. Piles of ribs, skull pieces, and the jaw. Teeth, some fallen out. The hip bone, which we'll use to determine the gender. The hard ridge above the eye socket—only men have that. We'll check the vertebrae, up and down, that can tell us the age. Here is the all-important femur. They take a sample from each left femur they find, and try to match it to one of the thirteen thousand identified family-types now waiting in the FAFG-created Victims and Families' National Gene Bank of Forced Disappearance. FAFG has created six categories of remains, from "A," evidence of death by firearm, to "F," a body partially putrefied, but not skeletonized, no sign of autopsy—someone thrown fresh into a pit.

I work all morning with Candi, cleaning bones with a little stick and brushes. She tells me about the dreams that followed her night after night when she first started working here. Her friends and family wonder why she is wasting her time and career—shouldn't we all just forget what happened and move on? Did it even really happen? We dust, pick, rub, clean, measure, and record. We saw off a piece of femur, put it in a paper bag, mark it, then go back to the black table, on to the next pile of bones. Five in a day, says Candi: that's good.

The people who work here have a kind of bravura mixed with tenderness, and an unspoken respect for the dead. Foul language and jokes abound, but never about the bones, the bodies. No one I met talked much about faith, but each one seems to work from the ethical conviction that human life cannot be simply discarded, destroyed, or erased. They balance loving compassion for the human remains before them with a determination to keep working. They forge on through the bone piles, creating order and meaning out of nothingness and oblivion. Their actions—methodical, scientific, stubborn—threaten the house of terror that was built out of these bones. These dead were never meant to speak again. But they do.

My dreams this night are thick and worrisome. The interior landscape of my imagination is being reshaped; I embrace the cracking bones, and I love them in wordless, tearless grief.

> O dry bones, hear the word of the Lord. Thus says the Lord God to these
> bones; I will cause breath to enter you.
> —Ezekiel 37:4-5

It was hoped that the first well, which dates closest to the years of highest horror, would produce matches. Four thousand Guatemalan families had their DNA recorded at that point, now more than thirteen thousand. Now, as of February 2020, the FAFG has achieved thirteen identifications from La Verbena.[12] I peered down into the deepest shaft, Well #2; I can't see the bottom, even with a flashlight. It goes down forever.

According to US historian Greg Grandin, "disappearing" political opponents was refined in Guatemala in the late 1960s under the training and direction of the CIA.[13] Later this technique was exported around the continent, and horror stories abound in Argentina, Chile, and El Salvador. But Guatemala continues to hold the grisly record.

Each of the forty-four thousand Guatemalans who vanished ("disappeared," usually by state forces) during the war was a human being, with a family, dreams, and plans. Most are now just bones waiting to be found. Most never will be. But the work of Fredy, Jorge Mario, Raul, Candi, and the rest carries on anyway. Whether or not they identify anyone, they are restoring dignity—life—to these bones and to all the disappeared. They are claiming them out of the dark earth of forgetfulness, and—in the face of ongoing threats of violence and the national official insistence on oblivion—saying that these, our dead, all of them, have a place in Guatemala's story.

What happened was the highest kind of crime, by a state apparatus committed at all costs to the preservation of the perverse power of a few violent and wealthy people. Many of the disappeared defended the outcast and the poor—and their deaths reflect the way of the Holy One of Peace, he who died on the hill at the place of the skull.

When my third and final day in the cemetery ends, I leave quickly and walk alone back up the road. I wait, wistful and distracted, at the fast-food chicken joint Pollo Campero on Roosevelt Boulevard for my taxi driver from the Quiché who arrives late through a snarl of traffic. We head out on the three-hour road home to Santa Cruz, the ground zero of the horrors of war, down the road from where my sister-in-law Beatriz is buried. I have nothing left to feel, or say, but he talks, as I nod, and then jerk awake and listen. My driver, my friend, knows where I have spent the last few days, and he starts to tell me his own story. They were fifteen years old when his best friend's head was blown off by a military man. Most everyone from the region where I live has stories like this. My tears for the dead fall quietly in the dark. A full moon rises as we turn north through the corn fields.

Thus says the Lord God: I am going to open your graves, and bring you up from your graves. O my people . . . I will put my spirit within you, and you shall live.

—Ezekiel 37:12-14

Figure 3. CREOMPAZ, Exhumation in Cobán's former military base. Mass grave number sixteen inside the Guatemalan military base known as CREOMPAZ (UN's Regional Centre for Training in Peacekeeping), formerly known as Military Zone 21, reveals dozens of bound, tied, and blindfolded human remains. The exhumation, which took place during 2012 and was carried out by the Forensic Anthropology Foundation of Guatemala (FAFG), rendered the human remains of 533 people, dozens of whom were women and children. Cobán, Alta Verapaz, Guatemala. May 29, 2012. Photo: James Rodríguez.

Chapter 2
Mining in the Wake of Genocides

In Guatemala, it is not possible to operate a large-scale mine (let alone just about any large-scale economic "development" project in the sectors of hydro-electric dams, garment sweatshops, for-export production of African palm, sugar cane, bananas, and more) without participating in and benefiting from human rights violations and repression, corruption, and impunity. Put another way, violating human rights, using repression, and acting with corruption and impunity are how businesses operate in Guatemala, particularly large-scale businesses.

In her contribution, journalist Sandra Cuffe explains why and how "the history of mining in Guatemala over the past sixty years is . . . a history of transnational mining companies doing whatever they need to in order to advance their interests, working with every government administration along the way, whether with genocidal military rulers or with administrations so corrupt that most top officials are now sitting in prison cells." Human rights accompanier and writer Jackie McVicar shares from her perspective the ongoing violence of uncertainty even when a mine closes down. McVicar documents the ongoing violence even when one Canadian-owned company, Goldcorp, Inc. closed down operations at their Marlin mine in 2018 but neglected (or purposefully chose not) to share an official closure plan with affected communities. Community members wonder, of course: could it start up again?

As one grasps the systemic nature of the harms and abuses that repeat decade after decade, from one company to the next, from one sector of the economy to the next, one then understands that transnational mining companies are not benefiting from "Guatemalan" corruption, repression, and impunity—the companies themselves are corrupt, are repressive, and are acting with impunity.

Mining in the Guatemalan Mafia State
Sandra Cuffe

A military coup clears the way for mining interests. Exploitation licenses are granted by military rulers. A mining company is directly involved in attacks and assassinations. A mining law is written by future mining company personnel. Exploitation licenses are granted by corrupt government officials. A transnational mining executive becomes a fugitive. Company and government officials coordinate police and military action to quell dissent. People's homes are burned to the ground. People are killed.[1]

The history of mining in Guatemala over the past sixty years is one of violence, corruption, and impunity. It is a history of transnational mining companies doing whatever they need to in order to advance their interests, working with every government administration along the way, whether with genocidal military rulers or with administrations so corrupt that most top officials are now sitting in prison cells.

It is not an exaggeration. Guatemala has had eight presidents since the 1996 Peace Accords formally ended a thirty-six-year armed conflict. Six of the eight have faced, or are facing, some form of legal proceedings related to corruption, and it's unlikely the other two were exceptions to the rule. Mining companies have worked with all of these presidents and their administrations.

Prior to the Peace Accords, companies worked with successive military rulers engaging in horrific crimes against the civilian population.

Mining companies, the majority of which have been Canadian, have benefited and continue to benefit from this systemic violence, repression, and corruption. Attention to the links between mining companies and impunity tends to focus on particular human rights violations against community leaders and anti-mining activists. However, impunity is tied to all aspects of mining from A to Z, with corruption and/or violence at every stage, from the creation of pro-mining laws and granting of concessions and licenses to land acquisitions, to operations, to closure, and beyond. Some of these dealings are questionable at best. Others are criminal.

"Mining companies have been acting as criminal structures, hand in hand with the government," CALAS (Centro de Acción Legal, Ambiental y

Social de Guatemala / Centre for Environmental and Social Legal Action) lawyer Rafael Maldonado said in an interview with the Business and Human Rights Centre.[2]

A full examination of the issues and history would require a multi-volume encyclopedia. This is not that. This text traces how Canadian-owned INCO (International Nickel Company) / EXMIBAL's (Exploraciones y Explotaciones Mineras Izabal, SA / Explorations and Exploitation Mining Izabal, SA) activities and state atrocities coincide with decades of state repression and genocide; gives an overview of the rise of new mining legislation and projects, particularly Goldcorp Inc.'s Marlin mine, during administrations wracked with corruption allegations; and focuses on the links between mining companies, security forces, repression, and corruption scandals in the past five years.

I do so briefly, in an overview comprised of snippets to illustrate patterns over the modern era of mining in Guatemala, from 1954 to present. Much more in-depth and specific research and reporting has been undertaken by Guatemalans, particularly Luís Solano[3] but also Francisca Gómez Grijalva[4] and many others, including reporting by the Centro de Medios Independientes de Guatemala, Nómada, and Plaza Pública. And ultimately, the work is only made possible by the communities and organizations that have been documenting their own history and struggling for justice for decades.

Mining, Crimes against Humanity, and Impunity

"What the company does is send police to kill people," Jorge Xol said following the burial of his son-in-law, Carlos Maaz Coc.[5] A twenty-seven-year-old Maya Q'eqchi' fisherman, Maaz Coc was shot and killed by police on May 27, 2017 during the violent eviction of a road blockade set up by local small-scale fishers to reiterate their demands for investigation, transparency, and action with regard to Lake Izabal pollution related to the Fénix nickel mine in eastern Guatemala. The following day, some government officials stated that no one had died. Over a year later, no one has been brought to justice. It was but the latest killing related to the mine, the history of which is inextricably linked to violence.

The Fénix nickel mine, located six kilometres west of the town of El Estor along the northwestern tip of Lake Izabal, has been tied to killings and repression for decades. Now owned by the Solway Investment Group, headquartered in Switzerland, the mining project was previously owned from 1965 to 2011 by a series of Canadian companies: INCO, Skye Resources, and Hudbay Minerals.

For more than half a century, the history of mining in the area has been a history of state and company violence, spanning Guatemala's entire thirty-six-year armed conflict and beyond. The decades of violence and impunity accompanying every stage of mining, from legislation and concessions to operations, closure and re-opening, were initially rooted in a US-backed military coup.

A US-Backed Coup Sets the Stage for Mining

In 1954, the United States government supported a military coup in Guatemala to overthrow the government of Jacobo Arbenz, who had enacted sweeping agrarian reform and expanded political rights and freedoms. The country soon descended into decades of state repression against the general population and armed conflict between left-wing guerrilla forces on the one hand and US-backed state armed forces and paramilitary groups on the other. The horrific human cost was overwhelmingly borne by the country's Indigenous Maya population. Between 1960 and 1996, an estimated two hundred thousand civilians were killed, tens of thousands of people were disappeared, and one million people were displaced. The Comisión para el Esclarecimiento Histórico / Commission for Historical Clarification (CEH), Guatemala's UN-backed truth commission, later concluded that agents of the state carried out acts of genocide in four regions of the country.[6]

It was in this context that INCO, at the time a Canadian corporation, was able to set the stage for its nickel mining operations in the municipality of El Estor, in the Izabal department in eastern Guatemala. The extent to which mining corporations have colluded with the state over the decades to engage in human rights violations and suppress dissent should not be underestimated. In the case of INCO and its subsidiary EXMIBAL, company personnel participated directly in war crimes.

In 1955, one year after taking power in the US-backed coup d'état, de facto ruler Lieutenant Colonel Carlos Castillo Armas issued Decree 272, which encouraged investment in mining. During General Miguel Ydígoras Fuentes' presidency in 1960, the same year the country's thirty-six-year armed conflict is considered to have begun, EXMIBAL was formed and major exploration work began. The company was majority owned by INCO. Colonel Enrique Peralta Azurdia came to rule the country via military coup in 1963 and went on to suspend the constitution, dissolve congress, prohibit political association, and essentially assume absolute control of the state. In 1965, his government enacted a new mining code, allegedly written by an engineer hired by INCO. That same year, the government issued EXMIBAL a forty-year, 385-square-kilometre concession.

As INCO's mining plans advanced, the human rights violations and war crimes committed with impunity by state and paramilitary forces that would become staples of the armed conflict increased during Peralta Azurdia's rule. The state used torture, political killings, and death squad activity to stifle dissent, targeting anyone it deemed a threat.

Peralta Azurdia was part of the National Liberation Movement (MLN), an extreme right-wing political party with a paramilitary wing that was responsible for some of the uptick in disappearances and extrajudicial executions in the late 1960s and 1970s. The MLN's power endured for decades following the 1954 coup, and figures from the right-wing, military-linked movement continued to crop up in positions of power even after the party was formally disbanded in 1999.

For example, Alejandro Maldonado Aguirre, who became president without a single vote being cast in his name when President Otto Pérez Molina was forced to step down and was subsequently arrested in 2015, was an MLN congressman from 1966 to 1970.

Political Repression against INCO's Opponents

Colonel Carlos Arana Osorio was also tied to the MLN. He became president in 1970 and promoted Efraín Ríos Montt, who would later be convicted of genocide, to Army Chief of Staff. "The regime of Arana Osorio was characterized by actions targeting not only the armed insurgency but also students, workers, and legal political opposition," the Commission for Historical Clarification wrote in *Memory of Silence (Memoria del silencio)*, a twelve-volume report released in 1999.[7] "During the first year of his government, there were widespread searches, numerous detentions, expulsions of political leaders from the country, and also reports of politically motivated deaths and disappearances," the commission noted.

A few high-profile cases of repression in that first year of the Arana Osorio government were directly connected to INCO's nickel mining interests in El Estor. Two members of a high-profile ad hoc commission of lawyers, academics, and politicians, established in Guatemala City to investigate the issue of mining rights in the area, were killed in 1970 and

1971; another commission member was wounded, and a fourth was forced into exile. Following the killings, INCO and its subsidiary EXMIBAL were given the green light by Arana Osorio.

Killings and attacks against people questioning and opposing the mining project only worsened during the period the nickel mine was in production, from the late 1970s through 1982. This period overlapped with time in power of three presidents, under whose rule some of the worst atrocities were committed against civilian, and particularly Maya, populations around the country.

In the area around the nickel mine, killings and attacks targeted local Maya Q'eqchi' community leaders and members struggling for rights to ancestral lands claimed by the company. The perpetrators were no longer just state armed forces or paramilitary death squads. The direct involvement of INCO subsidiary EXMIBAL personnel in several cases was documented by the Commission for Historical Clarification.[8]

In 1974, another MLN-backed military general, Eugenio Laugerud, took over the presidency from Arana Osorio, under whose administration he had been army chief of staff and defence minister. Towards the end of Laugerud's rule, in 1978, there were attacks on and a massacre of Maya Q'eqchi' community members working for the recognition of their collective land rights in the Izabal and Alta Verapaz departments, including in areas claimed by the mining company.

The Panzós Massacre

On May 26, 1978, civilians travelling in private vehicles and an INCO/EXMIBAL company truck opened fire on residents of Chichipate, ten kilometres west of the main mining company installations and plant. Two local men, Miguel Sub and José Ché Pop, were injured.[9]

Three days later, the first large-scale massacre of the scorched earth era took place in Panzós, twenty-five kilometres west of Chichipate. Hundreds of Q'eqchi' from communities throughout the region mobilized to Panzós for a march for land rights culminating in the central plaza. The army opened fire on the crowd, killing dozens and possibly even upwards of one hundred people. According to some reports, prior to the massacre, Q'eqchi' travelling on foot from El Estor and Chichipate to join the mobilization in Panzós were shot at by men in INCO/EXMIBAL trucks along the way.[10] The following month, in June 1978, military commissioners and

INCO/EXMIBAL employees shot and killed four people in a village in the municipality of Panzós.[11]

In July 1978, General Romeo Lucas García took office. During his presidency—which coincided almost completely with the period in which the nickel mine was in production in El Estor—counterinsurgency operations, attacks on civilians, and massacres of Indigenous communities became the national norm.

In communities around INCO's mine, attacks against and disappearances of local Maya Q'eqchi' leaders continued, with at least one more documented case of direct mining company involvement. On January 31, 1981, judicial police travelling in an INCO/EXMIBAL truck executed Chichipate community leader Pablo Bac Caal.[12]

Mining operations shut down the following year due to prices and politics, but the project was suspended, not abandoned, and conflicts, killings, and disappearances related to disputed lands continued throughout the reign of General Ríos Montt and beyond.

Mining Company Crimes against Humanity

In armed conflicts, whether of an international character or not, "intentionally directing attacks against the civilian population as such or against individual civilians not taking direct part in hostilities" is a war crime, according to the Rome Statute of the International Criminal Court.[13] According to the same statute, murder and enforced disappearance, "when committed as part of a widespread or systemic attack directed at any civilian population, with knowledge of the attack," are crimes against humanity.[14]

An armed conflict was going on for decades between guerrilla and state forces. Parallel to the conflict, however, was a near-endless commission of war crimes and crimes against humanity by state forces against the civilian population, including in Q'eqchi' lands, in and around the area of nickel mining.

To the extent that INCO/EXMIBAL personnel or resources, such as company vehicles, were involved in the attacks documented by the Commission for Historical Clarification, the company participated in war crimes and crimes against humanity.

Even when the company did not directly participate, it benefited from war crimes and crimes against humanity both against Q'eqchi' communities in the area and against critics in the capital. It benefited from the generalized state terror that stifled dissent and unarmed community struggle. It worked with military rulers and genocidal dictators engaging in genocide. They had shared interests. INCO and the Guatemalan state were directly in business together. INCO was the principal force behind its subsidiary EXMIBAL, but it was not the sole owner. The Guatemalan state had a significant stake in the company: originally closer to half, the state stake in the subsidiary was still at 20 percent at the time of its sale in 2004. For decades, INCO shared ownership with a succession of repressive military and autocratic rulers engaging in horrific crimes against the population.

Neither EXMIBAL/INCO nor individual executives have ever faced justice for the company's role in extrajudicial killings and attacks. Laugerud, Arana Osorio, and the military rulers who preceded them never faced justice. Lucas García faced potential legal proceedings for genocide and other crimes against humanity such as the 1980 Spanish Embassy fire that resulted in thirty-seven deaths, but he managed to evade prosecution until his death in exile.

Lucas García's successor, General Efraín Ríos Montt, who took power in a 1982 coup d'état, did eventually face justice for genocide in the Ixil Triangle region. A military commander in the Ixil region at the time, Otto Pérez Molina, would also later face justice, though for corruption during his presidential campaign and administration, not for genocide. And not for decades to come. In the meantime, Ríos Montt, Pérez Molina, and others would go on to hold positions of power during a subsequent rise in foreign-owned mining interests and projects.

A New Era of Peace Begins . . . for Investors

In the years leading up to the 1996 Peace Accords, military officials in charge of genocide remained in government. In 1989, Ríos Montt founded a new political party, the Frente de República Guatemalteca / Guatemalan Republican Front (FRG). He attempted running for president in 1990, but his candidacy was rejected due to a constitutional prohibition that does not permit anyone who has taken part in a coup d'état to become president. He was elected to Congress instead and remained a congressman from 1990 to 2004, serving in Congress again from 2008 to 2012. During the latter part of the peace process, from 1994 to 1996, Ríos Montt was President of Congress.

In the early 1990s, Pérez Molina was national director of military intelligence. He is accused of being the intellectual author of war crimes and crimes against humanity committed by military intelligence officers, such as the longstanding torture and eventual disappearance of Efraín Bámaca, a guerrilla commander and prisoner of war.[15]

In January 1996, Álvaro Arzú of the PAN (Partido de Avanzada Nacional / National Advancement Party) won the presidency, narrowly defeating FRG candidate Alfonso Portillo in a runoff election. Both men would later face legal proceedings for corruption. Arzú's electoral campaign centred on his promise to see the peace process through. Early talks led to the declaration of a ceasefire within Arzú's first two months in office. A series of agreements, including measures such as an amnesty law, were made over the course of 1996, leading to the eventual signing of the Peace Accords on December 29. Reaching far beyond simple disarmament, the accords attempted to address historical and structural roots of the conflict, including inequality, land tenure, and racism.

As is often the case, once the Peace Accords were signed and the opposition guerrilla forces demobilized, there was little compliance with the accords thereafter. In fact, efforts to intentionally stifle the implementation of many of the peace accord commitments were made, by way of parallel talks and deals between representatives of the government, companies, and international institutions to implement reforms and a neoliberal framework that would soon exacerbate some of the very issues that had been at the root of the decades-long conflict.[16]

A New Law Ushers In a New Wave of Mining

The 1997 mining law was one small part of those efforts, and its passage flew in the face of substantive parts of the Peace Accords. "Its debate and passage coincide with a period of promotion and application of reforms tending towards liberalization and privatization," note the authors of a 2014 study by the Instituto Centroamericano de Estudios Fiscales / Central American Institute for Fiscal Studies (ICEFI).[17] The law reflects the tendency at the time to promote primary extraction to attract foreign direct investment, they explain.

The 1997 mining law permitted 100 percent foreign ownership of mining projects, gave companies tax breaks, and reduced royalties on revenue to 1 percent.

Two people who would later go on to benefit from the law through their employment with Montana Exploradora, a subsidiary of a series of Canadian companies eventually owned by Goldcorp, were involved in devising and drafting the law, Guatemalan researcher and economist Luís Solano explained in his book *Guatemala petróleo y minería en las entrañas del poder*.[18] Milton Saravia, who worked as a government official in the early 1990s, including for a directorate and a unit within the Ministry of Energy and Mines, participated in the development of the mining law.[19] He would later become, in 2003, the general manager of the mine eventually owned by Goldcorp. Jorge Asensio Aguirre, later a legal advisor for the same company, also helped draft the law, Solano notes.[20]

The revolving door between the government and mining companies, and in particular Goldcorp's Montana Exploradora, was not limited to Saravia, CALAS executive director Yuri Melini pointed out in an interview.[21] Years later, a subsequent general manager of the company would obtain the position following years as a government official in two administrations, first as director of mining and later as vice minister. "There's a conflict of interest," said Melini.[22] "They worked for the government. They're people who had access to privileged information."

The 1997 mining law ushered in a new wave of mining investment, exploration, and exploitation, but things did not really pick up until the 2000s. Montana Exploradora was ahead of the pack. The company was constituted in Guatemala in mid-1996, while negotiations for the Peace Accords were still underway. According to the current owner's history, the Marlin mine deposit was first discovered in 1998.[23] Montana Exploradora obtained an exploration license for the area in 1999, covering parts of the municipalities of San Miguel Ixtahuacán and Sipakapa, in the department of San Marcos. Originally a subsidiary of Montana Gold, a Canadian mining company, Montana Exploradora was bought out by another Canadian company, Francisco Gold, in 2000, and advanced exploration work was already underway by the end of Arzú's presidency at the beginning of that year.

A few years after his presidency, Arzú went on to be elected mayor of Guatemala City, a post he had occupied in the 1980s. Arzú became mayor of the capital again in 2004 and was continually re-elected as mayor until he died on a golf course in 2018. The year before his death, however, he was formally accused of corruption. Instead of attempting to avoid the spotlight, Arzú showed up to the October 2017 press conference and stood at the front of the room, literally staring down the Attorney General and the head of the UN-backed Comisión Internacional contra la Impunidad en Guatemala / International Commission against Impunity in Guatemala (CICIG) as they announced the results of their investigation.

The alleged corruption took place during Arzú's 2015 bid for re-election as mayor, but the central figure involved is a blast from his past, from a high-profile assassination that occurred during his presidency.

President Arzú and the Assassination of a Bishop

On April 24, 1998, Guatemala City bishop Juan José Gerardi presented *Guatemala: Nunca Más*, the four-volume report by REMHI (Proyecto Interdiocesano de Recuperación de la Memoria Histórica / Interdiocesan Recovery of Historical Memory Project) that he directed.[24] The report was the result of years of investigation, thousands of testimonies from witnesses and victims, and the documentation of more than fifty thousand human rights violations during the 1960-1996 conflict. The vast majority of victims were Indigenous civilians, and the vast majority of abuses were perpetrated by state armed forces, the report concluded. The UN-backed Commission for Historical Clarification (CEH), aided in part by REMHI's documentation, would present similar conclusions a year later, in its 1999 report *Guatemala: Memoria del silencio / Guatemala: Memory of Silence*.

Two days after he publicly presented the REMHI findings and report, the night of April 26, 1998, Gerardi was viciously beaten to death in a parish garage in downtown Guatemala City. Then-President Arzú initially denied a political motive and obstructed investigations. Alejandro Maldonado, the former MLN congressman, also attempted to impede investigations from his position as a Constitutional Court magistrate, Francisco Goldman reports.[25]

Despite their efforts, the assassination was eventually tied to the military. Retired colonel Byron Lima Estrada; his son, captain Byron Lima Oliva, a military intelligence officer serving in the Estado Mayor Presidencial / Presidential Security Service (EMP); and EMP military intelligence officer José Obdulio Villanueva were charged in 2001 as the material authors of the assassination of Bishop Gerardi. Villanueva was killed and decapitated in prison in 2003. Lima Estrada was granted an early release in 2012 after serving half of his twenty-year sentence. His son Lima Oliva became known as the king of the prison, with powerful connections inside and out. Despite his bulletproof vest and bodyguards, he was shot and killed in prison in 2016, sparking a gunfight that left more than a dozen people dead.[26]

Before Lima Oliva was killed, a cooperative he ran from prison was contracted by Arzú for mayoral re-election campaign materials, and the deal was accompanied by blank cheques, pseudonyms, and illegal campaign financing. According to prosecutors and CICIG, Arzú's municipal administration also had "ghost positions"—posts with salaries but no actual work—for Villanueva's widow, as well as Lima Oliva's partner and her mother.[27]

When Lima Oliva's partner Alejandra Reyes testified for the prosecution, the assassination of Gerardi came up. Approximately two months before he was killed, Lima Oliva told her that he had altered the crime scene at Arzú's request, Reyes said. Lima Oliva told her that he was tired and that he didn't feel his loyalty to Arzú had been properly repaid, she testified.[28] Arzú's involvement in Gerardi's assassination had always been rumoured.

More than a dozen people are behind bars in connection with the aptly named Pandora's Box case, including Lima Oliva's brother, his lawyers, a former penitentiary system director, and a government minister who was already in jail on other corruption charges. However, many government positions in Guatemala entail immunity from prosecution for the holder of office, and mayor is one of them. There are established procedures that may strip this immunity, but in March 2018, two of three appeals court judges ruled to maintain Arzú's immunity from prosecution. The Attorney General announced she would appeal the ruling. New steps in the investigation into Bishop Gerardi's murder were taken in late 2017 and in April 2018.

April 26, 2018 marked the twentieth anniversary of the killing. The next day, on April 27, 2018, Arzú died.

More Mining Licenses, More Corruption

The President following Arzú, however, did face prosecution and prison in his lifetime. Alfonso Portillo of Ríos Montt's FRG party took office in 2000, and during his four-year administration, Ríos Montt was president of Congress. Portillo fled the country almost immediately after he left office in 2004 and his immunity from prosecution was revoked. Audits showed $15 million in illegal transfers to the Defense department. He was extradited back to Guatemala in 2008, but in 2011 he and his associates were acquitted of embezzlement. In 2013, he was extradited to the US and pled guilty to laundering $70 million through US banks, but he did not serve much time in prison.

Montana Exploradora made significant progress with its Marlin gold mine project during Portillo's administration, obtaining its exploitation license in 2003. At that point, Glamis Gold was the Canadian parent company, though it was taken over by Goldcorp in 2006. Construction of the Marlin mine began in earnest in 2004, after Óscar Berger from the Gran Alianza Nacional / Grand National Alliance (GANA) party became president of Guatemala. He was a vocal champion of the mine, publicly insisting on the need to protect investors as he sent security forces to violently evict protests. During Berger's administration, an exploitation license was granted to another Goldcorp subsidiary, Entre Mares de Guatemala, for the Cerro Blanco silver and gold mine in the Jutiapa department.

Berger's government also granted an exploitation license for the Fénix nickel mine in El Estor, Izabal. Dormant for more than two decades, the nickel mine formerly owned by INCO was on its way to resurrection. The subsidiary EXMIBAL became the subsidiary CGN (Compañía Guatemalteca de Níquel / Guatemalan Nickel Company), and Skye Resources bought the project in 2004. It was granted a renewed exploitation license in 2006, and promptly initiated a series of violent evictions of Q'eqchi' communities in the area.

Unlike his two predecessors and the two presidents who followed him, Berger has not been formally accused of corruption. Yet.

Berger's successor, Álvaro Colom of the Unidad Nacional de la Esperanza / National Unity of Hope (UNE) party, took office in 2008, when Goldcorp's mine production was in full swing, despite ongoing conflicts and community opposition. In 2010, the Inter-American Commission on Human Rights granted precautionary measures to eighteen communities in the area of the mine who, among having other complaints, had not been properly informed or consulted, and ordered the Guatemalan government to suspend operations at the Marlin mine.[29] Neither Colom's government nor Goldcorp complied.[30]

The Colom administration also granted an exploitation license to EXMINGUA (Exploraciones Mineras de Guatemala, SA / Exploration Mining of Guatemala, SA), a subsidiary of Canadian company Radius Gold, later sold to US company Kappes, Cassiday & Associates (KCA), for the highly contested and so far successfully blocked El Tambor gold and silver mine.

Figure 4. Eviction of Barrio La Revolución. Hired men from the nearby community of Mariscos burn homes at Barrio La Revolución. On January 7, 8, and 9, 2007, the Guatemalan Nickel Company, local subsidiary of Canadian Skye Resources, ordered the forced eviction of five Maya Q'eqchi' communities around Lake Izabal in both El Estor and Panzós. Over eight hundred State security forces carried out the forced eviction, destroying and even burning many huts in the Indigenous communities who claim the territory as ancestral land. Barrio La Revolución, Chichipate, El Estor, Izabal, Guatemala. January 9, 2007. Photo: James Rodríguez.

In February 2018, Colom and ten of his former cabinet members were arrested. Former Vice Minister of Energy and Mines Alfredo Pokus was among them, as were ex-ministers of the Environment, Defense, and the Interior. Nearly three years later, the case continued in court, though Colom had been granted house arrest and exempted from attending hearings for medical reasons. They are accused of corruption and fraud in connection with the financing of the Transurbano public transport project in Guatemala City during Colom's administration.[31]

Initial Cracks in the System

With the exception of Portillo, who was charged and acquitted early on in Guatemala, all of the recent major corruption cases against former presidents, government officials, and companies have come to light in the wake of the 2015 court cases and mass protests that brought down the government of Otto Pérez Molina.

Pérez Molina is first and foremost a military man. He has been an officer of the Kaibil special forces, director of military intelligence, and a military commander in the Ixil triangle region during the Ríos Montt military regime when genocide was being carried out against the Maya Ixil. As Pérez Molina rose in the ranks, he was viewed as a progressive element in that he supported peace negotiations over the endless war favoured by hardline factions, and he became a military representative to the peace negotiations that resulted in the 1996 Peace Accords. He left the Army in 2000, founded the Patriotic Party (PP) the following year, and successfully ran for Congress in 2003. Following his time in Congress during the Berger administration, Pérez Molina ran for president, but lost to Colom. He ran again and won in 2011.[32]

Pérez Molina took office in 2012. Less than a year into his term, a historic verdict shook the foundation of the country and was heard around the world. As soon as his congressional term ended in January 2012, Ríos Montt no longer had the immunity from prosecution bestowed by the office, and he was indicted on charges related to a series of massacres in the Ixil triangle during his 1982-1983 military rule. On May 10, 2013, Ríos Montt was convicted of genocide and crimes against humanity. He was sentenced to eighty years in prison. It was the first and and remains the only time a former head of state has been convicted of genocide in the domestic court system of their own country.

The sentence, conviction, and a chunk of other trial proceedings were later voided by way of technicalities, and a partial retrial was ordered by the Constitutional Court. The ruling sparked accusations of bias and corruption. A separate court determined that Ríos Montt would no longer be required to be present in court due to his age and health, and that he would not have to serve time in prison if convicted.

To many survivors and relatives of victims of genocide, the importance of the fallout paled in comparison to the importance of the initial verdict: genocide had occurred, and Ríos Montt was guilty.

Efraín Ríos Montt died on April 1, 2018. Relatives of the dead and disappeared, survivors, activists, and supporters gathered in the central plaza to remember and honour his victims. The retrial continued, and though Ríos Montt's former head of intelligence was ultimately acquitted later that year, Ríos Montt likely would not have been. The tribunal was unequivocal: the military committed genocide during his rule.

Figure 5. San Rafael Mine Signing. Then-Mining and Energy Minister Erick Archila (left) whispers to then-President Otto Pérez Molina during the signing of the official agreement between the Guatemalan government and Tahoe Resources and Goldcorp's El Escobal silver project via its local subsidiary Minera San Rafael. The signing came two days after six local men were shot by the company's security guards. Guatemala City, Guatemala, April 29, 2013. Photo: James Rodríguez.

The Mafia State Brought to Light

President Otto Pérez Molina, his Vice President Roxana Baldetti, and most of his cabinet ended up in prison before the end of his administration, on charges related to corruption during both Pérez Molina's presidency and the electoral campaign leading up to his election.

Pérez Molina's government wasted no time in taking action in favour of mining companies after he took office in January 2012. Over the course of the year, it issued eight mining exploration licenses for projects around the country to various individuals and companies, including two that had long been at the heart of conflicts. Goldcorp's subsidiary Entre Mares was granted a new exploration license in Sipakapa, in the area of the Marlin mine, and Tahoe Resources' subsidiary Minera San Rafael received the Juan Bosco exploration license that would later be the target of both fierce community resistance and legal action.

The Pérez Molina government's facilitation of mining projects was not limited to exploration. The following year, in 2013, it issued the exploitation permit in the Santa Rosa and Jalapa departments for the

Escobal silver mine. The license came through for then-owner of the mine, Vancouver-based Tahoe Resources, at a time of massive local opposition and a crackdown by security forces.* Years later, that opposition continues stronger than ever and mine operations have been paralyzed by both Constitutional Court legal action and community resistance camp blockades.

The Pérez Molina government also granted an exploitation license in 2013 to CGN for the Niquegua Montufar II nickel mining project in Los Amates, Izabal, across the lake from the company's Fénix mine. The latter was reactivated by the Solway Investment Group in 2014, more than thirty years after its initial production phase. Meanwhile, Goldcorp's Marlin mine was winding down during the Pérez Molina administration amid ongoing local conflict and despite the lack of anything resembling an adequate closure plan.

During the entire time the Patriotic Party government was granting mining licenses and dealing with mining companies, it was plagued to the core by corruption. The first massive corruption scandal hit in April 2015, when the Public Prosecutor's Office and CICIG executed arrest warrants and announced an ongoing investigation into what CICIG dubbed La Línea, a far-reaching criminal network both in and outside the government. Stemming from old military networks, La Línea involved a graft scheme within the customs authority. It would eventually bring down most of Pérez Molina's cabinet, his Vice President Roxana Baldetti, and later that year, Pérez Molina himself.[33]

The La Línea case was just the first of many corruption cases that would be revealed over the next several years, and investigations are far from over. It became increasingly clear that all three branches of government were involved in corruption, as were corporations across many sectors, including mining.

One of the ensuing criminal cases, dubbed Co-optation of the State, is particularly important in that regard. The case, which deals with private sector financing—including by mining companies—of Pérez Molina and the Patriotic Party electoral campaign in exchange for favours once in power, illustrated two key truths, as Nómada journalists Martín Rodríguez Pellecer and Gabriel Woltke wrote: "The PP wasn't a party, it was a criminal mafia. And mafias don't exist in a vacuum. They're nothing without

---

* The mine is now owned by Vancouver-based Pan American Silver.

their national associates."[34] But as subsequent CICIG investigations into political party financing across the spectrum and including the current government have shown, the Patriotic Party clearly is not alone, they wrote: "Corruption is the unifying force of the Guatemalan political system."

The Vices: Baldetti, Maldonado, and Extractive Industry "Good Governance"

Pérez Molina's Vice President Roxana Baldetti was one of the central figures of La Línea. However, during her time in power she was, among many other things, the coordinator and champion of the Extractive Industries Transparency Initiative (EITI) in Guatemala.

In 2014, Guatemala became the second country in all of Latin America to be designated a compliant country by EITI, "the global standard for the good governance of oil, gas and mineral resources."[35] Much of the initiative focuses on the transparency of government revenue, which in the case of mining in Guatemala is primarily collected by the Ministry of Energy and Mines and the customs authority, SAT (Superintendencia de Administración Tributaria / Superintendent of Tax Administration), which was home to the La Línea graft scheme. Baldetti's EITI efforts were supported by the World Bank, the United Nations Development Programme (UNDP), and the Deutsche Gesellschaft für Internationale Zusammenarbeit / German Society for International Cooperation (GIZ), among others.

Goldcorp became an industry representative in the Guatemalan EITI working group, and Tahoe Resources, whose Escobal silver mine in Guatemala has since been taken over by Pan American Silver, has partnered with EITI as well.

Amid massive nationwide protests, Baldetti was forced to resign in 2015, was subsequently arrested for her pivotal role in the La Línea case, and now also faces further charges related to other corruption schemes. In February 2017, she was indicted by a US court on drug trafficking charges, and the US is seeking her extradition, though that will remain on hold while she serves out a prison sentence in Guatemala for another corruption case and awaits a ruling in the La Línea trial.

When Baldetti was forced to step down in 2015, Alejandro Maldonado was appointed Vice President. "One heartbeat away from the presidency and not a single vote cast in my name. Democracy is so overrated." The words were uttered by the Frank Underwood character from the Netflix series *House of Cards*, but they ring just as true for Maldonado. After Pérez Molina was forced to resign and was arrested in September 2015, Maldonado became President of Guatemala without a single vote cast in his name.

Over a span of four decades, Maldonado held top positions in all three branches of government. He was a congressman affiliated with a coup-linked political party with a military wing while INCO was working on setting up its nickel mine. He was a Constitutional Court judge on two occasions, during which time he was accused of endeavouring to ensure impunity in high-profile cases such as Bishop Gerardi's murder and Ríos Montt's role in genocide. And ultimately, he became president.

Ministers of Corruption and Violence

Erick Archila was among the many government figures to go down for corruption. He was the Minister of Energy and Mines during the Pérez Molina administration, which granted licenses for mining projects owned by Canadian companies Skye Resources, Tahoe Resources, and Goldcorp, among others. His initial charges were related to the media corporations he owns, but the corruption was directly linked to the administration of which he was a part. He has also been subject to further legal action and investigations, including by the Comptroller's Office for corruption linked to energy contracts he authorized. Facing charges and a warrant for his arrest, Archila slipped out of the country and became a fugitive. Reports later indicated he was actually living in Miami. In January 2017, Archila was detained in the US on an immigration-related infraction, but was soon released on bail. In December 2020, anti-impunity prosecutors unveiled a new case, "Mechanisms of corruption in the Ministry of Energy and Mines," accusing Archila of orchestrating a corruption ring while Minister and taking more than $10 million in bribes from oil and energy companies in exchange for contracts and concessions.

Mauricio López Bonilla, Pérez Molina's Minister of the Interior, on the other hand, was indicted on drug trafficking charges by the US in February 2017, but is currently in jail in Guatemala. He was forced to resign in 2015 amid the corruption scandals and was later arrested. He was sentenced to more than thirteen years in prison in 2019 for fraud and faces ongoing proceedings in other corruption cases. During his time in office, he oversaw the national police force, which has been involved in countless crackdowns against community residents organizing to oppose imposed mining projects in their lands.

In 2013, the government decreed a state of siege in three municipalities around Tahoe Resources' Escobal silver mine. Previously used to quell opposition to hydroelectric dams in other regions of the country, the state of siege is a state of explicitly institutionalized impunity involving the suspension of certain constitutional rights and freedoms, including some related to detainees and due process. The region around the Escobal mine was suddenly overrun by security forces, which engaged in arbitrary raids of residents' homes, among other actions. Although the state of siege was clearly instituted to crack down on protest and opposition to the mine and to enable further criminalization and intimidation of community leaders, López Bonilla claimed the state of siege was related to terrorism and drug trafficking.[36]

A Goldcorp Executive Is a Fugitive from Justice

In a nutshell, the Co-optation of the State case involves illegal campaign financing of the Patriotic Party by individuals and corporations paying for future favours from the government. When the CICIG and Public Prosecutor's Office first announced the case and initial wave of arrests in 2016, one name among the list of people with arrest warrants that authorities had not yet been able to execute stood out to organizations and communities involved in resistance to mining.

"When the Public Prosecutor's Office report appeared, we heard a name: Eduardo Villacorta. Who is that? Could it be the guy who was a manager for Goldcorp and for the Marlin mine?" That's what Sipakapa community leader Aniseto López thought when he first heard the news. He said this news helped him and others who had been organizing resistance to the mine better understand the strong ties between mining companies and political parties and why the mining business always advanced so quickly and with such support from government figures.

Villacorta started out with Canadian mining company Glamis Gold in 2001, as the manager of the San Martin gold mine in Honduras. After Goldcorp took over and the Marlin mine in Guatemala got going, Villacorta became the company's executive director for the region. In 2009, Goldcorp appointed him Senior Vice President for Central and South America.

According to the Co-optation of the State investigations, Villacorta was to be arrested because he was involved, on behalf of Goldcorp subsidiary Montana Exploradora, in the corruption scandal through illegal financing of the Patriotic Party's campaign in 2011.[37] Goldcorp has been fairly silent about the case, and nearly all traces of Villacorta's name have simply been removed from its website. The company did state that with regard to Villacorta, the case concerned him as an individual and was unrelated to the mining company. According to the Public Prosecutor's Office, however, there is a direct connection. Villacorta stands accused of corruption in his role as a representative of Goldcorp subsidiary Montana Exploradora, a spokesperson for the Public Prosecutor's Office confirmed in 2017.

"Goldcorp financed political parties. It was the cash box of which government officials asked for favours. It had real political power," said Yuri Melini during his tenure as CALAS director.[38] While Villacorta was not technically the company's legal representative in Guatemala, he actually did have the key role with regard to the government. "Eduardo Villacorta was the one to do all the political and diplomatic work" and was the one to make deals with the government and private sector, said Melini. "What he wanted was the mine and for the mine to operate, and he made deals with god and the devil to obtain that outcome," said Melini.

Villacorta, Goldcorp's former Senior Vice President for Central and South America, evaded arrest and remains a fugitive.

Police at the Service of Mining Companies

Transnational mining companies in Guatemala have long relied on state security forces to crack down on opposition, suppress conflicts, and facilitate extraction. In many regards, the relationship between mining corporations, the police, and the military under Pérez Molina's administration was nothing new.

What is new, however, is the paper trail. On the one hand, evidence of corruption piled up against López Bonilla, who ran the Ministry that commands the country's police force, and the case against Villacorta illustrates the direct involvement of at least one mining company in the illegal campaign financing behind the corrupt Pérez Molina government. On the other hand, official documents reveal company requests for police intervention in mining areas both during and following López Bonilla and Pérez Molina's time in power.

Documents I obtained from the Ministry of the Interior via freedom of information requests under Guatemala's Access to Public Information Law illustrate the correspondence and coordination between mining companies and the government for police support and defence of mining company interests, particularly in the case of community conflicts and protests.[*]

In May 2013, CGN nickel mining company president Dmitry Kudryakov formally requested police intervention in El Estor "to offer security in the face of possible acts of vandalism." López Bonilla instructed one of his vice ministers to coordinate the requested support, according to inter-departmental Ministry of the Interior correspondence. Earlier that year, in January, the same Vice Minister of the Interior had informed Kudryakov that police personnel at the local police station in El Estor would be increased to twenty regular police officers and twenty police special forces, in response to actions "taken by local residents due to discontent."

Goldcorp has had similar interactions with the Ministry of the Interior over the years, requesting police intervention in the face of local discontent and protests. In January 2014, Goldcorp subsidiary Entre Mares de Guatemala general manager Julio Mérida requested a police contingent due to local opposition in certain communities in Sipakapa, in the area of the company's Marlin gold mine. "We have received information that this time the opponents don't plan to stop and the lack of police presence facilitates their actions," Mérida wrote. The request was approved.

The prompt facilitation of public security forces for private mining company interests was not limited to the Pérez Molina administration. In May 2017, during the government of Jimmy Morales, who was elected president after Maldonado's transitional time in power, Goldcorp subsidiary Montana Exploradora general manager Alfredo Gálvez Sinibaldi wrote to Francisco Manuel Rivas, the Minister of the Interior. Gálvez Sinibaldi requested police support to deal with local conflict in El Salitre, a community in San Miguel Ixtahuacán, the municipality home to the Marlin mine. The company offered to pay the costs of transportation to the area, "by air if necessary," and food, and offered to "facilitate a space" for the national police officers to stay while in the area. The request was granted.

---

[*] As part of the author's ongoing investigations into mining and governance in Guatemala, she submitted a request to Guatemala's Ministry of the Interior on May 26, 2017 under the country's Public Information Access Law, and on June 23, 2017 she received documents from several units and offices within the Ministry of the Interior in response to the request. The author has kept copies of all relevant documents.

General manager Gálvez Sinibaldi, who made the 2017 request, came to his position through the revolving door between mining companies and the government. Gálvez Sinibaldi was the General Director of Mining during Óscar Berger's government and then Vice Minister during Maldonado's administration.

"There's a conflict of interest there," Melini pointed out, adding that Gálvez Sinibaldi's role in the Berger administration and now directly in a Goldcorp subsidiary is likely no coincidence. "Who was the biggest PR person for Marlin? Who was the greatest promoter of the Marlin project? Óscar Berger," said Melini.

Co-optation of the State Continues

From the decades of working with military dictators engaged in crimes against humanity to relationships with administrations wracked by an explosion of corruption scandals in recent years, mining companies waver very little. They work with whomever needed to secure and advance their projects and profits, regardless of violence, corruption, or impunity—or all three, which is often the case.

The Morales government that came to power following Maldonado was soon implicated in corruption scandals, including accusations of illegal campaign financing against the president himself. In response, Morales and his allies launched a sustained campaign to shut down CICIG, the body leading investigations and prosecution of high-level corruption cases. The Guatemalan Special Prosecutor's Office against Impunity / Fiscalía Especial contra la Impunidad (FECI), which worked alongside the international commission, continues its work, but has also been subject to sustained attacks. FECI's investigations into Morales continued when he left office in January 2020, but Morales regained immunity from prosecution hours later when he was sworn in to the Central American Parliament.

CICIG's work to dismantle clandestine networks of corruption and parallel power was far from over when it was shut down. The Cuerpos Ilegales y Aparatos Clandestinos de Seguridad / Illegal Clandestine Security Apparatuses (CIACS) that developed and set down roots under military rule have co-opted and captured the Guatemalan state, CICIG noted upon presenting one of its final thematic reports.[39]

"CIACS have nested in the majority of State entities, including the executive, legislative, and judicial branches; many municipalities and even in the bodies in control of the State. To achieve this, they have distorted and utilized democratic institutions to their own benefit, perverting elections, the political party system and various mechanisms of participation and representation," according to CICIG.[40] In that ongoing context, Alejandro Giammattei took office as president in 2020 and his administration is expected to continue to back transnational mining companies with political, economic, and security support. A decade before taking office, Giammattei spent ten months in pre-trial detention for extrajudicial executions of inmates during his tenure as director of the prison system under the Berger administration, but he was ultimately acquitted. After his election, he chose an ex-military official as his Minister of the Interior and a former president of the country's powerful private sector alliance, Comité de Asociaciones Agrícolas, Comerciales, Industriales y Financieras / Coordinating Committee of Agricultural, Commercial, Industrial, and Financial Associations (CACIF), as his Minister of the Economy.

Many Guatemalans expected Giammattei to be more of the same after Morales, but Guatemalan law professor Oswaldo Samayoa viewed the change in government differently. Giammattei's administration will be something Guatemala has seen twice before, specifically under Arzú and Berger, according to Samayoa. Giammattei's circle and especially his appointment of a former CACIF president represents the direct return of the private sector elite to power, not as a behind-the-scenes force but directly in control of the public administration to govern according to corporate interests, he said.[41]

Despite it all, communities and local movements continue to mobilize against mining, mounting legal challenges, organizing road blockades and resistance camps, and demanding justice for criminalization, attacks, and murders against them.

At the national level, there have been cracks in the system of corruption and impunity, but so far, that's all they are: cracks in the system. On the ground, communities have to confront both the immediate projects threatening their lives and lands and an entire system that considers them collateral damage standing in the way of profits. As such, their struggle is both one of local resistance and a part of broader collective struggles for systemic change in the country, and that will continue no matter what.

When You Benefit from Destruction: United Church of Canada Pension Fund and Goldcorp

Jackie McVicar

In January 2019, I visited Marlin mine–affected communities where the Maritimes Conference "Mining the Connections" Committee and United for Mining Justice donated more than $6,000 that was raised through a Restitution Project that was created in 2018 for victims of Goldcorp Inc.'s Marlin mine.[42] This was a small, symbolic contribution raised by churches, United Church Conferences, and individuals who felt compelled to respond to the crisis that Indigenous Maya communities are facing after close to fifteen years of gold and silver extraction without consent in their territory.

The communities were never meaningfully consulted prior to, nor throughout, operations of the mine. Not surprisingly, when I visited, the communities had not been told of the recent sale of Goldcorp or what long-term impacts, if any, that would have on the mining-affected communities. At the Marlin mine, Goldcorp processed an average of 6,500 tons of rock per day, turning out higher than expected amounts of gold and silver at the mine that started extraction in 2005.

Throughout its operations, locals repeatedly and adamantly reported the negative impacts and severe human rights violations happening near the Marlin mine. The story of some thirteen years of corporate harms and violations, corruption, and impunity were well documented at the mine, the first large scale open-pit mine in Guatemala, a country ravaged by genocidal war against Indigenous nations by economic and military powers, both national and international, keen on accumulating wealth through the dispossession of territory.

During the genocides of the 1980s, hundreds of thousands of Indigenous Maya people were displaced from their territory and collective property rights were privatized by force. Land and water were illegally bought and sold and ended up in the hands of large agribusiness, mining, and hydroelectric companies. The genocides that result from colonialism and capitalism have been particularly harsh in Guatemala in the cruelty of the massacres in the early 1980s, but the legacy, and system, of destruction, dispossession, and annihilation go back centuries.

Thirteen Years of Violence, Human Rights Violations, and Environmental and Health Harms

For more than a decade, unions, universities, grassroots organizations, international human rights organizations, and churches have condemned the way that Indigenous peoples were tricked into first accepting Goldcorp's mine into remote villages in the northern highlands, and later the series of negative environmental and social impacts it had. Falling-down homes, social conflict and violence, family breakdown, water contamination, skin rashes and never-seen-before illnesses, drying up springs and water sources, destruction of ancestral and ceremonial sites and medicines, and air contamination were just some of the serious complaints that were documented.

Assassination attempts, increased military and police presence, and criminalization of land defenders all intensified. People began to feel that they were not safe in their homes or on roads where they would normally greet their neighbours. People who spoke out against the mine would hide in their homes when trucks drove by and were afraid to go to the local market for fear of verbal or physical violence. With few options, many were forced to migrate to the south coast or to the USA. The open pit where gold mining once happened is now full of dirt and trees, but the deep connection to the earth, its medicines, its life-force, has been deeply changed.

Mining and Corruption

Local and national governments and the company downplayed their corruption and collusion from the start, even though it was well documented and denounced by locals and the Public Prosecutor's office with the help of the UN-backed International Commission against Impunity in Guatemala (CICIG). And the deceit and lack of transparency that served as the company's way of working continue. According to locals, the company has not adequately informed the communities surrounding the Marlin mine of the closure plans, or who is even responsible for their implementation. The long-term environmental and health impacts created by contamination have been left to the community to remedy. The "state of the art" hospital, that Goldcorp at one point showed off to investors with the help of the Canadian government as an act of corporate social responsibility, has closed up; it now houses the most basic of health services with no regular doctors, nurses, midwives, medicines—or, at times, even electricity. Through Inter-American Development Bank loans received by the State to entice the mining company—not company good will—the once dusty road to San Miguel Ixtahuacán is now paved, but the communities keep paying the price for the so-called development they received.

Investor Complicity and Profiteering

The United Church Pension Plan refused to divest from Goldcorp for more than ten years, even after knowing of the devastating impacts that the Marlin mine has had on church partners and allies in Guatemala. They chose to engage in dialogue with the company—not the impacted communities—which led to no visible or tangible change for the better. They argued "fiduciary duty" and chose to invest in a project that sought to destroy the lives and livelihoods of local communities. The resistance never gave up though; the voices of dissent were never completely silenced, and though there is deep injustice and deep sadness, they never gave up on their spirituality, their connection to Mother Earth. They are recuperating their ceremonies, coming back to who they are, because the mine also led to breakdown of the culture and identity of the people.

"Wake up, humanity, there is no time left!"

On May 1, 2019, over fifty international organizations sent a letter to the World Bank, urging the financial institution to prioritize recycling, circular economy, public transit, and other non-mining solutions as the primary components of its agenda—not business as usual and the promotion of the mining sector.[43] The letter noted, "Metals mining is currently one of the world's dirtiest industries, responsible for at least 10% of anthropogenic greenhouse gas emissions, and over 50% of all toxic solid wastes in many producing countries."[44] Quite simply, mining is not the way forward. We simply cannot count on it as a sustainable way to build the world we need.

As Berta Cáceres, a Lenca leader who was murdered for her opposition to extractivism in her territory, warned just months before her death, "Wake up, humanity, there is no time left!"[45] Greta Thunberg, Autumn Peltier, and people around the world are urging us to heed Berta's call. As Greta says, "Act like your house is on fire. Because it is."[46]

The tragedy at the Marlin mine is heartbreaking. It is also completely unjust and racist that Maya Mam and Sipakapense territory has been destroyed by a Canadian company, thanks to investments from the Canada

Pension Plan (CPP), churches, unions, and "ethical funds," while those who are left to pick up the pieces are the very people who never wanted the project in the first place.

As we struggle to live in a right way and in a relationship with all our relations, we know that we need a new relationship, not a "reconciliation"— for as Indigenous rights activist, spiritual teacher, and transformational change maker Sherri Mitchell argues, colonial and Indigenous nations have never had a conciliatory relationship.[47] We must start anew. We need to imagine and live in a way that deeply reflects our values of love and justice for the earth and each other. As we witness the devastating impacts of Canadian colonialism, glaringly evident through the mining sector, we must urgently use our power to change.

Chapter 3

Confronting Goldcorp at Every Step of the Destruction and Repression

T he writings included in this chapter—Annie Hylton's comprehensive overview piece to mining struggles in Guatemala, Jeff
Abbott's piercing look at the aftermath of Goldcorp's Marlin
mine after it was closed in 2018, along with an interview with and *testimonios* of four courageous Maya Mam community defenders—set out how, for
over thirteen years (2005-2018), courageous Maya Mam women and men,
young and old, waged a dignified, visionary community defence struggle
against the illegal, violent, and harmful mining operation of Goldcorp Inc.,
which was at the time one of the three wealthiest, most powerful gold mining companies in the world. (Goldcorp has since merged with Newmont
Mining, the most powerful and wealthiest gold mining company in the
world.)

These writings, interviews, and *testimonios* show how over the course
of this struggle, community members suffered and lost in just about every
conceivable way in terms of human, community, and environmental
well-being.

Entire mountaintops and forests were destroyed to make way for
Goldcorp's open-pit, cyanide leaching operation. Hundreds of people were
illegally and sometimes violently evicted from their homes and communities. Humans and animals suffered health harms, including death, due
to mining-related contamination of water sources. Women and men were
shot, some killed, and otherwise attacked and wounded, and many had
trumped-up criminal charges filed against them. Hundreds of homes were
cracked, and some crumbled to the ground due to the use of explosives.
The local agriculture-based economy was destroyed. Families and communities were divided and rent asunder. Some community members were

forced to flee into exile, trying to cross Mexico and enter the US and maybe scratch out a living there.

The flip side of this on-the-ground lived reality is that over the course of these thirteen years, Goldcorp's management, board of directors, shareholders, and investors benefited massively in the only way of concern to them: personal and institutional financial gain.

There is no silver lining—let alone justice or reparations—for the suffering and loss experienced by local Mam communities. Yet it needs to be clearly acknowledged that their environmental and territorial defence struggle helped expose the blatantly pro-mining role of the Canadian government through its embassy in Guatemala, a role which included openly using Canada's political leverage to promote Goldcorp's interests while ignoring or sometimes outright denying the widespread harms, violence, and suffering. The courage and resolve of Mam communities helped further expose the oftentimes illegal, violent, and rapacious nature in which Goldcorp chooses to operate its businesses in places like Guatemala, which seem far away to Canadians.

Their human rights defence struggle helped educate people across

Figure 6. Protest During 2007 Goldcorp AGM. People protesting Goldcorp's mining-linked violence and harms in Guatemala and Honduras gather outside the offices where Goldcorp's annual general meeting is taking place with a sign that reads: "Goldcorp: No more mining terrorism!" Vancouver, Canada, May 2, 2007. Photo: James Rodríguez.

Canada and the US—many of whom came on fact-finding delegations to the Goldcorp-harmed communities of San Miguel Ixtahuacán, many of whom heard Maya Mam community defenders on speaking tours across Canada and the US—as to the harmful, violent, and oftentimes illegal policies and actions of the Canadian and US governments and companies like Goldcorp in places like Guatemala.

Is Canada to Blame for Human Rights Abuses in Guatemala?
Annie Hylton

Rosa Elbira Coc Ich says she was cooking at home when the men with guns came on January 17, 2007. The women and children of her village were busy preparing food and tending to domestic tasks, while the men farmed in the fields.

In a signed affidavit, Coc Ich describes seeing the men with guns before: about a week prior, hundreds of them swept up the remote region of eastern Guatemala, burning homes down to charred rubble while evicting at least five Maya Q'eqchi' communities. Coc Ich's community of Lote Ocho, a small farming village about a six-hour drive northeast of Guatemala City, had been targeted. The Guatemalan Nickel Company (CGN), a subsidiary of Canadian mining company Skye Resources, which amalgamated with Hudbay Minerals in 2008, claimed to own those lands.

Coc Ich, a Maya Q'eqchi' woman, had spent all of her life on those ancestral lands before the mining company security guards, police, and military came to destroy close to one hundred wood and thatch houses. She fled with her neighbours farther up in the mountains, to hide in the highlands. A few days after the eviction, when the armed men left, the villagers returned to rebuild. They collected plastic, nylon, string, and bamboo to repair their huts, and they tended to their fields of beans, corn, squash, and cardamom.

The armed men then paid the village a second visit, on January 17. As the vehicles approached, filled with hundreds of military, police, and mining company security guards, some villagers began to run while others tried to gather their belongings. Coc Ich, twenty-two at that time, says she stayed inside her home, the hut she had begun to rebuild.

Coc Ich describes how the men barged in, and a police officer pointed a gun at her head, asked where her husband was, and threatened to kill her. Coc Ich replied that she didn't know. The men began smashing things, including her bowls and cooking utensils. Then she was thrown to the ground, and her clothes, a traditional Maya blouse and skirt, were ripped off. She was held down; her mouth was covered. But she says she could see, affixed to some of their uniforms, chest patches that read "CGN" (though Hudbay argues that there were no CGN personnel or private security contractors at the scene that day); others were military men, dressed in fatigues, and national police officers, in black uniforms. "I thought only one of them would rape me, but instead all nine men raped me, one after the other, on the floor of my home," she says in the affidavit.

Coc Ich is one of eleven women in the community of Lote Ocho who say they were gang raped that day, in similar circumstances, and are suing Hudbay Minerals. Two of the women were pregnant—one suffered a miscarriage, the other gave birth to a stillborn baby. (Coc Ich had a number of miscarriages, after the rapes, until she was able to conceive a baby daughter in 2017.) We return to this case in chapter 4.

Canadian Government Mining Push

Coc Ich lives in the northeast of the country near the Fénix mine, but her story is not exceptional. Diodora Hernández, a woman who lives in the remote western highlands, near Goldcorp's gold mine in San Miguel Ixtahuacán, was shot in the head. And seven men from the southwest, near Tahoe Resources' silver mine, also claim to have been injured when security personnel shot at them. All are victims of the Canadian government's failure to regulate and standardize corporate behaviour abroad.

The year 1996 marked the formal end of three-and-a-half decades of state repression and genocides against the mainly Maya population and a small armed conflict in Guatemala. It also marked the beginning of a more aggressive neoliberal development agenda, partly through licenses with Canadian extractive companies. A year later, Guatemala amended its national mining law to encourage foreign investment, a decision that would fuel conflict between companies and communities for decades to come.

According to geographers Catherine Nolin and Jacqui Stephens, who studied the work of Canadian mining companies in Guatemala from 2004 to 2008, Canada's "pro-business, pro-mining stance, through its embassy's activities," has shaped Guatemala's development model and, in turn, has helped plunder the resources of Indigenous and local communities.[1]

Documents received through Access to Information requests show that the embassy was active in creating a favourable environment for the operation of Canadian companies.* This included forming ties with Otto Pérez Molina, Guatemala's president from January 2012 to September 2015 who was imprisoned in 2015 for his alleged involvement in a multi-million-dollar customs corruption scandal (see Cuffe in chapter 2).

Pérez Molina is an ex-military and intelligence officer, trained at the US Army School of the Americas. The school trained several of Latin America's dictators over the past fifty years, and it has since closed—though a very similar institution is now open in the same location. According to the National Security Archive, Pérez Molina was allegedly involved in "scorched earth campaigns," which annihilated entire Indigenous villages during the country's war.[2]

In 2011, a couple of weeks after Pérez Molina was elected president, an embassy attaché sent an email to then-Canadian ambassador Hugues Rousseau about a meeting with the future Guatemalan mining minister, which included: "The recently elected government and the current conjuncture is being seen by the mining sector as a good momentum to move forward on the discussions about the mining law and its implications. Apparently, the extractive sector . . . is showing genuine interest to initiate dialogue with the government." Rousseau responded, "I spoke with opm [Otto Pérez Molina] tonight about a request [redacted]. I also told him we were eating with his chosen mining minister. Very happy with our approach."

About a year later, in February 2012, the vice president of corporate affairs of Canadian mining giant Goldcorp—one of the first Canadian companies to operate a mine in Guatemala's post-conflict period—went before a Canadian parliamentary committee meeting and described what appeared to be the expectation of a close level of co-operation between the Canadian and the Guatemalan governments:

> In Guatemala, I would like to see them modernize their mining regulations. That would add to the stability of the environment within which we deal in Guatemala. Can I go as Goldcorp and start training the Ministry of

---

* As part of the author's ongoing investigations into mining and governance in Guatemala, she submitted a request to Guatemala's Ministry of the Interior on May 26, 2017 under the country's Public Information Access Law, and on June 23, 2017 she received documents from several units and offices within the Ministry of the Interior in response to the request. The author has kept copies of all relevant documents.

Energy and Mines? I can't do that. The credibility behind that is not right. However, I think it makes a lot of sense to have a government institution come in to take our experience here in Canada—Natural Resources Canada in terms of their experience—and bring that experience to Guatemala.

Documents shared by Shin Imai, an emeritus law professor at York University and director of the Justice and Corporate Accountability Project, suggest that the embassy played a key role in these industry gatherings.[3] At one point, over the issue of land confrontations between Maya communities and Canadian companies, the embassy, in its internal communications, even referred to the Indigenous people as "invaders."

At least four security groups hired at Canadian-owned mining sites in Guatemala have been accused of having questionable human rights records. Some of their members are said to have trained in counterterrorism, to be operating without weapons licenses or registration with the state, or to have ties to the Guatemalan military during the country's war.[4]

The UN-backed Commission for Historical Clarification, set up after the war to investigate human rights violations, found that state forces and related paramilitary groups committed 93 percent of documented violations during the state-sponsored terror and genocide; now, some of these same forces are working privately in the mining industry.[5]

Hudbay Minerals Repression

Mynor Padilla González, for example, is a former lieutenant-colonel in the Guatemalan army who later headed security for Hudbay/CGN. He did so as part of the security company whose personnel were allegedly involved in the gang rapes of Coc Ich and other women in Lote Ocho. Padilla is on trial in Guatemala for the murder of Adolfo Ich Chamán, an Indigenous community leader and teacher who was allegedly hacked with a machete and shot in 2009 by Hudbay/CGN's security personnel (see chapter 4). One of Ich Chamán's five children, José, witnessed the incident and described it in a sworn court document:

> Approximately 10 or 15 security personnel surrounded my father, and continued to lead him away. . . . My father began to resist. He didn't want to go with the security personnel, so they started to hit him with their guns. My father raised his arm to defend himself, and one of the security personnel struck my father in the arm with a machete. The machete blow almost cut

my father's right arm off. Mr. Padilla then shot my father in the head, and he fell to the ground. . . . I could see that he was dead.[6]

The day Ich Chamán was killed, protests erupted related to land disputes with Hudbay, which had amalgamated with Skye Resources in 2008. Padilla González allegedly led a group of men with bulletproof vests, machetes, guns, and tear gas to curb the protests. Padilla González is also charged with shooting a man named German Chub Choc, who had been watching a soccer game and was allegedly shot without provocation; German survived, but he is now paralyzed and has lost the use of his left lung.

Although Guatemala is formally on the other side of the conflict, it remains a country in which seeking access to justice comes at a cost. According to Human Rights Watch, "98 percent of crimes in Guatemala do not result in prosecutions."[7] In a later report, Human Rights Watch concluded, "corruption within the justice system, combined with intimidation against judges and prosecutors, contributes to high levels of impunity."[8]

Canadian mining companies around the globe, some listed on the Toronto Stock Exchange, have also escaped any kind of reckoning. They have been at the centre of controversies involving allegations of environmental damage, slavery, child labour, mass sexual assault, and murder—and have even been accused of indirectly financing terrorism. According to Washington-based think tank Council on Hemispheric Affairs, "the Canadian government actively assists the extractive industry without requiring that their mining companies respect the environment and human rights."[9]

Hudbay Minerals Lawsuits

To date, only the new ownership of Tahoe Resources has worked to settle one of these cases. In July 2019, Pan American Silver issued a formal apology on behalf of Tahoe Resources and arrived at a legal settlement.[10] Otherwise, none of the companies has been held legally responsible for corporate or employee misconduct abroad, nor are there any effective mechanisms in place to investigate such complaints. That may soon change. With the help of Canadian attorneys at the Toronto-based Klippensteins law firm, German Chub Choc, Angélica Choc (the widow of Adolfo Ich Chamán), Rosa Coc Ich, and ten other women from Lote Ocho are suing Hudbay in Canada for negligence, and seeking damages.[11]

The case is the first of its kind in Canadian courts. In a 2013 decision, an Ontario Superior Court Justice, for the first time in Canadian legal history, opened the possibility for a Canadian company to be held accountable for the human rights abuses of its subsidiaries abroad. The attorneys for the victims hailed this as an unprecedented step in Canadian corporate accountability: "Corporations be warned—this case clearly shows that Canadian companies can be sued in Canadian courts for alleged human rights atrocities committed at their foreign operations."[12]

Scott Brubacher, director of corporate communications for Hudbay, had a different opinion. In an email, he wrote the same text that is posted on Hudbay's website: "The ruling did not make any determinations with respect to the facts of the cases, does not set any legal precedent and simply said that, if the facts as pleaded by the plaintiffs are true (which Hudbay vigorously disputes), it is not plain and obvious that the cases would fail."

As the plaintiffs await their day in court, ten years on and counting, their situation remains difficult. The women of Lote Ocho claimed they have been threatened, intimidated, and called "prostitutes." On a Friday evening, in September 2016, just after midnight, Angélica Choc, the widow of Ich Chamán, was sleeping at home in El Estor with two of her children when two unidentified assailants fired shots at the cinderblock wall of her home. "We interpreted that as a clear threat and warning to her, and we think it's motivated entirely by this lawsuit," said Cory Wanless, co-counsel for the plaintiffs.

The town of El Estor is surrounded by mountains and sits on the northern shore of Guatemala's largest lake, Lago de Izabal, a 320-kilometre drive from the capital. One hour west of El Estor, from the main road, it takes Rosa Coc Ich more than two hours to walk up the mountain to Lote Ocho.

Like those in Lote Ocho, the Maya Q'eqchi' who inhabit the municipality of El Estor have been in conflict with Canadian mining companies for years over contested land. The Indigenous people had already been evicted from their ancestral territory during the war by the dictatorial military government, in part to make way for mining. But in 2011, according to several statements of claim against Hudbay, Guatemala's highest court ruled that Maya Q'eqchi' communities have valid legal rights to those contested lands.

INCO and the Panzós Massacre

Near El Estor, the land around the Fénix nickel mine has been passed from one Canadian company to another since the 1960s. The original land concessions, which included the Lote Ocho territory where Coc Ich lives, were granted by the military regime following a US-backed coup in 1954. Six years after the coup, the Canadian International Nickel Company (INCO) began negotiations to build an open-pit nickel mine; the same year, an armed conflict erupted between the Guatemalan military regime and leftist groups. INCO was granted a mining lease in 1965 through its subsidiary, EXMIBAL.

A movement soon emerged to block the contract. The Commission for Historical Clarification (CEH) report on state violence says that the contract was seen by intellectuals and political opponents as a business deal meant to fill the pockets of the political and military elite.[13] The report found that, in the early seventies, Guatemala's former president, Colonel Carlos Manuel Arana Osorio, suspended constitutional guarantees and used mass detention and death-squad executions to quell opposition—some of which purportedly involved INCO/EXMIBAL employees. Arana Osorio was already known colloquially as "the butcher of Zacapa" for his earlier brutal counterinsurgency campaign.

On May 29, 1978, approximately seven hundred Indigenous Q'eqchi' people from neighbouring villages gathered in the town square of Panzós, a town not far from Lote Ocho. They were protesting the land sales to INCO and their ousting from the land their families had lived and worked on for around a century. According to Amnesty International, soldiers encircled the town square and opened fire on them.[14] It is estimated that more than one hundred people were killed, and some may have drowned as they attempted to flee. The casualties, however, are difficult to count: the army sealed off the town, and the dead bodies were dumped into a mass grave. According to Amnesty International, some observers said that the killings were connected to the fact that nickel and oil had recently been discovered in the area.[15]

The massacre incited some of the survivors and their descendants, including those of Coc Ich's generation, to become involved in land disputes with INCO's successors, Skye Resources and Hudbay, decades later. "On any given day you can go into the community of Lote Ocho and say, 'How many of you have family members who were killed in Panzós?' and a significant number of people will raise their hands," says Grahame Russell, a Canadian activist and attorney.[16]

INCO's operations were halted in the 1980s, in the midst of the country's three decades of conflict. Between 1960 and 1996 the CEH estimates that more than two hundred thousand people, mainly Indigenous, were murdered or disappeared, and many more were displaced in Guatemala's counterinsurgency operations and scorched earth campaigns.[17] The Commission found that it was Maya women who bore the full brunt of institutionalized violence.[18] "Rape of women, during torture or before being murdered, was a common practice aimed at destroying one of the most intimate and vulnerable aspects of the individual's dignity."[19]

Doing Business with the Military—Past and Present

The conflict formally ended in 1996 with the signing of the Peace Accords, but for the people in Lote Ocho, some of the same land disputes and violent conflicts continued, with many of the same political and military figures still active in the country—including Padilla González and Pérez Molina.

The collaboration between large multinational extractive companies and former military officials is common in Guatemala. According to Otto Argueta's 2013 book on the proliferation of private security in Guatemala, private security guards outnumber police by approximately five to one.[20]

Coc Ich's legal complaint against Hudbay for negligence and for the sexual violence she and other women suffered asserts that the company "knew or should have known, that individuals who were former members of the Guatemalan military and paramilitary groups during the Guatemalan Civil War were employed as part of Skye's Fenix Security Personnel."[21]

As confirmed by military documents, Mynor Padilla González, the head of Hudbay/CGN's security, was in the Guatemalan army from 1981 until 2004. Hudbay/CGN also contracted with a company called Integración Total, whose personnel allegedly carried weapons without licenses and registration, and were hired without background checks, according to the Ontario civil claims case (which Hudbay disputes).[22]

Scott Brubacher, the director of corporate communications at Hudbay, says that publicly available documents report that nobody was present in the village the day of the evictions, meaning the alleged sexual assaults never occurred—and did not involve Hudbay/CGN security personnel. What's more, "Hudbay did not have any ownership position in CGN at the time these alleged events are said to have occurred."

After Skye Resources purchased the Fénix project from INCO in 2004, it amalgamated with Hudbay in 2008. According to the Ontario court's judgment, Hudbay is legally responsible for Skye's legal liabilities after its amalgamation.

Voluntary Accountability

In a response to the court cases posted on its website, Hudbay said its former subsidiary, CGN, had approved a formal human rights policy. Brubacher confirms that Hudbay had committed to the *Voluntary Principles on Security and Human Rights* in 2011, which calls on companies to do a risk assessment of the environment in which they operate, to "consider the available human rights records of public security forces, paramilitaries, local and national law enforcement, as well as the reputation of private security."[23]

These are the same principles to which other Canadian mining companies have signed on, but they are entirely voluntary, and critics say that the Canadian government does not require adequate oversight or accountability for their violation. The government prefers, instead, to allow companies to adhere to voluntary guidelines under its Corporate Social Responsibility (CSR) framework.

Canadian officials in Ottawa and the embassy in Guatemala declined numerous interview requests to speak over the phone or in person about mining in Guatemala, answering questions only by email. "It is Canada's view that voluntary CSR initiatives advance public policy objectives in a more flexible, expeditious, and less costly way than regulation or rigid legislative regimes," Amy Mills, former spokesperson for Global Affairs Canada, explained.[24]

Two other Canadian mining companies in Guatemala—Goldcorp Inc. and Tahoe Resources—have adopted those same voluntary principles, while their private security companies have also been caught up in alleged human rights abuses.

Diodora Hernández Is Shot in the Head

Around four hundred kilometres west of Coc Ich's home, Diodora Hernández is embroiled in a similar struggle. In the mountainous northwestern highlands of Guatemala, a few hours' drive from the Mexican border, Goldcorp, headquartered in Vancouver, operated an open-pit mountaintop removal gold mine from 2005 to 2017. The Marlin mine and its industrial facilities are located in San Miguel Ixtahuacán and neighbouring Sipakapa, where Indigenous people live in scattered villages.

Hernández, an elderly Mayan Mam woman, is an outspoken opponent of the mine. Like others in the remote region, she subsists on farming. She is in her mid-sixties; her face is weathered, some of her teeth are missing, and she has one functioning eye—but she has the energy of someone half her age. She describes, in Mam, how her land has been passed down through her family for generations. While others in the region sold off their lands to the mining company, Hernández refused.

On July 7, 2010, two men shot Diodora in the head at point-blank range, just outside her small adobe hut. The bullet entered her right eye and exited her skull near her right ear. She lost sight in the eye and hearing in the ear, and half of her face is partially paralyzed.

When asked about the incident, Goldcorp's director of corporate affairs, Dominique Ramirez, told me, "In all cases we co-operate with local police for investigations and I'm sure that was the case in this case as well."[25] After years of pressure from the human rights activist group Rights Action, Goldcorp admitted in a letter that one of the suspected men was a former employee of Goldcorp's subsidiary and the other worked for a mine contractor. Yet, despite international and local pressure, the public prosecutor did not advance an investigation into Hernández's case. Hernández still lives on her property tending to her cows and sheep.

Nearby in the municipality of San Miguel Ixtahuacán, on a warm afternoon early in 2016, nearly forty people from a group opposing Goldcorp's Marlin mine met to share similar stories. Elderly women in bright traditional Maya clothing, men in straw cowboy hats, mothers breastfeeding their newborns, and children eating mango pops gathered in a building on the outskirts of town. It was the same type of meeting mine opponents have been organizing for over a decade, since the mine began construction in 2004 under the ownership of Canadian mining company Glamis Gold, which merged with Goldcorp in 2006. They spoke of physical attacks, excessive use of force, and kidnapping attempts. In their view, each was the cost of speaking out against the mine.

In 2004, Indigenous communities in San Marcos declared that the mining license violated "the collective rights of the [I]ndigenous peoples who inhabit our territories." An Indigenous group in a community 150 kilometres away from the mine then blockaded the Pan-American Highway to prevent equipment from entering the mine. The government response, according to press reports, was to deploy more than one thousand soldiers and police. Up to twenty people were allegedly injured and Raúl Castro Bocel, an Indigenous farmer, was killed.

A few months later, Alvaro Benigno Sánchez López, a twenty-three-year-old, was attacked and killed after attending a concert in San Miguel Ixtahuacán. Employees of the Golan Group, the mine's private security contractor, allegedly shot and killed him, then pressured his father not to bring charges. To date, it seems nobody has been charged for either incident, even though Goldcorp's 2010 own independent human rights assessment report confirmed the existence of the killings.[26]

An organization drawing on communities around the mine presented a report to the Canadian Embassy detailing a number of issues with Goldcorp's behaviour. The embassy received it on March 28, 2012. "We did not hear back," said one member of the group. "We are still looking for justice in our communities."[27]

Tahoe Resources (Child of Goldcorp)

On a map of Guatemala, a third Canadian mining site completes a triangle between where Coc Ich and Hernández live, each of them representing disparate places, but similar struggles, across the country. In 2013, in the south of Guatemala, locals had assembled outside of the Escobal mine to protest the presence of the Minera San Rafael company, a subsidiary of Tahoe Resources, which at the time had deep ties to Goldcorp (see chapter 5).

The company's private security personnel—employed by the Golan Group, the same company used by Goldcorp—allegedly opened fire on them. The head of security, Alberto Rotondo, was caught on wiretaps calling the protestors "faggots" and "sons of bitches," and discussing the shootings.[*] They fired pepper spray, buckshot, and rubber bullets, according to a legal complaint filed in the Supreme Court of British Columbia in 2014.[28]

Seven men suffered injuries, the most severe being the shooting of eighteen-year-old Luis Fernando García Monroy in the face and back. He needed facial reconstruction surgery.

Rotondo then ordered his men to falsify accounts of the shooting. "We're saying, 'Nothing happened here,'" he said. "The version is: they entered and they attacked us. And we repelled them, right?"[†]

---

[*] See the affidavit at miningwatch.ca/sites/default/files/affidavit_wiretap_transcripts_filed_23jan15.pdf.

[†] See the affidavit at miningwatch.ca/sites/default/files/

In June 2014, some of these victims lodged a civil complaint in Canada for battery. The British Columbia Supreme Court initially dismissed the case because it would be too expensive to conduct the trial in Canada, and Guatemala would be the "appropriate forum."* But with the help of Canadian attorneys Joe Fiorante and Matt Eisenbrandt, the decision was successfully appealed in January 2015. The Court of Appeal found "there is some measurable risk that the appellants will encounter difficulty in receiving a fair trial against a powerful international company whose mining interests in Guatemala align with the political interests of the Guatemalan state."[29]

Tom Fudge, vice president of Tahoe Resources' Guatemala operations in 2016, concedes the company made mistakes, but says a lot of the conflict around the mine had been driven by "power plays and efforts at extortion"[30] by local leaders. Fudge, who has decades of experience in the mining industry, believes in the positive impact that his industry can have on communities. "I'm not a monster, but I believe in mining," he said. In mining, when things are good, "you probably have too easy an access to capital," he said.

Fudge said the company has always had an active CSR program, which now includes the standards set out in the *Voluntary Principles on Security and Human Rights*, among others.[31] The Canadian government's CSR program promotes a number of different voluntary frameworks, including those established by the United Nations, the International Finance Corporation, and the Organisation for Economic Co-operation and Development. According to Fudge, the company's policies largely align with the Canadian government's CSR vision, but, he said, following so many guidelines is confusing. "Sometimes I get a little dizzy trying to remember what we are complying with and what's the difference between them," he said.[32]

In April 2013, Ambassador Rousseau was photographed with President Pérez Molina as an honorary witness for a royalty agreement between the Guatemalan government and Tahoe Resources in Guatemala City. The signing happened two days after private security officers at the mine allegedly shot and injured the locals who later brought the case forward in Canada.[33]

"They have been criminal. How they've acted in Guatemala has been criminal," says Pedro Rafael Maldonado Flores, referring to the role of the

---

affidavit_wiretap_transcripts_filed_23jan15.pdf.
* See bccourts.ca/jdb-txt/ca/17/00/2017BCCA0039.htm.

Canadian Embassy.[34] As the then-coordinator of the Guatemalan Centre for Environmental, Social and Legal Action (CALAS) he represented communities in lawsuits against Tahoe's mining operations in Guatemala. He says he heard gunshots outside of his office, had his apartment broken into, and received numerous death threats—so he keeps his security guard close by. In November 2016, one of CALAS's employees was assassinated (no one appears to have yet been charged for the incident).

* * *

In May 2015, Rosa Elbira Coc Ich, Angélica Choc, and German Chub Choc, some of the plaintiffs in the Hudbay lawsuits, travelled to Toronto from Guatemala to address Hudbay's directors and shareholders at the company's Annual General Meeting. Angélica Choc shared the story of her husband's death. "My question for you is: Do you acknowledge the harms suffered by me, Rosa, German, and our families and communities? And what will you do to address these harms?" So far, those calls have not been answered to anyone's satisfaction—not by the company nor by the Canadian government.

After Coc Ich and her community were evicted from their lands in Lote Ocho, they returned to their homes. They fear more violence, and the ownership of their lands is still in dispute. Despite roughly ten years of reliving her experience before Canadian courts, Coc Ich has said she has little faith in the legal system in Guatemala—a system that evicted her community from the land of which they say they are the rightful owners. Her only chance for justice, she says, is in Canada.

Diodora Hernández and Goldcorp Inc.: A Stark Contrast

Grahame Russell, Catherine Nolin, and James Rodríguez

On May 14, 2016 we hiked across open fields in the Maya Mam village of San José de la Esperanza to where Diodora was tending to her cows and sheep, as she has always done. We stood in the shade of an adobe hut with Diodora Hernández, her daughter and granddaughter, and with Aniseto López of Frente de Defensa San Miguelenese / San Miguel Ixtahuacán Defense Front (FREDEMI) who translated for us from Mam to Spanish.

With no right eye, no hearing in her right ear, no water running through the one tap in her home, no investigation or justice for the murder attempt on her life, Diodora will still not sell her land to Goldcorp, Inc. Her land sits in the path of where Goldcorp—and its Guatemalan subsidiary Montana Exploradora—had hoped to expand their initial open-pit mining operation; now, tunnels snake underground.

On July 7, 2010, two Goldcorp mine employees tried to assassinate Diodora, shooting her in the right eye. The bullet exited by her right ear, permanently blinding her right eye and causing loss of hearing. A couple of weeks before the assassination attempt, company employees had told local men, in a meeting at the mine, that they could not expand their open-pit mine because Diodora would not sell her plot of land. Men in the meeting said, "We'll take care of that." Some apparently tried; Diodora survived.

On July 20, 2010, David L. Deisley, Executive Vice President of Goldcorp, and General Counsel, wrote to Rights Action and ADISMI (Association for the Integral Development of San Miguel Ixtahúacan):

Figure 7. Goldcorp's Marlin Mine in San Marcos, Diodora. Diodora Hernández looks for a calf while shepherding her cows. On July 7, 2010, Diodora Hernández, who refused to sell her land, was shot point-blank in the face outside her home only a few metres from a fence that delimits Goldcorp's Marlin mine. She asserts her refusal to sell is the reason she suffered the assassination attempt. The operations of Goldcorp's Marlin gold mine in Guatemala's western highlands have caused serious internal conflicts within the local Maya Mam communities, as well as causing repression, trumped-up legal charges against community defenders, and widespread environmental and health problems. San José Nueva Esperanza, San Miguel Ixtahuacán, San Marcos, Guatemala, May 14, 2016. Photo: James Rodríguez.

> I understand that the two men who allegedly committed the assault have been identified and were detained by the police, but were subsequently released. . . . Both men are residents of San Miguel Ixtahuacán. One of the two was employed by Montana, but his employment was terminated more than one year ago. The other man is employed by a contractor that provides underground mine development services to Montana at the Marlin mine. . . . Both Goldcorp and Montana Exploradora de Guatemala condemn this violent attack and offer our sincere condolences to Ms. Hernandez and her family.

With condolences like these, who needs human rights violations?

With Diodora's cows ambling about eating grass, Diodora spoke of the complete lack of justice in her case. Though Goldcorp knows who the men are, they apparently have done nothing to support the investigation of the Attorney General's (AG) office. After the assassination attempt, criminal investigators never again contacted Diodora and her family.

Diodora and FREDEMI's Aniseto explain to us how in early 2016 they went to the AG's office in the nearby town of San Miguel Ixtahuacán and were told to go to the AG's office in San Marcos. From there they were told to go to the AG's office in Guatemala City. Once there, they were told that nothing had been done to investigate her case, but that it was an open file.

Water and Justice for Diodora

And it seems to be an open file as to when or if local community leaders (some of whom have jobs in the mine) will turn on her water again. "Since 2011, they cut water to the one tap at my house." Diodora and Aniseto discuss the next steps they need to take, beginning with making yet another formal denunciation with the local AG's office, to try and achieve the pressure necessary to ensure that her local community leaders turn her water back on.

As Goldcorp's mine churns on and on, above ground and now through some 147 kilometres of underground tunnels, as North American investors (public pension funds and private funds) review profit margins on their investments in Goldcorp (and mining operations around the world), we promise to do what we can to help Diodora get her water back and perhaps, just perhaps, help kick-start the investigation into the two former Goldcorp/ Montana workers who tried to assassinate her and, more importantly, who put them up to it.

Goldcorp Inc.'s Marlin Mine—A Family's Pain:
Death of Jaime Otero Pérez López

Catherine Nolin, Grahame Russell, and James Rodríguez

San Miguel Ixtahuacán, Guatemala: We met with the family of twenty-four-year old Jaime Otero Pérez López who spoke out for the first time exactly one month after his death in a collapsed Goldcorp Inc. tunnel. On April 14, 2016, Jaime was trapped and killed in one of the Marlin mine's 147 kilometres of tunnels that have spread out in all directions under the municipalities of Sipakapa and San Miguel Ixtahuacán, since the date of Goldcorp's first open pit mountaintop removal operation in 2005.

Vancouver-based Goldcorp Inc. is at the centre of ongoing structural and everyday violence, exploitation, and environmental destruction in the Maya Mam and Sipakapan communities in and around the mine's operations. Since 2004, repression, human rights violations, and environmental harms have been widely documented and denounced, and yet no legal measures, no international condemnation, no orders to cease operations have stopped Goldcorp in their efforts to continue to maximize profits.

Jaime's parents, Julian Gerardo Pérez and Margarita López Bámaca, his brother Nelson Marino Pérez López, and his two sisters Marta and Eva Aracelia Pérez López invited us into their humble home to speak about and denounce the death of their son and brother while on the job at Goldcorp's mine. Jaime started working at the mine on August 4, 2014, and his job was to place explosives in holes perforating the tunnels that would then be detonated to expand the underground network. Jaime was paid approximately Q2,500 per month (approximately US$300) for this dirty and very hot, difficult, and dangerous work, so as to support his family.

Though the family is not entirely clear on what happened that day to Jaime, they are clear on their pain related to the company's very slow body recovery efforts, the lack of communication with them by Goldcorp, the lack of explanation of how this accident occurred, and of his body's transportation to a morgue, five days later, without advising them. "It is a real pain in my heart, the way they treated my son," cries his mother, Margarita.

Jaime's father, Julian, denounced the discriminatory way in which the company's lawyers treated him during three meetings the family had, weeks later, with Guatemalan authorities and Goldcorp lawyers. Julian was referred to as "Julianito," as one would refer to a child, and asked if he needed help with translation, even though he understands Spanish perfectly well. The family are poor Maya Mam people; they speak Spanish very well. "They did not respect my dignity at all. We are all humans!" he states.

In complete contradiction to claims made by proponents of global, neoliberal resource development, and by Goldcorp about "bringing development" to Guatemala, Julian's father closed out our meeting by saying:

> There is such economic need [in our country] that one has to risk their life for 2,500 Quetzales a month. Then [when one is killed], we are discriminated against and there is no support from the company.[35]

In Guatemala's well-documented context of racism, exploitation and repression, corruption and impunity, and staggering mining profits, incidents of mining-caused repression, rights violations, harms and indignities—so widely documented since 2004—continue with no end in sight. It must stop.

Something in the Water: The Lasting Violence of a Canadian Mining Company in Guatemala
Jeff Abbott

A twenty-minute drive from the centre of San Miguel Ixtahuacán, in the western highlands of Guatemala, sits an open wound. Giant holes scar the earth where two open-air mines, owned by the Canadian company Goldcorp, lay. What we could not see was some additional 147 kilometres of tunnels snaking beneath the ground. In the distance, the processing plant, where the company sifted through millions of tons of earth to extract the gold that lay under the Indigenous Maya Mam and Maya Sipakapense communities of the department of San Marcos.

At the time, the company was in the process of closing the mine, yet the plant remained a hub of activity. "Twenty years ago, this was a mountain," Humberto Velásquez, a Maya Mam resident of San Miguel Ixtahuacán and member of the resistance to the Marlin mine, tells me as we stand over one of the pits. The pieces of construction equipment down below look like tiny toys. Nearby, a truck from the Guatemalan National Police sits empty as four officers stand in the brush on the other side of the road. Velásquez comments, "It is amazing: even after the mine closes, the police are still protecting the company."

In February 2017, Goldcorp announced that the company was closing the controversial Marlin mine—Guatemala's first large-scale gold mine—after twelve years of production. In the month following the announcement, residents of San Miguel Ixtahuacán blocked the entrance to the mine with tires, rocks, and their own bodies, insisting on a dialogue with the company to address damages to their community—the environmental effects, houses damaged by explosions, and the health impacts caused by production at the site.[36]

According to members of the resistance like Velásquez, the protests escalated after three government-mediated meetings between protesters and the company between April and June 2017, in which Goldcorp refused to pay for damages.[37] "Our demand at the protest was that the [company] has to pay for everything they have left in our community," says Velásquez as we drive around the community. "They have to pay for the impacts to the water, [our] health, and the tunnels they have left."

Francisca Pascual is a fifty-seven-year-old Maya Mam resident who was born in the village of Ixcail, which sits in the municipality of San Miguel Ixtahuacán, and she is a member of the local resistance to the mine. "We want to recuperate everything that we have lost," she says. "Our ancestors left us this land. They left it to us to protect. But now, what will we leave our grandchildren? Our grandchildren are going to suffer."

The conflict over the Marlin mine reflects the violence of Canadian mining operations across the world. Canadian mining firms are frequently the cause of intense social conflict over resource extraction—from the murders at Banro's gold mines in the Congo to gang rapes by security personnel at Hudbay Minerals' nickel mine in eastern Guatemala (see chapter 4). It is estimated that 75 percent of the world's mining and exploration companies are based in Canada.[38]

Between Profits and Investments

Since Goldcorp acquired Glamis Gold and its Guatemalan subsidiary, Montana Exploradora, in 2006, the Marlin mine has been incredibly profitable for the company and its investors. Between 2006 and 2010, the highlands of western Guatemala generated over $594.3 million in profits from the exploitation of the Marlin site. As international gold prices rose, so too did Goldcorp's earnings. In 2013 alone, the mine generated $447 million.[39]

Goldcorp has maintained that they are dedicated to resolving the social conflicts in the area around the mine as part of their corporate social responsibility policy. According to the company, $130 million was invested in infrastructure projects across the region since the beginning of the mine's operations—which included paving roads, providing communities with potable water, and building infrastructure at the mining site. But the latter is in service of the mine, not the local communities, and served as a point of contention when power lines were run across private lands.

"The only development that arrived stayed only with them," notes Margarita Sebastian Castellan de Leon, a thirty-two-year-old community leader and a current auxiliary mayor of the village Chilive, which sits to the west of the mine. "The company managed to pave some roads, improve some schools, what else? In my community, we have not had a potable water project until now." Castellan de Leon says that residents were largely left out of the conversation about how to allocate the funds.

Researchers and community members point out that even though 97 percent of the mine's 1,582 employees were Guatemalan residents, only a tiny fraction of Goldcorp's money has trickled down to the community. "The mine is leaving practically nothing," laments Julio González, an activist from the environmentalist collective Madre Selva. "If you look at the people who live around the mine, they have very little, and a profound social division."

"[The Marlin mine] is generating significant economic benefits in the operating phase in the form of wages in highly impoverished, subsistence-based local communities," write Lyuba Zarsky and Leonardo Stanley in a report for Tufts University.[40] "However, local benefits are a tiny fraction of total mine revenues and earnings, the bulk of which flow overseas to the company and its shareholders." They conclude that the economic benefit will abruptly cease and all evidence of economic development will disappear once the mine closes because Goldcorp failed to invest the revenues in sustainable industry.

International experts also raise concerns that Goldcorp is not closing the mining site in compliance with industry standards. A report by Comisión Pastoral Paz y Ecología / Pastoral Commission on Peace and Ecology (COPAE) and Unitarian Universalist Service Committee (UUSC), prepared by international mining and engineering experts, noted that the reclamation bond of only $1 million that the company paid to the Guatemalan government was "trivial" in comparison to international standards.[41] The document estimated that the actual cost of the reclamation would be $49 million.[42] The report also flagged that since the reclamation plan has not been made public, it lacks oversight that would guarantee proper closure of the site and therefore poses the additional threat of environmental contamination.

Goldcorp has left a trail of contaminated water and land in the wake of their prior mine closures. In 2009, a year after Goldcorp closed their San Martín mine in Honduras, an independent review of that shutdown raised concerns about the threat of acidic runoff due to the secretive nature of the reclamation plan and the potential for improper closure of the site.[43] Those concerns proved true in 2011 when it was revealed by Karen Spring and Grahame Russell that the Honduran government had been covering up widespread sickness in the communities around the old mine.[44] Residents showed high levels of arsenic and lead in their blood and urine.

Back in Guatemala, the lack of transparency of Goldcorp's plan for closing the Marlin mine raised red flags in the community. Many residents told me that they do not believe that the mine is actually closing, or speculate that it might just be moving to another site. "I've heard that they are going to close the mine, but I don't know if they are going to close or continue working," says Pascual.

Leaving a Divided Community

Goldcorp is also walking away from deep social divisions that they created in the once tight-knit Indigenous communities of San Miguel Ixtahuacán and surrounding areas. The mine has driven a wedge between supporters of the project and those who are concerned about the impacts of the mine. "Little by little they divided the community, the churches, the municipality, and even the catechists [of the Catholic Church]," explains Pascual. "This is horrible for us."

These social divisions have turned deadly. In 2005, Álvaro Benigno Sánchez, a twenty-three-year-old resident of the village Pie de la Cuesta, Sipakapa, was shot near his home by security guards of the mining site. Another attack occurred in 2009, when workers from the mine burned an anti-mining activist to death.[45]

To dismantle the resistance movement, the government issued arrest warrants for activists protesting the mine, accusing them of sabotage. González points to the case of Gregoria Crisanta Perez, a community leader who faced arrest due to her refusal to permit electric lines to pass over her land.[46] According to González, the criminalization of activists in San Miguel Ixtahuacán set the precedent for how the state responds to other social conflicts in Guatemala. The Public Prosecutor's office has since routinely filed criminal charges against leaders of social movements—such as Rigoberto Juárez Mateo and Domingo Baltazar, two community leaders in Huehuetenango who were detained and charged with instigating criminal activity in 2015.[47]

The mine has also disrupted the social organization of Indigenous communities, often eroding residents' sense of collective responsibility to the community. This has especially affected the practice of communal work that is foundational to Indigenous communities across Guatemala. "The company taught the people that when there was a project in the community, such as a school or community salon, that they would be paid [for their work]," says Velásquez as we drive to one of the villages near the mining site. "Before, people would provide their time and work together. Now the people think that they should be paid when we go to repair or clean a road."

On the national level, critics of the mine point out that Goldcorp and the mining sector in general have perpetuated corruption, including embezzlement and bribery, in the Guatemalan political system. In 2016, as detailed by Sandra Cuffe (chapter 2), the Guatemalan Public Prosecutor's office issued an arrest warrant for Eduardo Villacorta, the former Goldcorp senior vice president for Central and South America. Villacorta is accused of being one of the illicit financiers of the 2011 campaign of Guatemala's former president, Otto Pérez Molina, and his Partido Patriota (Patriotic Party, a conservative political party in Guatemala).[48] The Partido Patriota was cancelled following the arrest and prosecution of Pérez Molina for overseeing a criminal network that stole millions from the Guatemalan government.[49]

It's because of such corruption, critics say, that the company has faced little regulation and oversight of the mining location. "The expansion of mining firms in the country is one of the pillars of corruption in Guatemala. This is one of the major impacts of the mining sector," says González. San Miguel Ixtahuacán sits along the Cuilco River, which feeds into southern Mexico. The region was once known as Tejutla and is famous for being an abundant source of water. Yet the mining operation guzzled over 250,000 litres of water per hour—far greater than the amount a family will use in twenty years.[50] Soon after, wells began to run dry across the region. "At least twenty-eight water sources have dried up," explains Velásquez. "The families have no place to get water. They have no water to drink, or for their animals."

At the height of production, Goldcorp was importing two hundred tons of cyanide a month for gold processing. The Catholic Church and residents have long accused the mine of poorly managing waste at the mining site, threatening the surrounding communities with cyanide contamination in the water. According to the company, the cyanide facilities at the Marlin mine have been decommissioned following international standards and protocols.[51]

"We heard that the company was going to bring development, but this is a bunch of lies, as we have never seen development," says Pascual. "The development that the company has left is sickness." As frustration grew over the lack of access to water and rampant human rights abuses, the communities took the mine to the Inter-American Commission on Human Rights (IACHR). In 2010, the commission ordered the Guatemalan government to suspend the mine's license due to concerns of environmental contamination. In addition, the commission asked the Guatemalan government to decontaminate the water sources of the eighteen beneficiary communities and to ensure their members access to water, as well as "to adopt any other necessary measures to guarantee the life and physical integrity of the members of the 18 aforementioned Maya communities."[52]

The next year, the IACHR would withdraw their orders for the closure of the mine following intense pressure from Goldcorp. In their revised decision, the IACHR ordered the Guatemalan state to further guarantee access to clean water. In response to these orders, Goldcorp began to construct potable water systems in several communities. The company and the Guatemalan government have also taken steps to monitor communities' water.

Yet this has not calmed the concerns of residents. In 2012, a resident near the mining site took her animals to drink from the Cuilco River, and on the way home her animals began to vomit and eventually died. Six years later, the Pastoral Commission on Peace and Ecology / Comisión Paz y Ecología issued a study of water quality to coincide with the closure of the mine.[53] Their findings revealed high levels of toxic metals in the three rivers in the region, and stated that the water is not fit for human or animal consumption—or even irrigation—due to the levels of contamination.

Today, residents look upon the rivers and other water sources with suspicion. "Many people close to the mine have grown sick, in part because they avoid bathing due to the lack of confidence with the water," says Castellan de Leon. "Why? Because the mine has led to the contamination of our water, and because the many springs have disappeared."

Unfortunately, the businesses that have benefited most from the mining activities in San Miguel Ixtahuacán are apparent in the town centres. Cantinas, or small bars, dominate nearly every street, with names such as "Gift from God" and "The Miracle." Velásquez estimates there are at least 128 cantinas that have opened across town since 2005. The rampant consumption of alcohol by workers has proven to be a frustration for the Maya Mam community.

"This is the type of development that the mine has brought," Velásquez explains to me as we drive through town. "The mine workers cash their cheques and go and buy alcoholic drinks."

Interviews / *Testimonios*: Thirteen Years of Resistance with FREDEMI Members

Interviews with and *testimonios* of three FREDEMI members, gathered over several visits, are shared below. We met with Alfredo Pérez on May 16, 2017 in Sipakapa (located in the municipality of the same name) in the San Marcos Department in a confidential location as he emerged from several days of arbitrary police detention for his role in the resistance. One year later, on May 9, 2018, we travelled to Salitre in the San Miguel Ixtahuacán municipality (Department of San Marcos) to meet with Miguel Ángel Bámaca of FREDEMI and later met with FREDEMI leader Aniseto López on a site overlooking the Marlin Mine tailings pond to hear from them about their thirteen-year long struggle of resistance against the actions of Goldcorp, Inc. and the Guatemalan government in their communities, to learn about what they are defending, why, and at what cost.

Interview: Alfredo Pérez, FREDEMI
with Grahame Russell and Catherine Nolin

Question: Alfredo, after thirteen years of struggle resisting human rights violations, environmental harms and repression caused by Goldcorp Inc.'s mining operation here in Maya Sipakapan and Maya Mam territories, what would you like to say to Canadian politicians, to the directors and shareholders and investors in Goldcorp, and to the Canadian public?

I would like to say a few things about the struggle of the Maya peoples of this region, the Sipakapan and Mam people who have suffered and resisted thirteen years of mining harms and destruction of Mother Earth and the environment, thirteen years of community and social divisions and conflict.

The company did not bring "development," as they stated. We call on the company and on the Canadian government to reflect, as human beings, on all that they have done here. Before Goldcorp arrived, we lived in peace in our communities, with significant social harmony—we did not have all the conflicts that we now have.

As Maya peoples, what we want to say to the companies and investors in this project of destruction—we do not call it a development project—is *ya basta!* [no more!]. The environmental and social destruction that the company has brought is deeply lamentable. What suffering the company has left behind, destroying our water sources, both our natural springs and aquifers, cutting off access to water that our communities depend on.

Now the company has closed its operation and says it has left things as they were before. This is ridiculous. How will the company repair the damages they have done to our water sources that are gone?

Ya basta, we say to the company and shareholders of this project of destruction. We need to stop destroying Mother Earth and our planet. Does the company, do the investors, think that one day all this destruction will not affect them as well?

In the name of my people, the Maya Sipakapan people, in the name of all peoples in Guatemala who have suffered mining harms, as human rights, territory, and environmental defenders we ask that the Canadian government and the company repair the damages that they caused. Some of this was set out in the order made by the Inter-American Commission on Human Rights that, based on ILO [International Labour Organization] Convention 169, ordered the company to provide communities all around the mine site with potable water and water for their animals and for irrigation.

After thirteen years, the situation in many communities is critical. Children are sick, there is no water. One can see huge fissures in the earth from the use of underground explosives. We don't need any more proof. Some communities around the mine have become unlivable.

Testimonio: **Miguel Ángel Bámaca, FREDEMI**
with Grahame Russell and Catherine Nolin

My name is Miguel Ángel Bámaca and I live in Siete Platos. I have lived in resistance to this monster since 1998. What does this monster mean to me? It is a big invader of our natural resources of San Miguel Ixtahuacán in Mam territory. That is why I said "no." They are endangering our existence, our health, our lives. This monster is a great violator of our human rights, who without consultation pushed through their project. They have violated us in so many ways. In 2010, they attacked Diodora [Hernández] and criminalized us. They wanted to kill me—on July 14, 2010. It was the same week as the attack on Diodora. They intimidate us in so many ways. Spying on us, following us. They are always there with their eyes on us.

On May 20, about four hundred of us blocked the road between San Antonio and Siete Platos. Well, that was the cause of the death threats we later received. At least thirteen *compañeros* were injured, probably more, but they didn't have the strength to present themselves, out of fear. I wasn't scared. I knew the truth. No, I won't hide myself.

We are trying to pressure the government to make Montana Exploradora [Guatemalan subsidiary of Goldcorp and name used most often by those in resistance] pay for their damages. So, we are pressuring our government. But, we are frustrated that we have to pressure our government to do the right thing, and act like a government and hold the wrong-doer accountable. Montana does not accept its errors. They do not accept that they have done anything wrong here. And the government is not doing anything to pressure them to accept that it has done things wrong here and provide reparation of some sort.

I am sharing with you some of all that we've lived through here, and because I have been so involved for so long, I am now part of the dialogue process at the municipal level. That is not going well. But that is my role today besides getting on with my life. I am a formal member of the dialogue process. I am also a member of FREDEMI which is one of the organizations that grew out of the resistance.

We have dozens of natural springs that have dried up, which the communities depend on, even in the dry season. 2015, 2016, 2017, 2018 . . . The natural springs are not coming back, even though the mine stopped a year ago . . . I don't know what will happen in the future. But they have not come back yet.

Land for us is our mother. Our mother gives us what we live off, the honey of our lives that we survive on. We are defending our mother. All these years we've been defending our mother. It is our mother who gives us what we eat. It is our mother who gives us what we drink. This mother, this land, is our home. This is our house.

Our continuing resistance and desire to defend our mother, even though it is hard, is because we have pride in ourselves. We have self-esteem in ourselves. And we have no other option. This is our home. We know that we have been dealing with a lot of people who sit in offices and wear suits and ties. That's their world over there. But they know nothing of our world here. We know that we belong here and that we have no options but to fight and defend this life.

We get strength also from other people in other regions and other parts of the country who are also resisting and fighting back. We are with them and they are with us. We get some of our strength from that. We are also thankful for support of some international organizations. We have some hope from the Inter-American Commission on Human Rights. Even though we didn't achieve what they set out for us, the people who work there were able to remind us that we are right in our struggle and that we are right to struggle for our land and our children's land and our grand-children's land.

We were not allowed to do a municipal *consulta* here in San Miguel Ixtahuacán nor even *consultas* at the village level—though some were done clandestinely. Our authorities didn't allow us to do it, like there were in other places like Sipakapa, Huehuetenango, other places. It is our right do this but what does the government say? They say that we "recognize your right to do consultations but they are not binding." How is it possible that our consultations are not binding?!

Repression against the resistance was all around, connected to the consultation demands, but all around the struggle. As I mentioned earlier, February 28, 2011, we did another roadblock to try to get our rights respected. There was very serious violence against a lot of us. We had a roadblock right down near the bridge over there at Siete Platos where I live. Now, those guys over there, the Mejía family who own the hotel over there [points across the road], at the time were hired gunmen for the company to divide communities. The Mejía brothers were part of the group who, with some company security guards, came down and started shooting up the place, beating up people, threatening people. It was a really terrible day of violence, trying to break our peaceful roadblock. Aniseto [López] suffered immensely. He was hit over the head with a pistol, kidnapped, and detained not even by the police but by people connected to the company. They forced him to sign documents, to denounce the resistance. There was a lot of blood spilled that day. But no one was killed that day.

And now this Mejía family are now aligning themselves with the resistance, demanding reparations from the mining company!

Now that the mining company is gone . . . the struggle, the threats, the criminalization . . . they haven't paid for any of the damages and this whole region is worse off than before. People like the Mejías want to join our demands for reparations. We don't all agree if they should or shouldn't be allowed back into our circle. Aniseto's position is that they were wrong, they committed errors, but it is our responsibility to see if we can open the door for them so that they can come back and join in. Let us learn together.

Through all this, the "official" dialogue process is not moving forward. And for all the damage and harms, there is no justice. Justice is a pending issue. We survive on what we sell in this little store. My wife is asking, "How will we feed the kids?"

Testimonio: Aniseto López, FREDEMI
with Grahame Russell and Catherine Nolin

My name is Aniseto López and I am the coordinator for the San Miguel Ixtahuacán Defense Front / Frente de Defensa San Miguelense, FREDEMI. Welcome to San Miguel and thank you for coming here and spending some time to learn more about our resistance and land struggle. So, this is the Marlin mine's tailings pond. This is a total destruction of this place. Over there, before, that was a forested mountain. The woods were eliminated by the company and now we are looking at a tailings pond. It is very painful to see this; it is a destruction of our own lives. This tailings pond represents for us the destruction of our life because we are of the earth. We cannot destroy what we are "of."

In addition to the destruction that is for us this destroyed space, we are even more worried about the tailings pond with all the mud and dirty water that came out of the leaching process for gold and silver. We worry about the seepage into the water table. Now, they are slowly growing some grass on top of this toxic, acidic waste dump. Over time, this mess will slowly leach down into the earth and the water systems.

The mine created serious divisions at the local level between people who wanted the mine and people who didn't want the mine. They co-opted the leaders of communities, they co-opted the mayor's office because these were all people who benefited financially from the mining operation. So, we've had these divisions ever since the mine got here. These divisions will remain in our communities for a long time to come, even though the mine is shut down now. The local political parties that were in favour of the mine are the wealthier political parties. And they are the ones that are dominating the elections and winning the municipalities, the municipal elections.

Though it doesn't mean much in some ways, we in the resistance feel a small satisfaction that we stuck to our principles and our vision of what we want here, from the beginning to the end of the mining operation. We didn't achieve much but we stuck to our principles. We get tiny bits of satisfaction when, now, some people who were in favour of the mine come up to us and apologize to us. They will tell us directly, "You were right, we were wrong."

Going back to the beginning when the mine got here, they hired local people as *sicarios* [hitmen] or local thugs. They were working for the mine and they would go around and sow divisions or carry out threats and harassment or even attacks against those of us in the resistance.

Specifically, in the case of the Mejías, they carried out some very serious violence on that day, February 28, 2011, including against me. The Mejía brothers were *pistoleros* [hired guns], *sicarios* [hitmen], working for the company or people connected to the company; they were the ones who used very serious violence to break up our roadblock protest in 2011. And they came after me, as one of the leaders, and they kidnapped me for a period of time. They had a gun against my head and they forced me to sign a document which denounced myself and the resistance leadership. These are some of the people who have come to me, now, quietly, and said, "We were so wrong, you were so right. Sorry."

We'll see what comes from these apologies. We're not sure if this will be just a little apology and that will be it, or will they support us in the future when we try to go forward and continue to demand change around here? Is this real and long term? Who knows? Many of these people were supporting the mine in one way or another. There are people who benefited from our struggle.

So, after all of our water sources dried up or were contaminated, we went through this complicated process with the Inter-American Commission on Human Rights and got these "precautionary measures" that ordered the provision of water for five different communities because the water had dried up. These people in those communities that were in favour of the mine got their water back because of our struggle. They got their water back even though they had supported the mine. So, now, some of them are saying "sorry" and slowly starting to support us because the struggle is not just about these five water projects. It's about the cracked houses, it's about the open fissures in our land, it's about the ongoing access for water and the drying up of our water springs, and so on.

This story here is your struggle as well. Through my work, I have been able to travel extensively and talk about these issues and learn about other struggles. I've been to Canada a number of times, coordinated with some of the work that Catherine [Nolin] is involved in out of Montreal. I've gone up to see Goldcorp's mine in northern Quebec. I've seen how Canadian mining companies are operating in your country and down here. I also now have connections with people in Peru, Argentina, and elsewhere where mining companies are operating. And this is a *súper monstro* [big monster]. This is not just one story. This is a big problem and the struggle is long term. This is a problem for all of us.

Even with the so-called closure of the Marlin mine, we don't have a single bit of information. The company has not shared a "closure" plan for Marlin and they are not taking the installations down. We have no clue of their plan. They haven't even presented a closure plan to us. They claim that, by law, they don't have to. They claim that, by law, from the beginning they said they would shut down the mine one day and that they don't have to do or say anything more about it. So, there are all kinds of rumours and stories going around. We hear that maybe a new company will come in here and offer jobs. Maybe they are going to do an eco-tourism site where people can come and do eco-tourism. We've heard stories that there will be a *maquiladora* garment factory put in here. We don't trust any of these stories. We don't know what is going to happen because they don't tell us, because they never did. We do know that if and when it is used again, the people who come in here will make all kinds of promises to the people once again, saying how they are coming here to "help" everyone. But, basically, all over again they will just be taking advantage of the poverty of the poor.

The dialogue table does not function. Not one bit. It is useless. It is worse than useless. It is an entity that is set up to make us waste time and make us waste resources. Nothing will come from the dialogue table. Will the company give us anything? Well, we hear stories that they might be willing to recognize that, yes, some houses have been damaged and they might come up with a little bit of money to repair some houses.

Will the people here rise up again in anger and frustration? If all the company is going to do is throw around a few crumbs to resolve a few cases of the damages but not come close to resolving the enormity of the problems, will the people rise up again? We are looking at lawsuits. Even with all the problems of the legal system, we're looking at lawsuits, and those would go on for a long time. But maybe we have to try lawsuits to try to hold them in some way accountable.

We all need a life of opportunity, all of us, not just here in San Miguel Ixtahuacán. What kind of country is Guatemala? What kind of country has Guatemala always been? All through history, the majority of people in Guatemala have never had any real opportunity to make a life for themselves so they could have a decent life. People need a minimum amount of capital or resources to make for themselves and their families and communities a decent life.

I work with a small NGO that gets funding from the government and I work as an agronomist in the countryside, all through this region doing agricultural capacity building and educational work. I work with communities to figure out how they can better use their land. Besides all of the history of oppression and corruption that this mine represents, it has created a culture of dependency. People have lost hope for so long. They have no hope, so they are just waiting for someone or something to come and help them resolve their problems. If any *campesino* family had enough land, not much, but enough land and irrigation, well, that takes care of that. They can grow everything that they need. They can sell locally what they don't need and earn a bit of money and take care of their family, buy them clothing, and so on. But there are two sides to this problem. One is the history of oppression and inequality and injustice that takes land away from people or doesn't give them access to capital, and two, the dependency. People have lived this way for so long that they are waiting for someone to come and help them out.

What would that life look like? Well, here in San Miguel, if we had community-owned businesses, clothing that we could produce ourselves, for example. Clothing that some people call *típico* [typical], we could produce that here. A company owned by the people, invest money in the people, produce their own clothing, use it, sell it. That could work here. What about energy? Look at all this wind. We could have our own wind energy projects going on here so that we wouldn't live at the whim of foreign hydroelectric dam companies who come in here, take our water resources away from us, produce energy and then sell it back to us or maybe not at all. These are just some examples. We are just having a chat here. But, they are examples of opportunities, of things we could do here if there were the right conditions to do so. If the right conditions exist, many more people would come up with many more ideas of what a nice life would look like around here and how they could get involved.

It is difficult to achieve ongoing, operative, healthy communication with other struggles. We haven't really been able to achieve that here within our own country. This struggle here though, well, everyone knows about it. But unfortunately, we're not really connected with other struggles in San Rafael with Tahoe [Resources], nor with our brothers and sisters in Izabal [with Hudbay Minerals]. I've been able to visit other struggles in other countries like with the Cree people north of Montreal in Canada. But we're not connected with those struggles. This needs strategy and resources to make it happen and we don't have either.

What motivates me to keep going in this struggle is that there is really no other option. Either you are going to resist this or not and it will go ahead. We understand very clearly the reality that the mining company and its business associates are the enemy. The government is the enemy. Our leaders are in collaboration with the business owners and government and they are our enemy.

Chapter 4

Q'eqchi' People Fight Back against Hudbay Minerals, in Their Own Words

> Underdevelopment is not a step towards development, but the historic
> consequence from foreign development.
> —Eduardo Galeano[1]

In the spirit of valuing *testimonio*, this chapter amplifies the voices of several key individuals in the struggle for justice in the context of decades of Canadian mining interventions in the El Estor region of Guatemala—we hear from them, in their own words. First came INCO/EXMIBAL in the 1960s, then Skye Resources / CGN in 2004, and then Hudbay Minerals / HMI in 2008, who in 2011 sold off their Fénix nickel mining project and the Guatemalan subsidiary CGN (Compañía Guatemalteca de Níquel / Guatemalan Nickel Company) to the Switzerland-based Solway Investment Group, sustaining a substantial financial loss.[2] Decades of struggle in the face of violent evictions, murders, rapes, burned homes, threats, and more.

Our connection with the Q'eqchi' mining-affected communities of this region began in 2004 when INCO's forty-year concession was about to expire. Community members up and down the mountainous region were nervous. Memories of EXMIBAL's intimate participation with the 1978 Panzós massacre (detailed in the 1999 UN Commission for Historical Clarification [CEH] report) were front and centre.[3] The CEH report documents the abuses carried about by military forces associated with INCO/EXMIBAL to force local people off mining concession lands, including the first in a long line of massacres associated with the town of Panzós, Alta Verapaz which is further down the main road that leads from El Estor to the Fénix mine site, and through the Polochic Valley.[4]

It was May 2010 when we started off on the most difficult task of collecting *testimonios* of violent evictions at the request of the community of the mountaintop village of Lote Ocho, near El Estor and on the mining concession land. We left the town of El Estor in the back of a pick-up truck, drove past the mine site itself, down the rough, gravel road until we reached Chichipate, turned north onto an even rougher dirt road to climb into the mountains. We reached the original site of the community—burned down during the violent evictions—where several community members met us to guide us up into the new site. Approximately sixty people awaited our arrival: men, women, children, infants, sitting in the open-air community meeting space. Community land and rights defender María Cuc Choc served as a translator from Q'eqchi' to Spanish. Beginnings are difficult, but once the memories turned to words, these strong and determined people spoke for more than an hour. Raúl spoke first: "Why do they treat us like animals? Like something they do not know?"

"It was on January 9, 2007, when they arrived," Raúl told us: hundreds of national police, Guatemalan military soldiers, and the company's private security forces fired tear gas and bullets, forcing them out of the village and into the surrounding woods, took their possessions and burned down all one hundred homes. And then Raúl turned to us and said, "And this was when the women were violated. It is time that their stories are heard." One by one the women around us stood up to tell of the outrageous trauma they experienced during the evictions.

Years have passed since that gathering and our connection with the people of Lote Ocho and El Estor remains firm. The gang rapes that eleven women suffered during that violent, illegal Skye Resources / CGN eviction of the village of Lote Ocho in January 2007 are now one of the three landmark lawsuits filed in 2010 and 2011 against Hudbay Minerals in Canadian courts. The other two lawsuits: Angélica Choc, widow of Adolfo Ich who was killed by Hudbay security forces in September 2009; and German Chub, shot and left paralyzed by Hudbay security forces that same day in September 2009. These three cases are discussed in some detail in chapter 6.

This chapter includes the formal human rights violation complaint that we, and a group of students from the University of Northern British Columbia (UNBC), submitted in person to the Canadian Embassy in Guatemala City and by mail to the Minister of Foreign Affairs immediately after this meeting. We made this decision to act, not on their behalf, but in response to their requests that we demand from our leaders to get the company out of there. We delivered that formal complaint and received only silence in reply. Yet, the work of Grahame with Rights Action, lawyers Cory Wanless and Murray Klippenstein, and a constellation of activists, journalists, filmmakers, university professors and students, community members, and photographers keep the Hudbay Minerals lawsuits moving forward, fourteen years after the Lote Ocho women were raped, twelve years after Adolfo Ich was killed and German Chub left paralyzed. Our connection to this place and these people is forever. The *testimonios* of María Cuc Choc, Angélica Choc, and José Ich, along with statement of German Chub and reporting by Heather Gies, follow.

Formal Human Rights Violation Complaint

Catherine Nolin, Grahame Russell, and University of Northern British Columbia 2010 delegation

October 19, 2010

Updated Human Rights Violation Complaint submitted to the Canadian government: Canadian Nickel Mining Companies Involved in Violent, Illegal Forced Evictions of Mayan Q'eqchi' Communities, Gang Rape of Women Villagers & Assassination of Community Leader

To All Concerned Parties,

On behalf of the University of Northern British Columbia's Guatemala Delegation & Rights Action, we submit this updated human rights violation complaint to the Canadian government.

As you know, we submitted earlier versions of this complaint to Mr. Lawrence Cannon, other government representatives and politicians, and investors. To date we have not received a reply from anyone, except (October 13, 2010) from Mr. Cannon, who sent us a letter that responds to almost none of the points we raise in this complaint.

The violations we have investigated and reported on have not been addressed or remedied. The underlying issues that led to this nickel-mining related repression have not been addressed and the harmed Mayan Q'eqchi' (Kek-chi, phonetically) communities may suffer more repression in the future, at the behest of Canadian (and other) nickel mining companies.

A Canadian Government Request for Complaints

In May 2008, after a previous delegation of UNBC students (and their professor Dr. Catherine Nolin) and Rights Action visited the nickel mining-harmed communities of El Estor, the UNBC delegation met with then-Ambassador Kenneth Cook in the Canadian Embassy. At that meeting, the delegation informed him—and other staffers—of serious violations that Mayan Q'eqchi' communities of El Estor had recently suffered at the behest of Skye Resources and CGN (Guatemalan Nickel Company, subsidiary of Skye Resources).

Ambassador Cook told the UNBC delegation that the Canadian government—via the Embassy in Guatemala—was "open to receiving human rights complaints related to Canadian mining in Guatemala," though they had never received one.

A Canadian Problem: Nickel Mining and Forced Evictions, Gang Rape and Assassination

As Canadian citizens, we demand the immediate attention of the Canadian government. This is a Canadian problem.

All of the major decisions affecting this mining operation are taken by then Skye Resources, now Hudbay Minerals, in Canada. Canadian shareholders and investors (including the Canada Pension Plan) benefit from this and many similar mining operations. Additionally, the Canadian government is promoting, as policy, a largely unfettered expansion of Canadian mining companies in Guatemala.

The Violations

Over the past few years, UNBC's Dr. Catherine Nolin has organized a number of delegations to visit, along with Rights Action, the mining-affected communities of El Estor. These commitments include two more visits in May and August of 2010.

We have visited the mining-affected communities of La Unión, La Revolución, Lote 8, La Paz, and Lote 9. We have received testimonies from eyewitnesses to, and victims of, the forced evictions; eyewitnesses to, and victims of, gang rapes; we have spoken with eyewitnesses (including family members) to the assassination of community leader and teacher Adolfo Ich.

October 19, 2010

UPDATED HUMAN RIGHTS VIOLATION COMPLAINT
SUBMITTED TO THE CANADIAN GOVERNMENT:

CANADIAN NICKEL MINING COMPANIES INVOLVED IN VIOLENT, ILLEGAL FORCED
EVICTIONS OF MAYAN-Q'EQCHI' COMMUNITIES, GANG RAPE OF WOMEN
VILLAGERS & ASSASSINATION OF COMMUNITY LEADER

(Mayan-Q'eqchi' women of Lote 8 & La Paz communities, El Estor, Izabal. The 12 women of Lote 8 were gang-raped by Guatemalan soldiers, police and private security guards hired by the Guatemala Nickel Company, wholly owned subsidiary of then Skye Resources, now HudBay Minerals. Photo: James Rodríguez, www.mimundo.org, August 2010)

To:
Mr. Lawrence Cannon
Minister of Foreign Affairs
509-S Centre Block, House of Commons,
Ottawa, ON, K1A 0A6, Canada
cannol@parl.gc.ca

& other government officials and politicians

To: the Canada Pension Plan and other investors

To: HudBay Minerals & CGN (Guatemala Nickel Company)

From:
Grahame Russell, co-director, Rights Action, info@rightsaction.org, 860-352-2448.
www.rightsaction.org.
Dr. Catherine Nolin, Associate Professor of Geography, University of Northern British Colombia,
nolin@unbc.ca, (250) 961-5875, &
the undersigned

Figure 8. Formal Human Rights Violation Complaint submitted to the Canadian Government. Catherine Nolin, Grahame Russell, and UNBC Field School participants, 2010.

The Violators

These human rights violations were committed by the Guatemalan army and police, and private security guards employed by Skye Resources and Hudbay Minerals via their Guatemalan subsidiary company—CGN.

Lote 8

An example: One of the most attacked and harmed communities is that of Lote 8, an isolated Mayan Q'eqchi' community on the mountain ridge north of El Estor (where much of the nickel ore is apparently located). After hiking into the Lote 8 community in May 2010, and meeting with community members elsewhere in El Estor (in August 2010), the UNBC delegation and Rights Action received substantial testimonies from the community members. The community members told us that these testimonies were one of the first public recounting of their shared experiences:

January 9, 2007: Hundreds of police, soldiers, and Skye Resources / CGN private security agents arrived in at least eighty police pickup trucks, two army trucks, and three nickel company trucks. They arrived with the intent of illegally and forcibly evicting the inhabitants. Community members were given five minutes to retrieve belongings from their small homes; they were offered 300 Quetzales to destroy their own homes.

Upon the community's peaceful refusal, the police, soldiers, and private security forces started shooting teargas; they robbed the villagers' homes and then set them on fire with gasoline. In total, one hundred small homes were destroyed. The villagers—from grandparents to newborns—were forced to flee into the forests. All of their belongings, including clothes, bedding, food, cooking implements, etc., were either destroyed or stolen.

With absolutely nowhere to go, the one hundred families of Lote 8 spent the next week rebuilding minimal shelter, attaching plastic sheeting to poles (for shelter), while scrounging for food and trying to recover some of the subsistence crops.

During this week, Skye Resources / CGN helicopters regularly flew over their remote community.

January 17, 2007: Hundreds of police, soldiers, and private security agents returned to Lote 8 to again illegally and forcibly evict the community, this time while male residents were away from the community. They carried out the same plan of destruction as on January 9.

Moreover, police, soldiers, and Skye Resources / CGN private security guards gang raped twelve female community members. At least two of the victims were pregnant at the time, and lost their babies due to the rapes. Another victim, a newlywed, has been told that she cannot have children due to the violent rape. (In an earlier version of this Complaint, we referred to a smaller number of women. Based on our August 2010 visit, we now have testimony that twelve women were raped, who also described to us their fear of coming forward publicly.)

In 2008, soon after the execution of these illegal and brutal evictions and gang rapes, Skye Resources sold its nickel mining interests (including CGN) to Hudbay Minerals.

Assassination of Adolfo Ich

On September 27, 2009, well-known Mayan Q'eqchi' community leader and teacher Adolfo Ich was captured and then killed by CGN (now owned by Hudbay Minerals) security guards under the direct orders of chief of CGN security forces Mynor Padilla. This event took place in the community of

La Unión, in the town of El Estor. Under orders of Mynor Padilla, heavily armed security guards came on the La Unión property, grabbed Adolfo Ich in front of other villagers, and took him back onto adjacent company properties—firing live rounds at community members who tried to follow them. A couple of hours later, after all the security guards were ordered to leave the premises, family and community members found Adolfo Ich dead inside CGN company buildings, with bullet wounds and machete cuts.

Deeply Entrenched Impunity

Because of Guatemala's deeply entrenched and well-documented impunity for the government and powerful sectors, no criminal legal proceedings were even initiated for these illegal forced evictions and gang rapes. A capture order is out for Hudbay / CGN security forces chief Mynor Padilla, though that order has not been acted upon. Mr. Padilla is often seen in the El Estor region driving in Hudbay / CGN vehicles and on CGN property.

Not surprisingly, Hudbay Minerals / CGN denies all of the above.

Demands for Concrete Actions from the Canadian Government

The UNBC group and Rights Action have photographic, video, and audio testimonies of all of the violations and repression summarized above.

Though we concentrated our recent efforts on the most remote community of Lote 8 and the killing of Adolfo Ich, similar serious charges—including rape—have been made against the police, army, and CGN private security guards that were carrying out violent and illegal forced evictions in at least four other nearby communities in 2006 and early 2007.

As Canadian citizens, we demand concrete actions from the Canadian government:

That the Canadian government carry out a full and impartial investigation into these allegations;

That the Canadian government notify the appropriate Guatemalan authorities of these extremely serious charges and of the Canadian government's investigation;

That, with the community's consent, international accompaniers are provided to ensure that the mining-affected communities are not subject to retribution for making these accusations and claims;

That the findings of the Canadian government's investigation be made known publicly;

That the investigation provide a complete summary of the human rights violations and property destruction and loss suffered by the Lote 8 community, as well as the other five Mayan Q'eqchi' communities that suffered similar illegal and forced evictions around the same time;

That the investigation provide conclusions and recommendations with respect to the actions and/or omissions of the governments of Guatemala and Canada, and the Guatemalan security forces, and with respect to Skye Resources (now Hudbay Minerals) and the company's security forces; and

That the investigation set out what reparations and compensation ought to be paid and made to the victims.

We believe the Canadian government must carry out this investigation, based on the facts that:

The very authorities responsible for ensuring justice and security in Guatemala—the police and the military—were the perpetrators, along with CGN private security guards;

That the owners of the Guatemalan Nickel Company—then Skye Resources, now Hudbay Minerals—are Canadian companies; and

That the Canadian government is playing a proactive role in supporting the expansion of Canadian companies into Guatemala.

We insist that this human rights violation complaint be taken seriously and trust the Canadian government will take every means necessary to ensure that the perpetrators of these human rights violations be prosecuted to the fullest extent of the law, and that full reparations and compensation be made to the victims of these crimes.

We look forward to hearing back from you about this serious human rights matter. We have extensive knowledge about the violations and harms caused by nickel mining interests in the El Estor region and look forward to sharing it with you.

Sincerely,

Dr. Catherine Nolin   Grahame Russell
Associate Professor of Geography, UNBC   Rights Action

plus UNBC students Claudette Bois, Nathan Einbinder,
John-Paul Laplante, Alexandra Pedersen, Dana Pidherny, Ashley Gill,
Erica Henderson, Stephen John Porter, and Miranda Seymour

Testimonio: María Magdalena Cuc Choc, Taking Claims to Canadian Courts

with Grahame Russell and Catherine Nolin, May 16, 2017

María begins by introducing herself in Q'eqchi'

My name is María Magdalena Cuc Choc and I was born here in El Estor and I am thirty-eight years old. I am of the Indigenous people. I am of the Q'eqchi' people in El Estor. These lands where I am seated now are lands that serve my life, that help me and my children in our lives. These plants help us. The sky above helps us. The rivers and Lake Izabal, we are part of this, they help our lives. So, I just repeat very clearly, I am of these lands.

My parents are the first inhabitants. They migrated here years ago from Alta Verapaz. Since that time, we have been owners of these lands. Here, where we are right now, where I live, these are the lands of my parents and this is where we grow our sacred corn, the sacred food of the Indigenous people.

Now, the utterly SCREWED UP situation of foreign-owned mining companies coming here and violating our lives has affected my ENTIRE life and the lives of everyone here. Why do I say violate? Firstly, because they never asked for our permission to come here and work. This is the first injustice.

What is going on here today in 2017 is not the first time. This is a CANCER in the region that goes back at least to 1901 when the United Fruit Company was here. Since then, there have been a number of military coups, always to put in power governments that sell our country—the land of eternal spring—to the companies.

In the decades of the 1950s, 1960s, 1970s, and 1980s, our parents suffered massacres and other violations of their rights. Many were forced to flee their homes. In 1978, there was the Panzós massacre. The roots of the Panzós massacre go back to the United Fruit Company, because it was the Canadian company INCO and its Guatemalan subsidiary EXMIBAL that came and took over United Fruit Company lands. INCO/EXMIBAL have everything to do with the Panzós massacre. Blood was running in the streets of Panzós and hundreds of people were killed, many were wounded.

This is a long, sad, and bitter history.

It all continues today. Again, the company is here operating on our lands, contaminating our rivers and Lake Izabal. This long and bitter

Figure 9. *Defensora* Documentary Film Poster (2013). *Defensora* is a moving and powerful documentary that sets out the context and backdrop to the precedent-setting Hudbay Minerals lawsuits. Filmmaker Rachel Schmidt completed *Defensora* just after the landmark decision of Superior Court of Ontario Justice Carole Brown, who ruled in July 2013 that Hudbay can be put on trial in Canada for gang rapes, a shooting-maiming, and a murder that Hudbay is allegedly responsible for in relation to their mining project in Guatemala. Photo: Rachel Schmidt, director, *Defensora Final HD* (6kidsProductions, 2013, vimeo.com/329494479).

history picked up again in 2004 when Hudbay Minerals arrived, again without asking permission. Violent evictions were again carried out against communities throughout the region.

And, in the context of these evictions that Hudbay was involved with, I always talk of the community of Lote Ocho. What did they do there? They violently evicted the people from the lands and they raped the women. It has all been covered up by COMPLETE impunity; it is the government of Guatemala that permits the impunity. It is the government that keeps selling our lands to these companies, that keeps on using repression against us.

Let's just go back a bit to 1996. That was the year that so-called Peace Accords were signed on December 29, 1996. What do I think the Peace Accords are and the signing of Peace? A lie. They were a strategy used by the "parallel powers"—organized crime, drug traffickers—so that they could take power and do business with companies like Hudbay Minerals that operated here.

What did Hudbay do? Hudbay assassinated a member of my family, my brother-in-law. I will never forget this. And it is worse. Now the

Guatemalan justice system has defended this assassin; the justice system has acquitted and released this former lieutenant colonel.

The images will never be erased from my eyes, when the security guards fired teargas at community members and when this man—Mynor Padilla—took out his gun and shot my family member. This image remains in my eyes, in my heart, and I will carry this forever. It is also an inspiration for me to keep going.

Listen to my words. Look at me. We are the ones who live here and who suffer this. We are assaulted on our lands; we are raped on our lands by these foreign companies.

What did Hudbay do after it carried out the evictions, after it shot and killed people, after it raped so many poor and illiterate women? Hudbay sold the company and got out of here. Hudbay sold the mining operation to Solway Investment Group, a Swiss company. What is the company Solway doing? Once again, the company is violating the rights of the El Estor community members.

They always say they are bringing us development. This is a lie—there is no development. This is what it is.

Mynor Padilla, Hudbay Mineral's Former Head of Security, Provided with Police "Security Detail" for Safety

Grahame Russell and Catherine Nolin

May 18, 2016: A Guatemalan judge ordered today that a police security detail be provided for Mynor Padilla, Canadian-owned Hudbay Minerals' former head of security who is on trial for the September 27, 2009 murder of Maya Q'eqchi' community leader Adolfo Ich and the shooting-paralyzing of German Chub, a young community member. Yes, that is correct.

Padilla, in jail without bail because he was a fugitive from justice for three years after the crimes, and his lawyers (Carlos Rafael Pellecer Lopez, Frank Manuel Trujillo Aldana, and David Antonio Barrientos) convinced Judge Ana Leticia Peña Ayala that Padilla's personal security was at risk because he was "harassed" by people when entering the Puerto Barrios court house on May 17, 2016.

The people Padilla and his lawyers referred to were members of our Mining Impunity Delegation.[5] As police escorted Padilla into the Puerto Barrios courtroom, at approximately 1:30 p.m. on May 17, we were standing—some with cameras, some with notepads—to one side of the building's entrance. At a given point Padilla walked calmly away from his police escorts and directly approached members of our group filming him.[6]

After Padilla entered the court building, we had no further interaction with him. This quiet and calm moment was the "harassment" as determined by Judge Ana Leticia Peña Ayala, which merited providing a detail of eight to nine police to provide security for Padilla.

Angélica Choc, widow of Adolfo Ich, responded to the unfolding situation in this way:

> It makes me so angry that the judge concludes that the man who murdered my husband is the one being threatened. His lawyers come to the trial with armed private security guards all the time; the CGN company [formerly owned by Hudbay] has had other armed men who have followed us at different times during the trial; there are police everywhere, always escorting [Padilla]; and we have no weapons at all and no security guards at all, ever . . . and yet she determines that it is [Padilla] who needs police protection! How can I get justice?

This judicial order would be amusing, if it were not indicative of how corrupted, manipulated, and racist the entire trial has been, a trial which—in many ways—is characteristic of much of Guatemala's legal system and the application of the rule of law.

Mynor Padilla and Impunity

Mynor Padilla is former head of security for Hudbay Minerals (CGN). He is on trial for the murder of well-known Indigenous rights, community, and environmental defender Adolfo Ich and the shooting-paralyzing of German Chub. This repression took place took on September 27, 2009, in the community of La Unión, that is next to mining company property on the edge of the town of El Estor.

Starting in 2005, right through to the killing of Adolfo Ich and shooting of German Chub, there were many cases of Canadian mining company-related repression in the El Estor region. The Mynor Padilla trial is the only case of mining repression in El Estor that is before the Guatemalan courts. Many people believe this trial is advancing—stumbling, with numerous irregularities—only because there is an international spotlight on it due to the precedent-setting Hudbay Minerals civil lawsuits advancing in Canadian courts (see Wanless and Klippenstein's contribution in chapter 6).

This trial in Guatemala is completely separate from the Hudbay civil lawsuits in Canada, though some of the issues and incidents overlap. Hudbay has no direct or indirect legal liability in Guatemala for the crimes committed by Padilla and other former security guards, yet Hudbay is intervening directly in the criminal trial proceedings.

In 2015, Hudbay, which is represented by the Fasken Martineau law firm in the civil lawsuits in Canada, contracted John Terry, a senior partner with the Torys law firm, to appear in the criminal trial in Guatemala and provide "expert testimony" concerning the civil lawsuits in Canada. Lawyers and human rights activists following the Padilla trial found Terry's remarks to be misleading in a number of ways. It is also widely rumoured that Hudbay is paying for Padilla's team of three high profile defence lawyers; Hudbay has not denied this, as far as we know.

Testimonio: Angélica Choc, Taking Claims to Canadian Courts
with Grahame Russell and Catherine Nolin, May 16, 2017

Good afternoon and thank you. As an Indigenous woman and as a Maya Q'eqchi' woman of Guatemala it is profoundly regrettable and sad when one has to seek justice in this country and it is even harder when one is a woman, an Indigenous woman. I have lived through this as I have been seeking justice for the assassination of my husband.

I was profoundly saddened on April 6 of this year [2017] when the judge in the criminal case came down with a complete acquittal and ordered the immediate freedom of the accused, Mynor Padilla, an ex-colonel in the Guatemalan army and ex-head of security for the Canadian company Hudbay Minerals and its Guatemalan subsidiary CGN.

This terrible decision is a great sadness for me. I had some hope that in Guatemala we might get justice in the courts in this case. I participated fully. I didn't lie. I told the truth about what happened here in our neighbourhood, what happened to my husband Adolfo Ich, how he was assassinated. The witnesses told the truth. My son is one of the witnesses—he told the truth. They all participated fully in the trial.

Now we know that the judge wasn't listening to us. She wasn't paying any attention. That's why it is so sad and so hard.

Perhaps the hardest moment was when we all participated in what is called the "reconstruction of the facts," which took place here in this neighbourhood where everything happened. I now think the judge never should have made us do the reconstruction of the facts. She only did this to make us suffer, to make me suffer, to watch me suffer. She must have gotten some sort of joy out of this.

I remain traumatized. It felt like a blow when I was told the judge acquitted and granted immediate liberty to the assassin. I asked myself, "Why have they done this to us? Why have they not heard us?"

So, it hurts. I cried all afternoon and into the night, after the decision. Around midnight I asked myself, "How am I going to recover spiritually from the effort I have put into seeking justice?"

And it is worse. All of this happens in our country, when these foreign companies come and abuse us and make a mockery of our rights.

We put so much into this struggle for justice. This took years in the courts. There were all kinds of irregularities in the criminal trial, all kinds of discrimination. The judge treated me in an offensive and racist manner. But I kept quiet, thinking, "Well, at least there might be justice." And yet, there was nothing.

Yet in my heart, I have strength. And we're not going to leave this struggle. Yes, I had some hope. And I think maybe I should never have had hope because you never get justice for the poor and Indigenous people in Guatemala.

The governments don't care about the Indigenous people, the poor. We are the people who have taken care of Mother Earth and the natural resources, but the governments care only about giving concessions to the companies without consulting us.

In my heart I know we are strong. We are going to continue with this struggle. I have not hurt anyone. They hurt me. I have been in a resistance struggle in defence of our lands and of Mother Earth, the resources and the environment. We will continue in this struggle, come what may.

The April 6, 2017 decision of the judge here in Guatemala—the acquittal and immediate liberty of Mynor Padilla—left us with even less confidence in the legal system. When we left the courtroom that day, the women from Lote Ocho who were accompanying us and German [Chub], we were all crying. We were broken and had sort of lost hope. We were saying to ourselves, "We Indigenous people can't get justice anywhere." The best that we can do is go home and take care of our families and our communities.

We don't have any money and that's the only way you get justice, is if you have money.

But after a few days, with time to reflect, the women of Lote Ocho came back to me and said, "No. We are not giving up this struggle for justice. Not only are we going to continue the cases in Canada to seek justice but we are going to file a criminal case in Guatemala against the company for the rapes we suffered here. We are going to do this because we have the right to do this and they can't tell us that we can't do this."

So, it was the women of Lote Ocho and German who gave the strength back to me so that we could continue. And it is not just us. We have received solidarity from across Guatemala and around the world. This solidarity gives us strength. People know this is a struggle for Mother Earth and defence of our lands and the environment. People value what we are doing, they value our struggle, and so we will continue with our cases in Canada.

I thank God that I, as an Indigenous woman, as a Maya Q'eqchi' woman, have the strength to speak out, to have my voice listened to and to raise my voice demanding justice.

It is well known that we are in a struggle in defence of the lands and territories of Indigenous people. Our rights and lands have been abused by hydroelectric companies, by mining companies, by the producers of African palm, and more.

In all this, it is regrettable the role played by Canada. It pains me to tell you that the image of Canada is severely damaged here in the Maya communities of El Estor. Canadian companies, like Hudbay Minerals, have violated our rights.

In the years 2007, 2008, 2009, there was a series of evictions carried out by Hudbay and its Guatemalan subsidiary CGN. They burned villages to the ground; women were raped; homes were burned. In 2009, there was the assassination of a Maya Q'eqchi' community leader, my husband Adolfo Ich, may he rest in peace.

What message do I want to say to the people in Canada? Firstly, I am seeking justice in the Canadian courts. I ask for the prayers and support of all those people who love Mother Earth and are involved in work and struggle to protect Mother Earth. Let us work together in solidarity, in this struggle.

I ask for support for our three cases in Canada: the rape of the eleven women of the Lote Ocho community; the shooting of the young man German Chub who lives now in a wheelchair, paralyzed; and for the killing of my husband, Adolfo Ich. These are violations committed by Hudbay Minerals in 2007, 2009, and we still have had no justice done.

We have faith that in Canada we might get justice, unlike in Guatemala as was recently demonstrated by the court that acquitted and freed Mynor Padilla. We know that there are sisters and brothers in Canada who feel our pain, who know about the violations that your companies have committed here in Guatemala against us.

And for you who are also defending lands and territories in Canada, I urge you to continue strong in your struggles because you are defending the well-being of the future of your children and grandchildren.

Testimonio: German Chub, Closing Remarks at Criminal Trial of Mynor Padilla, March 8, 2017
edited by Grahame Russell and translated by Rights Action

> Hearing, Puerto Barrios, Guatemala, March 8, 2017
> Guatemalan criminal case: #18002-2009-00796
> Against: Mynor Rolando Padilla González

Good morning Madam Judge and everyone present here. I just want to request that you turn off the air conditioning because I still have a bullet inside me, that affects me when I speak.

Judge: It cannot be turned off, but we can turn up the temperature two degrees.

I am here today, present in this courtroom. I know that the law allows me to say some things. As you have noticed, I am Q'eqchi', I speak my own language.

Judge: Do you need an interpreter?

I also speak Spanish. I will speak in Spanish, to try to make sure that every-one understands what I have to say.

Madam Judge, I just want to tell you that I am feeling frightened and concerned because I am in this courtroom. I was a young man, twenty-one years old, full of life, full of aspirations. I worked, I was a farmer, just like my parents and grandparents. We lived off the land, off what Mother Earth produced and what natural resources gave us. We were poor and we continue to be poor, but I was capable of maintaining my family.

It is very sad and difficult for me to remember September 27, 2009. That day, by chance, I was at the community soccer field in [the] La Unión [neighbourhood], close to the Hudbay Minerals / CGN hospital.

That day, my life changed without my provoking anything. I was victim of the acts of violence that occurred those days. It made me completely paraplegic. A bullet entered my lung and affected my spinal column, paralyzing me from the waist down. Since then, I am paralyzed as you see me now. I cannot move my limbs or stand up, I cannot work to sustain myself, and much less my family.

I am here now, but I remind you that I didn't come to seek what is called justice. My parents, my Q'eqchi' brothers and sisters, never look for justice in the courts. History has taught us that what is called "justice" is always there to favour powerful people, not people like us.

I understand that due to this problem I had, the Attorney General's office investigated my case. That is how I became involved in all of this. Ever since they told me to come to give my testimony, I have had security problems and so have my parents.

Although I was very afraid and concerned, and because of my very serious health situation, I went to give my testimony to the Attorney General. I told them the truth about what happened to me. I did not say lies. But because of the same fear that I had, at that moment I failed to give the name of the person who fired the shot, I only said that security agents from Hudbay Minerals / CGN shot me.

Years later, I came to the hearing here in court and I continued to tell the truth, and I gave the name of the person who shot me. In the reconstruction of the facts, I showed from where I was shot and who shot me.

Now that I am here in this courtroom, I want to take this opportunity to ask you that justice be done, and that the person responsible be punished.

When we hear the defence lawyers accuse me of being a liar, of being false, of being a criminal, as if I was a big criminal, I ask myself, Madam Judge, why would I come to seek justice if I, the victim, might be punished?

What I want to assure you, Madam Judge, is that I don't have any need to lie and to bargain with my life. I am suffering. My life, and the life of my family and my son, have all been destroyed. I cannot have more children and that is very serious. I am disabled and without hope of being a normal person as I used to be before.

Madam Judge, I don't know where to find justice for my case. If you are a conscientious and transparent person who makes judgment, I will leave the justice for my case in God's hands and in yours. I need to struggle to try to recover so that I can care for my family.

It really hurts me that here in court they are calling me a liar. I am not lying to you, Madam. I am not coming here to lie to you. I am coming here to tell the truth under oath, and I have to abide by that oath. If I was a liar I wouldn't be here, I'd be hiding somewhere, but I am not lying. I am here to tell the truth. The defence lawyers take my testimony and try to confuse people but that's not how it is. I told the truth.

I have a son who is suffering. What fault does this little boy have to be suffering? I have not been able to accompany him as he deserves. But I cannot do it, he is suffering. Where I get my strength and energy from is from my little boy, because he tells me, "Papa, when are you going to get out of that chair?" I tell him, son, be patient. I tell him I will get up soon so he doesn't get sad. I am not going to tell him that they completely ruined my life, not for just a year or two but for the rest of my life—Madam Judge, my entire life. But I cannot tell my son that I'll be like this for the rest of my life. He must forgive me for lying to him.

But I love him very much and he gives me energy to come to this court,

Figure 10. *13 Brave Giants versus Hudbay Minerals*, painting by Pati Flores. Patricia (Pati) Flores' painting represents the thirteen Indigenous Maya Q'eqchi' plaintiffs from Guatemala and their case against Hudbay Minerals. Used by permission.

and so I come here, and what I am saying here is the truth. I am not lying, Madam Judge.

You are seeing me—is this a lie, Madam Judge? Every time I come here, thankfully those who accompany me here, they must carry me up the stairs to where I am now. This is not a lie, Madam Judge. This is the truth. I am here thanks to God who has created a miracle in me. I am still alive.

We are suffering, my son and I. Whose fault is it? It's the fault of the CGN and Hudbay Minerals, of the person detained here [Mynor Padilla]. They should pay for it, for the suffering, not only what I suffered those days but for the rest of my life.

I don't know how many months or years God will allow me to continue speaking on this earth, continue living. I leave it to you, Madam Judge, I put my heart in your hands, so that you can make justice as the law allows, Madam Judge.

That is all I have to say. Thank you for your time, my thanks to all the lawyers who are here. I also need to struggle to attend to the needs of my family. I know that I have a boy, and I have to struggle for him, look for the daily bread even if I will never enjoy it, but at least to give my son the little I can give him. I don't know how but I am going to struggle. I am a person who has not gone to school, I can't get a job, but I am going to keep struggling.

Thank you, Madam Judge, that is all I have to say.

Murder of Héctor: Nephew of Maya Land and Rights Activist Beaten to Death in Guatemala

Heather Gies

Héctor Manuel Choc Cuz, the nephew of prominent land rights activists, dreamed of becoming a professional mechanic when he got older. But the eighteen-year-old Maya Q'eqchi' youth's aspirations were cut short [in March 2018] when he was beaten to death in an attack that family members suspect may have been an attempt on the life of his cousin, José Ich.

According to his family, assailants took Choc Cuz to the edge of the eastern Guatemalan town of El Estor and beat him between the night of March 30, 2018 and the early morning of March 31, 2018. He died that day in the hospital in Puerto Barrios.

"We demand justice and that the murder of my nephew be solved," Choc Cuz's aunt, Angélica Choc, told Mongabay in a phone interview. She added that Choc Cuz, whom she described as hardworking and studious, was like a son to her, just as her son, José Ich, is like a son to Choc Cuz's parents.

Angélica Choc is a human rights and environmental activist who has fought for years against the foreign-owned Fénix nickel mine in El Estor. She is known internationally for demanding justice for the 2009 murder of her husband, Adolfo Ich Chamán, a teacher and local social leader in the anti-mining movement.[7] According to witnesses, Ich Chamán was beaten, hacked with a machete, and shot dead by private security guards of the Fénix mine, which was then owned by Toronto-based mining giant Hudbay Minerals.

The Fénix mine, which Hudbay sold to Cyprus-based Solway Investment Group in 2011, reopened in 2014 after being closed for three decades. Initially concessioned to the Canadian International Nickel Company in the early years of Guatemala's bloody thirty-six-year civil war, the mine has been plagued for decades by longstanding land disputes with local Indigenous communities and other controversies.[8] High-profile incidents include the 2009 killing of Ich Chamán, the 2009 shooting and paralyzing of German Chub Choc,[9] and the 2007 gang rape of eleven Maya Q'eqchi' women in the community of Lote Ocho—all allegedly at the hands of Fénix security personnel.

Witnesses in Choc Cuz's beating last month told the family on the condition of anonymity that they overheard an assailant say, "It's not Ich, let's go," according to a statement released by the family.[10] Choc said her son José is known as Ich in El Estor. She also noted that he and his cousin are very similar in physical appearance. Family members suspect the perpetrators planned to target Ich, but beat and killed his cousin Choc Cuz instead. They fear Ich and other family members could be under threat and are considering additional precautions. "I do not know what the intention was or why my son was mentioned," Choc said, stressing that many questions remain unanswered. "That's why I demand an investigation."

A spokesperson for Guatemala's Office of the Public Prosecutor, Julia Barrera, confirmed in an email that the case is currently under investigation. "The investigation is in development and I cannot provide details because Guatemalan law does not allow it," she said.

Grahame Russell, director of Rights Action, a Toronto- and Washington, DC-based human rights organization supporting Choc and other Guatemalan plaintiffs pursuing legal cases for alleged mining-related abuses, believes the attack was politically motivated. "We suspect that this was because of the family's work in general and because José is a direct participant" in court cases linked to the mine, Russell said in a phone interview.

José Ich is a key witness in two cases dealing with his father's murder. In Canada, his mother is set to battle Hudbay in a civil lawsuit seeking damages for negligence.[11] An Ontario court has given the green light to the case, but a trial is expected to remain years away. The case is one of a trio of ground-breaking civil lawsuits against Hudbay over alleged abuses linked to the Fénix mine that have shaken the Canadian mining industry by setting a precedent of holding companies accountable on home soil for their actions abroad.

Meanwhile, in Guatemala, Ich is also a central witness in the criminal trial of the mine's former security chief, former military lieutenant colonel Mynor Padilla, accused of killing Ich's father. A judge acquitted Padilla of murder and aggravated assault charges in April 2017.[12] The judge simultaneously ordered criminal investigations of Choc and other accusers, including her children, for alleged obstruction of justice and falsifying information. An appeals court overturned the ruling in September 2017 and ordered a retrial. Choc and her family are hopeful that the retrial will come to pass, even though she contends Guatemala's judicial system, rife with corruption and impunity, according to rights monitoring groups, is often stacked against poor Indigenous people.[13]

Cory Wanless, a lawyer at Klippensteins Barristers & Solicitors, the Toronto-based law firm representing Choc and other plaintiffs in civil lawsuits against Hudbay in Canada, said the firm is both "saddened" and "concerned" by Choc Cuz's "apparent targeted murder." "Threats, violence and murders are one of the key reasons that successful criminal prosecutions are so rare in Guatemala," Wanless wrote in an email. "With the ongoing threats and violence against the Choc family . . . we are seeing in real time why achieving justice in Guatemala is next to impossible."

Hudbay Minerals declined to comment on Choc Cuz's death. "Speculation is neither helpful nor respectful, particularly when local media indicates the young man died in a motorcycle accident," Hudbay corporate communications director Scott Brubacher wrote in an email. Local news outlet El Puerto Informa reported that version of events on March 31.[14] When contacted, the outlet said it did not have any further information on the incident beyond the original three-sentence story about what the story's headline called an "apparent" accident.

For Choc and her relatives, Choc Cuz's death fits a decade-long pattern of criminalization and violence they suspect is linked to their activism. In the wake of her husband's murder, Choc has suffered repeated threats and attacks. In 2016, unidentified gunmen fired shots at her house while she and two children were asleep inside. (Choc has five children, including Ich, and also cares for a sixth child she and her husband took in as a young girl.) No one was injured in the gunfire, but the family interpreted the attack as an attempt to put a stop to Choc's activism.

While visiting Toronto last fall to support Maya Q'eqchi' rape survivors from Lote Ocho suing Hudbay for negligence, Choc made clear in an interview with this reporter she would not be bullied into silence. She said she was not afraid to put her life on the line in her quest for justice. According to Rights Action's Russell, such systematic attempts to silence those clamouring for justice for genocide and other abuses against Indigenous Mayans can be traced back to the civil war. "When you're involved in large-scale, politicized human rights trials in Guatemala, repression will happen," he said.

Other members of the family have also been criminalized for their activism. Choc's brother, Ramiro Choc, was sentenced in 2008 to six years in jail on charges of land theft, aggravated robbery, and illegal detention. His supporters contend the charges were manufactured to silence his fight for land rights for Maya Q'eqchi' peasants. More recently, another sibling, María Cuc Choc, was detained in January 2018 and accused of aggravated trespassing, threats, and illegal detention. The allegations were linked to her land defence activism in the Livingston area east of El Estor, but she has also worked closely with the Lote Ocho community where the rapes allegedly occurred in 2007.

Although Choc Cuz and his immediate family were not directly involved in Choc's and other family members' activism, they were always supportive, Choc said. "Personally, it inspires me to continue fighting for the defence of our rights, human rights, Indigenous peoples, and Mother Nature," she said of her nephew's death. "Even though I am still carrying out a long, very difficult, costly process and am very repressed, I believe that my nephew Héctor's rights to live and enjoy life are also worthy," she said, referring to trials over her husband's murder. "Even though I feel tired, weak, I pick myself up to keep moving forward to demand justice."

Testimonio: José Ich, This Is How Hard it Is

José Ich, son of Adolfo Ich and Angélica Choc
with the UNBC Geography and Rights Action Delegation (Grahame
Russell, Catherine Nolin, and student participants), May 8, 2018, while
driving through the western highlands of Guatemala

Well, I have something to share with you guys. My family is well known as human rights defenders in the El Estor region of eastern Guatemala. My mom is Angélica Choc. Me, I never wanted to be in a leadership role; I was not thinking of being a human rights defender. I had a chance to go to the United States and study high school when my dad was still alive. He was a well-known community leader. As a defender of our lands and territory, he often had meetings with the mining company, the mining security guards and managers.

I remember how he would tell us, when he came back home, that the head of the mining security company would say to him, "One day, I will kill you." It was always "One day, I will kill you." I was just a kid and heard him say this to my mom, "This is what the guy told me." My mom would say, "Don't listen to him."

My dad kept working for the Maya Q'eqchi' people, for our community. In September 2009, I was home from the United States. My birthday is in September and I was supposed to leave soon to go back to the United States to continue my studies . . . but I couldn't do that anymore because on September 27 of 2009, my dad was killed.

That was really, really . . . for me, at that age, it is something I will never forget. I was fifteen years old. A guy came to my mom and dad's house. He said "Adolfo, let's go. There is a protest blockade." My dad said to my mom, "I'll be back." When I followed him he told me to go home. I didn't do what he asked me. I turned around, but when I saw him walking away, I followed him. You will see where all this happened when you go to El Estor and my mom will show you the area.

For me it is beyond hard, because I was there, I saw everything that happened. I will never forget. It is always stuck in my mind. And some-times I . . . sometimes when I remember, at times like this, right now, here with you all, it comes quickly like this [snaps his fingers]. I just can't talk about it.

After a couple of years, I continued my studies in the US. Also, a few years later, we were able to finally try and get justice in the Guatemalan courts. But from then on, I started getting threatening messages on Facebook, by email . . . I got a number of threats. I shared with Grahame [Russell] some of those threats.

* * *

So, I had to continue with my life. My mom said, "Do you want to leave?" "No, I don't want to leave." My mom took on my dad's leadership role. She was not as involved as him before. Then, it was mainly my dad, mom stayed more at home.

After dad's death, my mom was really sad and . . . well, she continued with the leadership of the community. She is well-known and respected in our village, the community. And now, my mom now is facing these threats again. She always receives threats.

It is the same as what happened with my Uncle Ramiro [Choc]. He was a political prisoner for five and a half years. And he is innocent—he was not guilty of anything. Now he is out of jail and he's continuing with his community leadership activism. Ramiro says, "If I am not doing something wrong, why should I be afraid of our government?" So, he is speaking out for the rights of Indigenous communities and peoples.

My Aunt María [Cuc Choc] does the same thing. María was recently put in jail in February. That was really shocking. She went to Puerto Barrios to help the community of Chaa'bil Choch because they needed help with translation from Q'eqchi' to Spanish and to have someone with them who knows a bit about how the legal system works. So, she was in jail and my mom and I just started crying. "What's going on?" "Your Aunt María is in jail right now." A lot of people start calling to my mom to ask "Is that true? Is that true?"

We finally found out what jail she was put in. I wrote to Grahame. I sent him a document. We needed people in the international community to know that this is something illegal happening. María had committed no crime when they took her to prison. After hours of detention, she was told she had three criminal charges against her. We were trying to do our best to help her since she was also really sick.

This is just a little bit of what you will hear about in El Estor with Grahame and my mom. And they will share more of their stories.

So, what I am telling you is that my family is really involved in defence of territories and human rights and my family is facing all kinds of threats. And now, even I have received those threats.

Then, on March 30 of this year, my cousin was killed . . . I never expected that. It was Holy Week and I was out on Friday night with friends and then at 10 p.m. I went to help my sister-in-law because they were going to sell meat the next day, so I was helping them . . . but I couldn't stay awake, so I went home to bed.

At five or six in the morning, I heard people knocking on my door. I was like, "Who is here? Why are they knocking on my door at six in the morning? This is not usual." I went to the door. They said, "Whoa, you are here, you are not a ghost." I said, "What's going on?" They said, "Well, they found a guy dead up in the San Marcos neighbourhood." "So what?" because I didn't know who it was at that moment. They said, "Where is your motorbike?" "My bike is right there." I opened the door wide and they saw my bike. "Who is the guy who is dead?" I asked.

I drove my bike to the health centre. I tried to find out who it is but the guard said, "No, you cannot go in." And I was trying to get in there . . . but then I decided to go home.

I got a call from a friend saying, "That's your cousin." "No, it's not." "Yes, it's your cousin." "No, it's not." I even swore at him and I hung up the phone and went to my aunt's house.

My older cousin was there and I asked him, "Where is your brother?" He said, "He hasn't come home since last night." His mom came out—my aunt—and said, "What's going on? Where is Héctor?"

"He hasn't come home since last night." "Why, why?" she asked to me. "It was because they found a guy who is dead right now in San Marcos."

"What colour of shirt does he have?" And I started telling her . . . "That's my son," she shouted. And then my aunt was CRYING. And my cousins . . . and everything.

My mom called me, because she was about four hours away in Cobán at an activity. And then she called me to say, "Is that your cousin?" "Yes, mom, it's my cousin." So that was really, really, like for us, it was really sad. It had, once again, a big impact on us.

Even my mom now is struggling with health issues. She can't move her arm, I don't know why. She's struggling. Even me and my cousin and my little brother—we're struggling. We can't forget it. We are still waiting for him to come home. It's kind of like what happened when I was waiting for my dad. So, it is very hard.

I went to the Canadian Embassy. I gave this kind of speech to them and I said it is hard for me to remember all those events that happened in my life, that I have lived.

Even when we had the evictions and burnings of our communities in El Estor—done for the mining company back in 2006 and 2007, by the police, company security guards, and military—well, I was there when they were doing the evictions, shooting tear gas, burning, and everything. I was there, at my young age. It was kind of like living in a WAR. For me at that time it was like a war. I still remember running and running. All I had on were sandals and when I couldn't run anymore, I took off my sandals and ran barefoot.

Then, last year there was the killing of one of the leaders of the Gremial de Pescadores / Union of Q'eqchi' Fisherpeople—his name is Carlos Maaz. I was THERE that day; I watched this. I SAW everything. And I say to myself, "Why in my life am I still living this?"

I do this—I speak out like this, I share my story and our stories— because it is not that I want to be exactly like my dad or my mom, but I want to do something for my community, I need to.

But now, I know that I can't stay any longer in El Estor because I am being followed. I don't know who is sending people to kill me. That morning after my cousin Héctor was killed, one of the witnesses came to our house and talked to my brother and said, "They mentioned your little brother," naming ME. I have the same colour of motorbike as my cousin Héctor, the same model. And they mentioned me. Why? The witness said that the killers said, "It's not Ich. Let's go, just leave him there."

In El Estor, everyone knows me as "Ich," my last name. So, the question we want to know is why did they mention me? Why did they want to kill me? And why did they kill my cousin?

So, all these events that happened . . . and these things happen not just to my family, the Ich Choc family. But all this is happening to my family as well. My Uncle Ramiro, my dad, my Aunt María, my mom, and now it has involved my cousin Héctor. Now Héctor's parents are involved in all this as well.

And our question is: "Why is it always like this?" Maybe it is because of our resistance, our defending territory and rights. The government here has always violated the rights of Indigenous people, of us Maya Q'eqchi' people in my region.

Now, I am here with you guys, helping you on your school trip as you go and listen to other community defence struggles that are similar.

When I hear other people's testimonies, I compare them to our own. For example, the last time I went to the community of Río Negro with Lisa Rankin, I just couldn't hear any more testimonies. I was IMAGINING events that happened in the worst years of the internal conflict . . . and now in 2006, 2007, 2008, 2009, there are almost similar violations and repression taking place in different places.

So, I listen to the community stories, and I compare them with my life, the life of my community and . . . well, sometimes you will see me sitting quietly, but it is just that in my mind I am comparing stuff. For me, it is important that I keep busy—it is not to forget everything, but I have lived through this my WHOLE life.

Like, I'll be remembering . . . I can't even watch movies with killing. It's like this [snaps fingers]—in one second, I then remember still having my dad and grabbing him and saying to him the words I said back then, "Dad, let's go. They are gone." Those words, when I watch movies like some of these movies with killing in them, they come to my mind and then I can't keep watching it.

And now it has happened again in 2018, on March 30, my little cousin Héctor. I said to him, "You're going to be okay, you're going to the hospital." I saw him bleeding in the nose, in his mouth, ear, eyes. I saw the hole in his head. And I am like, "Man, this is . . . why me?" First my dad, and now my cousin.

Nine years later it's like just a small amount of time that has gone by. All these violent events that have happened to us, and they always have to do with defending territory and human rights, I guess, and because my family is very involved in that.

My Aunt María is working with a lot of remote Maya villages up in the mountains. My Uncle Ramiro is working with remote Maya communities in the area of Livingston. My mom is working in the area of El Estor. Maybe violence is the way that the people with power want to stop or shut our voices off.

That's why Lisa Rankin was telling me—she works for a group called Breaking the Silence—"Let's go to the Embassy. Let's do this. Let's have the Guatemalan government receive a little bit of pressure from the Canadian Embassy. Let's have the Public Prosecutor's office get a little bit of pressure from the Canadians. Because if we don't do this, the people with power will always act with impunity."

Right now, during the criminal trial for the murder of my dad, not only was the killer acquitted by the trial judge eight years after my dad's death, but the judge ordered a criminal investigation into my mom. During the entire trial, my mom was intimidated and threatened in so many different ways, and now he is free, the killer is free, and the judge wants a criminal investigation into my mom. What is this?

And actually, we were all criminalized. The judge said in her ruling that we—the eyewitnesses to my dad's killing, including me—had to be investigated criminally for our role in the trial. The government and the legal system work like that here in Guatemala, so that is one of the reasons we are looking for justice in Canada. And thank god we now have the lawsuits there in court.

So that's what my life has been like. It's not always like happiness and happiness. I am TRYING, I'm TRYING to find a way to be happy. Maybe you will see me smiling but behind my face, it is just sadness.

Chapter 5

Facing and Resisting KCA / Radius Gold and Tahoe Resources on the Ground

> Guatemala has taken a series of legal, discursive and policy initiatives to produce a mineral extraction space within its territory. The government and the elites have been involved in the production of such space. . . . The production of space does not happen without resistance from those whose lives will be affected.
> —Mariel Aguilar-Støen[1]

P lace-based resistance to Canadian- (and American- and Swiss-) owned mining projects—proposed or active—in Guatemala is as inspiring as it is heartbreaking. At every step, beginning with first warnings of the arrival of mining equipment or notice of the granting of a mining concession in their communities and territories, concerned community members have come together with creativity, strength, and courage only to be met with violence, brutal force, and criminalization. In this chapter, we interview lawyer Yuri Melini who was the founder and director of the Centro de Acción Legal, Ambiental y Social de Guatemala / Centre for Environmental, Social and Legal Action (CALAS) about the organization's work to call out corruption and impunity and support mining-affected communities in their call for proper consultation before mining projects proceed.

Simon Granovsky-Larsen and Caren Weisbart then take a deep dive into the violent years connected with the El Escobal silver mine near San Rafael Las Flores, initiated by Vancouver-based Tahoe Resources (a child of Vancouver-based Goldcorp Inc.) and recently purchased by Vancouver-based Pan American Silver. Together, they highlight Canadian and Guatemalan institutional processes which served to facilitate the operation of the mine as well as the successful legal challenges within Guatemala and Canada to hold accountable Tahoe Resources for crimes and violations as well as the Guatemalan government for lack of consultation with the Indigenous Xinca people in the first place. Alexandra Pedersen then documents the story of the inspirational citizen movement at La Puya, the nine-year-long roadside encampment at the entrance to the El Tambor mine situated between San José del Golfo and San Pedro Ayampuc, just north of Guatemala City.

Catherine Nolin, Grahame Russell, and James Rodríguez then recount the May 18, 2016 session at the Guatemalan Supreme Court when CALAS lawyer Rafael Maldonado petitioned for a definitive suspension of the El Tambor mine. The trio then travelled to La Puya to talk with community members about what they are resisting and what they are fighting for. Amalia, Alvaro, and Ana Sandoval all speak about resistance but more passionately about the positive fight "for Mother Earth and nature and for our natural resources."

Interview: Yuri Melini, ILO 169 and Community Defence

Lawyer, Founder, and Former Director of Centro de Acción Legal, Ambiental y Social de Guatemala / Centre for Environmental, Social and Legal Action (CALAS)
with Grahame Russell and Catherine Nolin, May 18, 2017

Question: Please comment on International Labour Organization (ILO) Convention 169 in terms of defence of communities. What is the importance of this legal mechanism?

Convention 169 is at the same time both a legal instrument and a political instrument; it has both legal and political ramifications. In CALAS, we have been using Convention 169 in our lawsuits to successfully make arguments about the self-determination of Indigenous peoples, about the legality of the consultation process, and about citizens' rights to effective participation.

Before, Convention 169 was not being used or recognized in courts and now it is. Today, many court decisions make direct reference to laws and principles set out in Convention 169.

In CALAS, we have at least three cases that have gone to the Constitutional Court where the Court referred positively to Convention

169 as part of its ruling. Two of these cases dealt with the legality of the consultation process and the court ruled that Convention 169 was the fundamental basis in law establishing the legality of the community and municipal consultations.

Question: Can you expand on how the Courts have recognized this mechanism?

Two concrete cases that we have been fighting in the courts have dealt with the right to consultation and the right to free and prior informed consent. In these cases, the courts resolved three fundamental legal issues: (1) the people do not have procedures in place to be consulted; (2) it is unquestionably the peoples' right to be consulted; and (3) the results of consultations are binding on local administrative matters for the municipal government and all community members. These court decisions are now accepted legal jurisprudence.

Another case we are involved with is related to La Puya. In this case, the court recognized the community's right to consultation and that there was an ongoing violation of this right.

Question: How does endemic corruption and impunity impact your work?

In Guatemala, confronting the structures of impunity and the coalition of economic and political powers has been one of the most difficult elements of CALAS's work. These are coalitions of political and economic power centres at the national and international levels, along with the impunity and corruption of the illegal parallel structures.

We have found ourselves in, and had to denounce, the complicated situations of corruption and impunity manifest in all aspects of the legal system; to denounce situations when companies bribe politicians and government officials; to denounce situations when companies co-opt the media so that what gets published is favourable to the companies.

Question: How do Canadian and American companies participate in and benefit from corruption and impunity in the country?

The co-optation of the State is a big problem that Guatemala has. This has been highlighted in recent years by the corrupt actions of mining companies in co-opting the State. Just in the last two years, we have seen three cases of managers of mining companies involved in acts of corruption.

There is the case of Eduardo Villacorta, vice-president of Goldcorp's Latin America division, involved in bribery of public officials. There is an international capture order pending against him. There is the case of Mynor Padilla, head of security for Hudbay Minerals accused of murder and assault. There is the case of Alberto Rotondo, the head of security for Tahoe Resources, accused of assault.

There are cases of mining company managers who previously had worked in the Guatemalan government. There is the case of Alfredo Gálvez Sinibaldi, the current general manager of Montana Exploradora, the subsidiary company of Goldcorp. He was previously vice-minister of the Ministry of Energy and Mines; prior to that he had been director of mining during the government of President Óscar Berger.

There is the case of Milton Saravia, lawyer for Montana Exploradora, the subsidiary of Goldcorp, who previously worked in the Ministry of Energy and Mines. Former Energy Minister Erick Archila is also now charged with co-optation and bribery of State officials in a criminal scandal.

This phenomena of trafficking of influences between the mining companies and government is widespread.

Tahoe Resources' Violent Mining Operation
Simon Granovsky-Larsen and Caren Weisbart

Introduction

On April 27, 2013, seven unarmed men were shot by security guards employed by the San Rafael mine, a Guatemalan subsidiary of Vancouver- and Nevada-based mining company Tahoe Resources. The seven men were part of a group of local community members that gathered that day near the entrance to Tahoe's San Rafael silver mine—the Escobal Project—in southeastern Guatemala, and video footage of the incident shows guards rushing the peaceful gathering with guns blazing, shooting some of the protesters from behind.[2] While all seven men survived the attack, including those with now lifelong injuries, the Escobal project has been the site of several other violent incidents, including the kidnapping and attempted murder of at least six community leaders, and the murder of four others: Exaltación Marcos Ucelo, Telesforo Pivaral, sixteen-year-old Topacio Reynoso, and Ángel Estuardo Quevado. Over one hundred community activists have faced legal persecution on trumped-up charges for their opposition to the mine.[*]

Demonstrations of collective opposition to the San Rafael mine—including fourteen *consultas* (municipal or community consultations) that largely rejected the mine, as well as a range of protest tactics—have been met with violence and criminalization over the course of these conflictive years.[3] The events of these years are complex and are only partially summarized in this chapter.[†] Most important for our purposes is to recognize that the mass shooting of April 2013 took place in the context of the legally questionable approval of Tahoe's exploitation license earlier that month by the Ministry of Energy and Mines (MEM).

Four incidents stand out as the most important surrounding the turbulent approval of the Tahoe license. First, a number of deaths took place in early 2013: four Indigenous Xinca leaders on their way back from a *consulta* related to Tahoe's operations on their territory were kidnapped in March and one was killed, two security guards employed by the mine were killed in January, and a police officer was killed in April. The guard and police deaths were blamed on community opposition, but activists deny involvement and the attempt to blame violence on protesters who have consistently shown themselves to be peaceful amounts to a further criminalization tactic.

Second, shortly before Tahoe's license was approved, the San Rafael mine was elevated to the category of "strategic natural resource" by Guatemala's National Security Commission.[4] The April 27 shooting of seven protesters represents the third major incident, and is the focus of much of this contribution. Finally, just days after that shooting, the Guatemalan government declared an *estado de sitio* (state of siege) round of localized martial law to suppress opposition to the recently-approved mine.[5]

---

[*] Criminalization of social protest has become common in Guatemala, with a clear pattern of baseless charges intended to burden activists with legal defence and to intimidate others. Amnesty International, *We Are Defending the Land with Our Blood: Defenders of the Land, Territory, and Environment in Honduras and Guatemala*, AMR 01/4562/2016, September 1, 2016, https://www.amnesty.org/en/documents/amr01/4562/2016/en/.

[†] Readers interested in a more complete documentation and assessment should look to Luís Solano's comprehensive report, *Under Siege: Peaceful Resistance to Tahoe Resources and Militarization in Guatemala*, International Platform against Impunity in Central America and MiningWatch Canada, November 10, 2015, miningwatch.ca/sites/default/files/solano-underseigereport2015-11-10.pdf.

While this contribution zeroes in on documentation of those events in 2013, it should be noted that the conflict continues: community leaders were again shot or killed in 2014, 2015, 2016, 2017, and 2018;[6] a civil case was filed against Tahoe in Canada in 2014 (and settled in 2019), and a criminal case was filed in Guatemala in 2013 against Tahoe's head of security; and legal injunctions filed against the mine in Guatemala led to its temporary yet ongoing suspension in 2017, requiring Tahoe to conduct a community consultation with the surrounding Xinca Indigenous communities, which is ongoing, despite numerous irregularities.[7] Since June 2017, community members have peacefully protested the movement of mining equipment to and from the project site, and in early 2019 Vancouver-based Pan American Silver purchased Tahoe Resources. Soon after this purchase, the plaintiffs reached a successful conclusion to their lawsuit against Tahoe Resources for human rights violations, a first of its kind in Canada.[8] Yet, the struggle over the San Rafael mine is far from over.

Over the following pages, we highlight some of the Guatemalan and Canadian legal and government processes which have served to facilitate the operation of the San Rafael mine and its associated repressive violence

Figure 11. San Rafael State of Siege. Checkpoint between San Rafael Las Flores and Mataquescuintla during the first day of the Guatemalan government's declared State of Siege in four municipalities in support of the mining operation of Vancouver-based Tahoe Resources. Numerous constitutional rights were suspended for thirty days. Mataquescuintla, Jalapa, Guatemala, May 2, 2013.
Photo: James Rodríguez.

and criminalization. Our analysis centres on this court case heard by the British Columbia (BC) Supreme Court, brought against Tahoe Resources by the seven survivors of the April 2013 attack, as well as on the Guatemalan state's monitoring of protests in 2013 and 2014. Through a reading of the over three hundred pages of publicly released documentation entered into the case, and two hundred pages of official Guatemalan documents obtained through access-to-information requests and other research, we point to a number of ways in which repression and extraction are shaped through both legal processes and the coordination of multiple state institutions and non-state entities.

Timeline of Events Mentioned

January 11, 2013: two private security guards employed by the San Rafael mine killed

March 17, 2013: four Xinca community leaders kidnapped, one murdered—Exaltación Marcos Ucelo

April 27, 2013: seven unarmed protesters shot by Tahoe Resources security guards

April 29, 2013: one police officer killed during a protest against the mine

April 2013: Guatemala criminal case filed against former San Rafael Mine Security Manager Alberto Rotondo

April 30, 2013: Rotondo arrested while trying to flee Guatemala

May 2–8, 2013: State of Siege: martial law and military operation in four municipalities surrounding the mine

April 13, 2014: Topacio Reynoso murdered; her father Alex Reynoso is shot and wounded in the same attack

June 18, 2014: civil case against Tahoe filed in Canada

April 5, 2015: community resistance member Telesforo Odilio Pivaral Gonzalez murdered

October 17, 2015: Alex Reynoso, Marlon Loy Dominguez, and Estuardo Bran Clavel survive shooting attack by unknown assailants

November 2015: BC court refuses to accept jurisdiction over the civil case against Tahoe, deciding that Guatemala is the better forum to hear the case

Late November 2015: Alberto Rotondo escapes house arrest in Guatemala and flees to Peru

January 22, 2016: Interpol captures Rotondo in Peru where he currently awaits extradition

November 12, 2016: murder of Jeremy Abraham Barrios, assistant to the General Director of CALAS, a legal defence association assisting the community opposition

January 2017: BC Court of Appeal overturns trial court decision and determines that case should be heard in Canada

June 2017: community protest against the movement of mining equipment begins

June 2017: Canadian Supreme Court denies Tahoe Resources' appeal; civil lawsuit can proceed to trial in BC

July 2017: Guatemalan Constitutional Court temporarily suspends San Rafael mine

September 2017: San Rafael mine suspension overturned by Guatemalan Supreme Court, under order to hold consultations with Indigenous communities and report on results within a year

February 2019: Pan American Silver purchases Tahoe Resources

July 31, 2019: Pan American Silver apologizes to four plaintiffs and strikes legal settlements

Violent Norms

Two distinct legal suits have been launched in response to the violent events of April 27, 2013. The first is a civil case against Tahoe Resources in Canada for negligence and battery,[9] and the second is a criminal case in Guatemala against former security manager Alberto Rotondo, who oversaw the April 2013 shooting. Rotondo has been charged with assault and obstruction of justice.[10] Together, these two cases provide important insight into how law operates in both countries through a variety of inter-related mechanisms to shield Tahoe Resources, at least temporarily, from responsibility and accountability. Responsibility for the complex mine security operations, discussed below, which resulted in the shooting of the seven men, is obscured in three interconnected ways: first, by Tahoe's legal arguments that Guatemala is the more appropriate forum* for the civil

---

* For more background on the *forum non conveniens* and its application in Canadian courts in relation to corporate abuses abroad, see Shin Imai, Bernadette Maheandiran, and Valerie Crystal, "Accountability Across Borders: Mining in Guatemala and the Canadian Justice System," *Comparative Research in Law & Political Economy. Research Paper 26/2012*, 2012, digitalcommons.osgoode.yorku.ca/clpe/28/; Liisa North and Laura Young, "Generating Rights for Communities Harmed by Mining: Legal and Other

case, as a BC court would originally decide in November 2015;[11] second, through information presented by Donald Gray, former Country Manager of the San Rafael mine, in his November 24, 2014 affidavit submitted to the BC court; and, finally, the failure of the Guatemalan criminal case to bring any form of meaningful justice to the victims of the violent shooting. This final point stands in stark contrast to the notion, as argued by Tahoe in Canada, that justice could be achieved through Guatemalan courts.

On April 30, 2013, Rotondo was arrested in Guatemala on charges of assault, aggravated assault, and obstruction of justice. According to the audio footage transcribed and submitted to the BC court as part of the civil case against Tahoe, Rotondo had allegedly ordered his subordinates to clean up all shrapnel and evidence of the April 2013 shooting.[12] When the case was finally brought to trial in Guatemala after a failed attempt to escape the country under his arrest warrant, the Guatemalan judge who presided over his case decided that Rotondo was not a flight risk and placed him under house arrest. On November 30, 2015, weeks after a BC judge in the civil case decided that Guatemala was the better forum to hear the civil case against Tahoe and that the court would not hear the case in Canada,* Guatemala's court system discovered that Rotondo had escaped house arrest, and it was eventually determined by Rotondo's former lawyer that he had fled to his home country of Peru.[13] While he was eventually captured by Interpol, his prosecution has been suspended while Guatemala seeks Rotondo's extradition from Peru, a process that lawyer Matt Eisenbrandt states has "stretched on for years."[14]

Distinct from the civil case for negligence and battery against Tahoe Resources in Canada, the Guatemalan criminal case against Alberto Rotondo provides invaluable insight into the ways in which private security

---

Action," *Canadian Journal for Development Studies* 34, no. 1 (March 2013): 96–110; and Charlotte Connolly, *Exporting Canada's Extractives Approach to Development: The Nexus of Law, Violence and Development in the Case of Tahoe Resources Inc. in Guatemala* (master's thesis, University of Northern British Columbia, 2019).

* A decision was made on January 26, 2017 and was later confirmed by the Supreme Court of Canada on June 8, 2017 when that court declined to hear Tahoe's appeal. Also, the former head of security Mynor Padilla for Hudbay Minerals / CGN was acquitted of the murder of Adolfo Ich Chamán, for the shooting of German Chub resulting in his paralysis, and for shooting and wounding six other men. Marina Jimenez, "Guatemala Murder Acquittal Could Have Far Reaching Consequences," *Toronto Star*, April 7, 2017, thestar.com/news/world/2017/04/07/guatemala-murder-acquittal-could-have-far-reaching-canadian-consequences.html.

guards can ultimately shoot to kill and almost never be held accountable. A subsequent case related to Rotondo's escape from police custody also highlights the ongoing influences of corruption over the judicial system in Guatemala and the resultant lack of access to justice for the men brutally attacked, highlighting the dangers of the case being heard in Guatemala. On June 1, 2017, a Guatemalan judge found the police officers involved in guarding Rotondo during his house arrest guilty for negligence and culpability. Testimonies from the trial point to the "tight control that Rotondo held over his own house arrest."[15]

In his November 24, 2014 affidavit, former Country Manager and Vice President of Operations Donald Gray seems to deny any responsibility on the part of Tahoe Resources for the actions perpetrated by private security contracted to the San Rafael mine.[16] First, he clarifies that the Grupo Golan Inc. private security contract was managed by Rotondo. He states that "as Security Manager, Rotondo was required to manage third party contracts related to security for the Escobal Project" and that Gray himself "took no specific direction from [CEO] Clayton regarding Minera San Rafael / Mining San Rafael [MSR] security activities."[17] He also asserts that the *Ley que regula la seguridad privada* [Law regulating private security]* demonstrates that private security officers receive "theoretical and practical training, in accordance to international standards applicable to the matter, on the use of force and the use of weapons."[18] With these statements, he seems to imply that because the law required third party contracted private security companies to train their officers, and Rotondo was responsible for managing these contracts, then Tahoe performed their due diligence regarding international standards and the use of force.

This reliance on the letter of the law as opposed to the law's application in the context of corruption and impunity that characterizes post-conflict Guatemala is Gray's straw man and certainly contradicts the company's commitment to the *Voluntary Principles of Private Security and Human Rights*.[19] The voluntary principles indicate that companies must ensure private security personnel follow international standards related to the use of force and firearms.† Yet, according to a concept note circulated during

---

* Access the law in Spanish at Centro Nacional de Análisis y Documentación Judicial (CENADOJ), "Ley que Regula los Servicios de Seguridad Privada," *Decreto Número 52-2010* (Guatemala: CENADOJ, December 9, 2010), ohchr.org/Documents/Issues/Mercenaries/WG/Law/Guatemala.pdf.

† There is much academic discussion about the binding impact of such voluntary

a United Nations Working Group panel on private military and security companies in Latin America, even if laws seem to be well-written and include human rights protections,

> a country with a more complete and adequate substantive law protecting human rights does not necessarily achieve more effective protections, because that depends on the degree of implementation and application . . . Because Latin America and the Caribbean is the region with the highest incidence of violence and homicides in the world, plus a lack of confidence in police institutions and the judicial system . . . it is clear that it is not enough to observe the quality of existing legal texts.[20]

It is well documented that private security companies operating in Guatemala fit this description. It is also no secret that former military and government officials, which have maintained their influence over particular army and security structures established in the 1970s and 1980s,[21] have been involved in the formation of private security companies and the contracting of international private security advisors with military experience and "mercenary roots in the Iraq and Afghanistan wars."[22]

Furthermore, top Guatemalan officials who have supported Tahoe Resources and ensured public "security" for the region surrounding the mine site, as elaborated on in the next section, include the former Minister

---

regulatory mechanisms. See Shin Imai, Landan Mehranvar, and Jennifer Sander, "Breaching Indigenous Law: Canadian Mining in Guatemala," *Indigenous Law Journal* 6, no. 1 (2007): 101–39, papers.ssrn.com/sol3/papers.cfm?abstract_id=1267902; Imai, Maheandiran, and Crystal, "Accountability"; Karyn Keenan, "Commentary: Desperately Seeking Sanction: Canadian Extractive Companies and Their Public Partners," *Canadian Journal of Development Studies* 34, no. 1 (2013): 111–21; Stuart Kirsch, *Mining Capitalism: The Relationship between Corporations and Their Critics* (Berkeley, CA: University of California Press, 2014); J. P. Laplante and Catherine Nolin, "Consultas and Socially Responsible Investing in Guatemala: A Case Study Examining Maya Perspectives on the Indigenous Right to Free, Prior and Informed Consent," *Society & Natural Resources: An International Journal* 27, no. 3 (March 2014): 231–48; MiningWatch Canada and RAID-UK, *Privatized Remedy and Human Rights: Re-thinking Project-Level Grievance Mechanisms*, Third Annual UN Forum on Business and Human Rights, December 1, 2014, miningwatch.ca/sites/default/files/privatized_remedy_and_human_rights-un_forum-2014-12-01.pdf; North and Young, "Generating"; David Szablowski, *Transnational Law and Local Struggles: Mining, Communities and the World Bank* (Oxford and Portland, OR: Hart Publishing, 2007); and David Szablowski, "Operationalizing Free, Prior, and Informed Consent in the Extractive Industry Sector? Examining the Challenges of a Negotiated Model of Justice," *Canadian Journal of Development Studies* 30, nos 1–2 (2010): 111–30.

of the Interior, Mauricio López Bonilla, and former President Otto Pérez Molina. Both are well known for their military leadership roles in the brutal counterinsurgency campaigns of the 1980s against defenceless communities and both faced charges and are in jail for their alleged involvement in major corruption scandals; López Bonilla was subsequently sentenced to thirteen years in prison in 2019.[23] * Due to their prominent positions within the Guatemalan government, however, these two men were naturally part of the contact list of the Canadian Embassy in Guatemala. According to a document released under an Access to Information request to Global Affairs Canada, López Bonilla was second on the priority list of who Canadian diplomats† should meet with after receiving accreditation in Guatemala because of his role in a "defense and security proposal from Canadian companies."[24]

The April 27 violent attack on protesters did nothing to curb Canadian government support for the Escobal project when, two days later, on April 29, then-Canadian Ambassador Hugues Rousseau presided over a Voluntary Royalties ceremony along with Otto Pérez Molina and then-Minister of Energy and Mines Erick Archila.[25] Like Pérez Molina, Archila later resigned because of corruption charges related to money laundering. Then, in 2015, the Guatemalan Centre for Environmental, Social and Legal Action / Centro de Acción Legal, Ambiental y Social de Guatemala (CALAS) filed a suit against him. CALAS argued that the granting of the license was both unconstitutional and a breach of duty because Archila had failed to consider 250 individual complaints submitted by community members to the Ministry about Tahoe's exploitation license. The complaints had raised serious concerns about the environmental impact of the project.[26] The Royalties ceremony is no different from Gray's straw man, when taken within the context of the suspension of Tahoe's exploitation license[27] for failure to consult impacted Indigenous communities living near the mine site: it is an empty ceremony that both obfuscates the violent reality of land defenders who resist Canadian mining companies'

---

* López Bonilla was also indicted by the District Court of the District of Columbia on drug-related charges. Héctor Silva Ávalos, "Guatemala Ex-Minister Used Police to Escort Cocaine Shipments: US," *Insight Crime*, June 28, 2017, insightcrime.org/news/analysis/guatemala-ex-minister-used-police-escort-cocaine-shipments-us/.
† It is not clear from the documentation provided for whom the list was generated. However, the assumption can be made that it was for the ambassador given that it refers to priority meetings before and after accreditation in Guatemala.

presence in Guatemala and ignores the clear opinions and persistent resistance of several Indigenous and non-Indigenous communities impacted by Canadian projects.

Extraction and Counterinsurgency

While documents and decisions entered into the Tahoe case show the many legal sleights of hand that have the effect of supporting Tahoe, research into the role of the Guatemalan state exposes a counterinsurgent strategy that took shape in response to protests. Documents created by a range of Guatemalan state institutions and obtained through our research point to the sustained and multi-institutional collection of intelligence on people and groups organized against the San Rafael mine.

Following four decades of US-backed Guatemalan state repression, characterized increasingly by the subversion of state institutions for counterinsurgent warfare,[28] the war on land defenders and other activists has intensified since the early 2000s. The techniques of counterinsurgency are today being mobilized against unarmed activists and communities that organize to defend their land, water, and resources from expropriation or contamination by extractive projects. In the national press, routine discussion of social movement opposition to extractive projects as "terrorism" is used to justify their violent repression.[29]

As part of this pro-mining counterinsurgent strategy, criminalization, defamation, militarization, and targeted physical and psychological attacks are used against activists on a near-daily basis,* with 2,226 incidents registered between 2013 and 2016, including fifty-one assassinations and another fifty-three attempted assassinations.[30] As an extractive operation of high strategic concern to the Guatemalan state, Tahoe's San Rafael mine revealed a level of counterinsurgent activity that serves as a window onto tactics being used across the country. Here we present just one element that comes to light in connection to the Escobal project: intelligence gathering that may be mobilized towards the strategic deployment of force by a range of state and non-state armed groups.

Intelligence gathered towards establishing control over a population is considered the key element of counterinsurgent operations.[31] In the

---

* The categories of threats and attacks listed here was first presented by the Network in Solidarity with the People of Guatemala in their report, *In Defense of Land* (Network in Solidarity with the People of Guatemala [NISGUA], 2017, 2).

municipalities surrounding the San Rafael mine, intelligence-gathering has occurred in a fashion that both coordinates a wide range of government and private sector actors and recalls the style of counterintelligence utilized during the armed conflict. As revealed in Luís Solano's comprehensive report, *Under Siege: Peaceful Resistance to Tahoe Resources and Militarization in Guatemala,* Tahoe management participated directly in a pilot project of intelligence coordination in 2013 through the creation of an "Interinstitutional Office for Comprehensive Development" in San Rafael Las Flores, linked to an "Interinstitutional Group for Strategic Natural Resources (Mining)."[32] The group and office brought together high-ranking officials from, among others, the Ministry of Energy and Mines, Ministry of the Environment and Natural Resources, Ministry of the Interior, and National Security Council. The group was created by the Guatemalan government's Secretariat for Strategic State Intelligence and was headed first by the Consejo Nacional de Seguridad / National Security Commission before its direction was passed in June 2014 to the Ministry of Energy and Mines.[33]

The minutes of twelve meetings of the Interinstitutional Office for Comprehensive Development between December 2013 and September 2014, obtained through Access to Information requests in Guatemala, suggest that the concern of the group lay primarily with the security and operation of the mine, and only with local development efforts as an afterthought. Among the stated objectives of the office are: to "generate the security conditions that guarantee investment and allow for the development projects to operate," "teach [*sensibilizar*] the local populations about the advantages of using natural resources," and "supervise the actions that generate legal certainty for the various projects and development plans."[34]

In order to ensure the operation of the mine, the meeting minutes suggest that the office involved the regular presence of security advisors from the National Security Commission—including at least two people identified as armed forces officers, who participated in one meeting each, and a presentation by the Jutiapa military brigade at a meeting earlier in 2013—and focused a significant proportion of its resources on monitoring the activities of opposition to the project. For example, a meeting on December 13, 2013 dedicated an agenda item to discussing the presence of the grassroots environmental association Colectivo Madre Selva, describing the group as one working to "create panic."[35] At the meeting of March 28, 2014, all agencies participating in the office were asked to contribute their existing information on opposition actors, including information already collected by the National Security Commission.[36] Minutes for six of the twelve meetings explicitly document discussion of opposition groups, protests, or community *consultas*.

It should be noted that available documentation begins in December 2013, but the Interinstitutional Group and office were created in March of that year. A review of activities from 2013 included in one document show that the group met nine times during 2013, including three times in the month leading up to a major military operation in May, and once after that same operation had been downgraded from an *estado de sitio* (state of siege) to an *estado de prevención* (state of prevention).[37]

The Guatemalan Policía Nacional Civil / Civilian National Police (PNC) have also engaged in strategic intelligence gathering in relation to the San Rafael mine. Documents found on a third-party website collect nearly one hundred pages of police reports on community organizers.* One document, which presents the results of an investigation into various instances of property damage and the abduction of police officers and company employees reportedly connected to the community resistance, includes detailed information on movement participants. In addition to outlining information collected on the incidents in question, the document presents details on people suspected of organizing protests against the mine, including photos of the individuals and their places of residence, along with their personal cellphone numbers. Headshots of supposed organizers fill three pages, complete with ages and personal identification numbers. A series of photos are shown allegedly from protests and community plebiscites related to the mine. Pages of photos with commentary outline an analysis of the role of local organizers and Guatemalan NGOs in the struggle against Tahoe. For those familiar with counterinsurgency and intelligence documentation collected illegally on thousands of disappeared, tortured, and murdered Guatemalan activists during the decades of US-backed state repression and genocide, the layout of these files draws an immediate and chilling connection to the recent wartime period of counterinsurgency.[38]

Intelligence gathered on people opposed to the San Rafael mine—which our research shows was collected by the Civilian National Police, the National Security Commission, and the Interinstitutional Office for Comprehensive Development between at least 2012 and 2014—may have

---

* Files were accessed in July 2015 but have since been removed.

been deployed to facilitate the use of repressive force and legal intimidation in order to quell community opposition. While the connection between intelligence gathering and repression cannot be proven, it seems likely that the information collected could be utilized in subsequent attacks and arrests. For example, during the state of siege surrounding the mine in May 2013—which represented one of the largest military operations since the 1996 formal end of the armed conflict, with at least 8,500 military troops and police officers imposing martial law across four municipalities during a period of seven days—at least two organizers profiled in the aforementioned police document were arrested.* One of these was accused in the police file of possessing a weapon, but the other was only included as a protest organizer; photos of both people were included in the pre-arrest documents, as were images of their homes.

Following the tumultuous period of early 2013, the use of violent force against activists has shifted away from police–military–private security and towards targeted assassination through hired gunmen. It is our opinion that the establishment of control through counterinsurgent intelligence gathering and military operations described above contributed to a new phase of violent repression through targeted attacks against community leaders and their supporters, flanked by ongoing crackdowns by police and military.†

As Guatemalan-Norwegian scholar Mariel Aguilar-Støen explains, "by prioritizing mineral extraction as a strategy to create income revenues, the Guatemalan government disregards local interests and recasts places into 'extractive spaces' that will always be met with resistance by those whose lives will be affected."[39] In this case, in collaboration with the Guatemalan government and local elite players, Tahoe directly participated in a pro-mining counterinsurgency campaign of population

---

* A list of people arrested during the *estado de sitio* was published in Guateprensa; we then checked that list against the names of organizers included in the police file. Guateprensa, "Estado de sitio en Jalapa y Santa Rosa deja 16 capturados," May 3, 2013, guateprensa. wordpress.com/2013/05/03/estado-de-sitio-en-santa-rosa-y-jalapa-deja-16-capturados/.
† The Guatemalan legal defense organization Centro de Acción Legal, Ambiental y Social de Guatemala / Centre for Environmental, Social and Legal Action (CALAS), which has worked closely with communities resisting Tahoe, has suffered severe intimidation including the murder of CALAS staff member Jimmy Barrios in December 2016 (UDEFEGUA, "Informe 2016: Exprésate con otro rollo sin odio," 2017, 49), as well as significant mention within the documents created by the police and the Interinstitutional Office for Comprehensive Development and discussed here.

control and repression. Evidenced through the Guatemalan criminal case against Alberto Rotondo, the Canadian civil case against Tahoe Resources in relation to the shooting of seven unarmed men, and the material we obtained through Access to Information requests, this particular violence was harnessed, resourced, and legitimized by corporate and state actors alike, to ensure a stable climate for the investment and smooth operation of Canadian mining companies in Guatemala. Tahoe's violent mining operation received the full support of both the Guatemalan and Canadian governments which enabled them to enrich their shareholders, deny any connection to murder at their project sites, and leave the country with an undisclosed settlement and an apology.

The Peaceful Encampment at La Puya
Alexandra Pedersen

It was another cold summer's night in the Guatemalan highlands when the phone rang with devastating news. "Yoli has been shot!" said a voice on the other end. Frantically, my colleague Emilie Smith and I gathered all the information we could: "Is she alive?" "Where is she now?" By the time we went to bed—not that I could sleep—we knew rights defender Yolanda (Yoli) Oquelí Veliz was stable and safe, at least for the time being.

Somos La Puya—We Are La Puya

We first met Yoli at the community encampment known as La Puya in May 2012. La Puya is a community of rights defenders located approximately thirty minutes north of Guatemala City. Vancouver-based junior mining company Radius Gold Inc. began moving large equipment into community territory when they acquired an exploitation license from the Guatemalan government in early 2012. By March 2, 2012 locals from the *municipios* (municipalities) of San José del Golfo and San Pedro Ayampuc assembled the encampment at the mine site's entrance; now occupied twenty-four hours a day, seven days a week. La Puya's community members are protesting what they say is a lack of transparency by the company regarding the use of water and impact on the environment, as well as patterns of impunity and corruption within the Guatemalan government that protect transnational company operations at the expense of citizens' rights. The Guatemalan Human Rights Commission–USA expressed worry over

Radius Gold's environmental impact assessment as the company "recognized that air quality would be affected, as well as flora, fauna, top soil, and the available quantity of water," and does not make clear "where the company plans to treat or dispose of chemical 'tailings' and what impact this will have on the local water and soil."[40] Communities in this area have access to water once, sometimes twice a week, making water a primary concern for farmers and other locals.

Inspired by their resistance, I set out to understand changing spatial and social conditions of the newly created encampment of La Puya, whose members first resisted this Canadian- and later American-owned mining company operating locally. My doctoral research findings indicate that resource extraction, called "development," promoted by the Canadian and Guatemalan governments, transnational business strategies, and relations in Guatemala have detrimental impacts on community life.[41] Conflicts related to resource extraction are increasing at local and regional scales across Latin America as mining operations expand into new territories.[42] The localized experiences of direct and indirect violence at La Puya explicitly demonstrate how governments and companies appropriate development discourse to further their own needs.[43]

Radius Gold's attempt to establish the El Tambor gold mine was met with powerful peaceful resistance by members of La Puya. Two months after Yoli's June 2012 shooting, Radius Gold sold what it called a "problematic asset" to Nevada-based company Kappes, Cassidy and Associates (KCA), but maintained financial stakes in the mine in the form of deferred payments and royalty interests to the sum of ten million US dollars.[44] Former military personnel, along with other local mine employees and state riot police made several attempts to remove protestors from La Puya in November and December 2012 and again in May 2014.[45] Despite the temptation to react with violence, community members at La Puya have not thrown one stick, not one stone. "We may be meek, but we are not stupid," Yoli told us. "We know our rights and we are going to fight for them."

Violence against Rights Defenders

Yolanda is one of many human rights defenders attacked in recent years. Research from the Unit for the Protection of Human Rights Defenders and Advocates of Guatemala / Unidad de Protección a Defensoras y Defensores de Derechos Humanos de Guatemala (UDEFEGUA)[46] documents the reporting of 5,350 aggressive attacks against rights defenders between 2000 and 2017; at least 130 of those incidents resulted in death. By the end of 2019, UDEFEGUA reported another 392 attacks against human rights defenders in 2018, with eighteen attempted killings and twenty-six murders of human rights defenders, of which twenty-one were recorded from May onwards.[47] In 2012, Yolanda was one of 305 human rights defenders in Guatemala attacked for defending communal land rights.[48] Attacks are directed principally against rights defenders—individuals or groups who are Indigenous Maya, community leaders, environmentalists, activists, academics, lawyers, journalists, or union representatives—who defend their own rights and the rights of others. UDEFEGUA's documentation confirms the increase in attacks against rights defenders since 2000 whose work is more difficult and dangerous over time.

Mining companies are often supported by the Guatemalan government, military, and police as they attempt to control, with violence, those who speak out against extractive projects. Physical violence and psychological terror aim to divide and dismantle campaigns against unequal forms of "development" and further marginalize those already disenfranchised through processes of criminalization. The practice of criminalization uses the criminal justice system against citizens as a means to delegitimize and demobilize the actions of those accused.[49] Criminalization does not address the social problems that cause conflicts, but rather makes political action an unlawful act, transforming defenders into criminals. Lawsuits, arbitrary arrests, illegal detentions, and campaigns of defamation—abuses of the judicial system for the advancement of economic interests—constitute common practices of criminalization in Guatemala. The Guatemalan state, Radius Gold, and later KCA pursued a relentless campaign of social stigmatization and criminalization against opponents of the El Tambor mine, causing lasting social divisions and harms within communities.[50] According to Centro de Acción Legal, Ambiental y Social de Guatemala / Centre for Environmental, Social and Legal Action (CALAS) lawyer Rafael Maldonado there are at least ten cases of criminalization against rights defenders from La Puya involving false charges and prolonged criminal processes that infringe on the livelihoods of community members.[51]

Violence against Community Members at La Puya

While the years-long resistance of community members at La Puya remains peaceful, interventions by state authorities are frequently violent. Arguably, the most violent incident at La Puya occurred on May 23, 2014.

At this point, La Puya's efforts had delayed exploitation at the El Tambor mine for over two years, leaving the company anxious to start production, generate revenue, and repay royalty interests to the Canadian company Radius Gold. López Bonilla, then Minister of the Interior and a former military leader, ordered hundreds of Policía Nacional Civil / Civilian National Police (PNC) and Fuerzas Especiales de Policía / Police Special Forces (FEP) to accompany KCA and Exploraciones Mineras de Guatemala, SA / Exploration Mining of Guatemala, SA (EXMINGUA, KCA's Guatemalan subsidiary) mining equipment into the El Tambor mine site. The actions of the minister demonstrate state backing of the implementation of the El Tambor mining project.[52]

On the morning of May 23, 2014 members of the Office of the United Nations High Commissioner, the Sistema Nacional de Diálogo Permanente / National Permanent System of Dialogue (SNDP), the Procurador de los Derechos Humanos / Human Rights Ombudsperson's Office (PDH), and several other rights organizations, Guatemala Human Rights Commission (GHRC) and Peace Brigades International (PBI) included, attempted to broker a solution between the police security contingent and the community. However, by the afternoon, police broke the peace, forcefully evicting protestors from the encampment.[53] Human rights organizations document that approximately three hundred FEP and PNC mistreated men, women, and children, beating them with batons as they attempted to flee the encampment.[54] Amnesty International recorded injuries to twenty-three protestors and fifteen police during the event.[55] Human rights organizations condemned the excessive use of force and failure by the PNC and FEP to follow proper protocols.[56] No court order was ever presented to justify the community's eviction.[57] Temporarily evicted from the encampment, community members returned two days later to reoccupy the roadside adjacent to the El Tambor mine entrance.[58]

The police maintain and reinforce power using tactics of physical and psychological abuse, harassment, and intimidation to foster spaces of fear and insecurity for rights defenders. The psychological and physical violence used at La Puya mirror tactics utilized during the genocide. As a result of this violence, mental health issues—anxiety, insecurity, frustration, and depression—resulting from direct aggressions diminish rights defenders' quality of life and overall well-being.[59] My experience during fieldwork pointed to the cumulative effects of indirect and direct violence amongst participants and community members more broadly. In particular, the gendered aspects of violence became apparent; men typically suffered criminalization and imprisonment, while women endured varying forms of social isolation, harassment, and intimidation for their participation at the roadblock.

Guatemala has the highest instances of violence against women rights defenders in all of Central America. In 2014, 313 women were attacked in Guatemala, nearly double the 126 attacks in 2012. In total, 633 women reported assaults during this three-year time frame. Alarmingly, women who are attacked are 50 percent more likely to be assaulted again in the future.[60] The Iniciativa Mesoamericana de Mujeres Defensoras de Derechos Humanos report finds that at the regional level, 22 percent of all assaults against women rights defenders are perpetrated by companies and businesses.[61] These incidences are particularly troublesome in Guatemala and are ongoing. Patterns of inadequate rights protection in the country are facilitated by structural inequalities designed by the political and economic elite to hinder social movements and maintain hegemonic control of the country.

Canadian Support for Transnational Mining Activities

Although El Tambor Mine is no longer Canadian-owned, what happened to Yolanda is emblematic of numerous community experiences with Canadian companies in Guatemala. The majority of the world's mining companies are headquartered in Canada, controlling more than eight thousand exploitation and exploration projects in 120 countries worldwide. Latin America alone accounts for 55 percent of Canadian mining assets abroad.[62] The Canadian government accepts that mining companies adopt voluntary industry initiatives rather than committing to formal regulations and potentially facing legal liability. Mining companies are left to police themselves regarding respect for human and environmental rights. The industry's own research showed that between 1999 and 2009, Canadian corporations owned 33 percent of the global extractive companies involved in mining conflicts, trailed by Australia and India at 8 percent each.[63]

The Canadian extractives sector is promoted abroad as the latest cure for "development" shortcomings, without acknowledging these practices as detrimental to the self-determined development sought by local communities.[64] Canadian extractive companies receive substantial financial support from Export Development Canada; the Canadian International Development Agency (CIDA), now a part of the Global Affairs Canada; the World Bank; investments by the Canada Pension Plan (CPP); and a range of supports via staff at Canadian Embassies. For example, in 2013 CPP investments into Goldcorp reached $217 million and $54 million went into Tahoe Resources, despite both Canadian companies then being under scrutiny for rights abuses in Guatemala.[65] Most Canadians remain unaware of their financial involvement in the mining sector and how their contributions fund abuses in the Global South.[66]

Whose "Development"?

The financial, political, and judicial pressure brought to bear against rights defenders and communities resisting Canadian mining companies is enormous. Based on my research with community defenders at La Puya, communities desire respect and dignity; they believe in a self-determined way of life in harmony with the earth rather than extracting precious metals for short-term gain. Those who benefit from mining are not locals, they told me, but corrupt government officials, the Guatemalan elite,[67] and transnational mining companies and their investors,[68] all of whom strengthen their economic and political power under the guise of "development." Jobs are limited and temporary, corporate social responsibility "gifts" in the form of healthcare or education dry up after the mines close (and often before), ecosystems are left destroyed, and community divisions are irreparable.[69] When resource extraction activities are understood from the perspectives of rights defenders, we are left to ask: How is this development?

What started as a small group of individuals blockading the El Tambor mine's entrance has emerged as a new community seeking validation for alternative visions of self-determined development. La Puya's story, while unique in and of its own terms, is not uncommon. Rural populations across Guatemala have declared a resolute "no" to mining in their territories.[70] Yet transnational mining companies continue their attempts to expand operations and control of local landscapes, with the support of the Guatemalan government.

For the community of La Puya and their supporters, the collective voice amplified through place-creation to challenge and counter hegemonic power represents a dignified local struggle for the protection of the environment, clean water, and the welfare of future generations. However, the continued violent repression of rights defenders who request respect for Indigenous, human, and environmental rights is deeply rooted in Guatemala's recent genocide and will continue to be exacerbated by the state's embrace of neoliberal policies.

Guatemalan Supreme Court of Justice: KCA (& Radius Gold) vs. La Puya Land and Environmental Defenders

Catherine Nolin, Grahame Russell, and James Rodríguez

The *La Sala de Vistas* courtroom of the Guatemalan Supreme Court of Justice was full for the May 18, 2016 hearing in which lawyers with Centro de Acción Legal, Ambiental y Social de Guatemala / Centre for Environmental, Social and Legal Action (CALAS), on behalf of the mining-affected communities, petitioned for the final, definitive suspension of the mining license for the El Tambor mine owned by Nevada-based mining firm Kappes, Cassiday & Associates (KCA).[71]

Radius Gold—which initiated this illegal and contested mining operation—sold its interests in 2012 to its junior partner KCA soon after an assassination attempt on the life of community member Yolanda Oquelí. On a deserted stretch of road near the mine's entrance, two hitmen on a motorbike shot Yolanda three times. She survived, with one of the bullets remaining perilously close to her spinal column. Radius Gold maintains a royalty interest in the mine's gold production.

No to Mining, Yes to Life

Our delegation joined with people from mining-affected communities throughout the country who attended in support of community members from the peaceful resistance of La Puya to say, once again, "No to mining, yes to life." Signs held by men from communities harmed by Tahoe Resources' gold and silver mine in San Rafael Las Flores read: "Mother Earth is not dying. She is being assassinated" and "San Rafael, Santa Rosa: We demand compliance with the Constitutional Court ruling that cancelled the El Escobal mining exploitation license of [Tahoe Resources'] Minera San Rafael."

"So Much Insecurity"

Daniel W. Kappes, President of KCA, attended the hearing. Mr. Kappes, who refused to give his name, directed journalists to defence lawyer Estuardo Ralón. When asked to confirm Mr. Kappes' identity, Mr. Ralón stated: "Since there is so much insecurity in the country, it is best to keep this gentleman's identity anonymous. But yes, he is a major investor in

KCA." Despite "so much insecurity," Kappes and KCA continue to push ahead with their mining interests.

During the hearing, CALAS lawyer Rafael Maldonado argued that the license for KCA's mine should be definitively suspended (revoked) on two grounds: (1) the lack of free, prior, and informed consent with the Indigenous people of the region prior to the development of the mine; and (2) the egregious behaviour of the company in ignoring the Constitutional Court ruling, more than one year previous, to cease operations.

La Puya (The Thorn)

From the court, we drove one hour outside of Guatemala City, to a place known as La Puya. Since March 2012, community members from San José del Golfo and San Pedro Ayampuc have maintained a permanent peaceful encampment—La Puya—at the entrance to the illegal mining operation.

Community members take turns staying, eating, and sleeping here, maintaining a permanent presence of protest to the illegal and unwanted mine. Since 2012, community members have been victims of repeated acts of repression by Guatemalan police and armed civilians; community members have been targeted with trumped-up criminal charges. Through all this, they remain clear and firm in their dignified resistance in defence of community, environment, and life.

A Message to North Americans about Their Companies

After being offered coffee, rice, and beans prepared in the La Puya kitchen, we asked Amalia Sandoval Palencia (a mother of four from San José del Golfo): "As you know, KCA is a US company and Radius Gold is a Canadian company. What might you like to say to North Americans?" Amalia Sandoval's response:[72]

> I would ask them to help us get the company out of here. Because here we live from corn and beans and with the company here, we're not going to have any more corn and beans. And we don't want our kids to get sick—we don't have money to cure them. And we don't want the mining company to take the water, because without water we cannot live. And [in the US] they don't want to accept us, because we'll all migrate there. If this land ends up sterile, we won't be able to live here and we'll have to migrate somewhere. So [in the US] they won't want us to migrate there. I ask [the people of Canada

and the US] to please help us if they can to help get the company out of here. We want to live and for our kids not be sick. We're doing this struggle for them. If we suffer repression, or if the company tries to get rid of us . . . but it's for the kids. You know, for a mother, the kids are the most important. It's for them that we're doing this. So, I ask [Canadian and American people] to reflect on this: they have kids and they wouldn't want anything bad to happen to them, either.

A few months later, in July 2016, the Guatemalan Supreme Court unanimously suspended the license for KCA to build the El Tambor mine and it remains closed today. The court found the license approval violated Indigenous communities' right to consultation. Local courts found that the mine never had a valid construction license to start with.[73] KCA remains combative and in December 2018 filed a $300 million claim with the World Bank's International Center for Settlement of Investment Disputes against the State of Guatemala. The La Puya resistance remains.

Testimonio: Alvaro Sandoval and Ana Sandoval, Dealing with Radius Gold / KCA

La Puya peaceful resistance leaders and community defenders with Grahame Russell and Catherine Nolin, May 17, 2017

The peaceful resistance struggle here in La Puya for the past five years is collective and is based in the community—this is what gives it its underlying legitimacy. There are other struggles like this across the country, where it is the community itself leading its own struggle against harms and violations caused by companies. The collective, community-driven nature of the struggles is what gives them their strength, dignity, and legitimacy. The companies and the government say we—in the communities—are being manipulated by outsiders. Our community-based struggles are proof that this is not so.

Here in La Puya, we have maintained our struggle for five years and a few months. In the beginning we didn't know how long this was going to be. We were surprised how long it was taking. Now we understand that while we know when the struggle began, we don't know when this is going to end. We now understand that as long as there are resources and riches in these lands and mountains, there will be business people and companies who want to come and profit from it. This is why we insist on getting youth involved, resisting the complicity of the transnational companies, the government, and corrupt local business people. The politicians and government lend themselves to the transnational companies by passing laws and regulations that favour their economic interests.

For us this is a completely unique process. We began it one day in 2012 not knowing how long it would go on. The people here began the struggle with a lot of heart and energy. Now that it has continued for five years and a few months, we have no idea how long God will give us the strength we need to continue with it. Part of the story has been written; but we don't know what the other part will be.

We are fighting for Mother Earth and nature, and for our natural resources. The most valuable resource we are fighting to defend is water—water is life. When we talk of water, we are talking of something that is indispensable for life—all life, not just human life, but of animals, plants, and all living beings. Here, where we live, there are annual water shortages—that is why we are in this struggle.

Figure 12. La Puya Resistance against Unwanted Gold Mine. Community defenders block the entrance gate to El Tambor gold mine, owned by EXMINGUA, local subsidiary of Canadian mining company Radius Gold (later of American company KCA). Since March 2, 2012, local neighbours from San José del Golfo and San Pedro Ayampuc have blocked the entrance to the proposed mining site. Residents from the communities assert the industrial activity in their territories is illegal since they were not appropriately consulted before the mine began operating. La Puya, San Pedro Ayampuc, Guatemala, July 19, 2012. Photo: James Rodríguez.

We need to be able to influence policies in this country so that these issues can be resolved democratically, so that communities can define their own development needs, so that others cannot impose their interests on us, whether it is the government or companies. Today, our governments are puppets of the companies. This is happening around the globe. The companies are governing, not those individuals elected by the peoples.

I would like to call on the people and politicians of Canada and the United States to reflect seriously on your way of life in your so-called developed countries; that your way of life is achieved at the cost of exploiting the natural resources in our countries that you call "underdeveloped."

We call on the Canadian and American people to investigate and learn about how your companies come here and violate our rights; how your companies participate in and take advantage of the corruption of our governments that serve the interests of your companies to then violate our rights and harm the wellbeing of our natural resources, our communities, and our people.

We call on your politicians and business leaders to reflect on how you do your work as politicians and business people; we call on you to do your work in an honourable way and not in a way that profits from the blood and tears of other people. Like you, we merit respect in life.

Chapter 6
Using Law and Democracy to Resist Predatory Mining

As argued throughout this book, mining with Guatemala's genocidal generals is characterized by violence and human rights
violations, by corruption and a fundamental lack of democracy, and by impunity and immunity from legal liability.

In Guatemala, the institutions of democracy (the electoral process,
executive and legislative branches of government) have long been characterized by corruption and manipulation by the wealthy and powerful sectors. All along, the democratic system has been characterized by repression
against opposition party members, from the national level through to the
municipal level.

In this chapter, J. P. Laplante describes the courageous democratic
process of *consultas* being carried out by Indigenous communities across
the country, trying to use the legally binding, democratic processes of "consultation" to defend their territorial and human rights, despite fundamental flaws and weakness in the institutions of democracy and the rule of law.

In Canada, Canadian mining companies have forever benefited from
immunity from liability in Canadian courts for crimes, human rights
violations, and environmental harms they cause in other countries. In
this chapter, Cory Wanless and Murray Klippenstein—co-counsel in the
precedent-setting Hudbay Minerals lawsuits—address serious efforts
to slowly but surely put an end to Canada's entrenched immunity from
liability.

Reclaiming Democracy, Realizing Self-Determination: *Consultas* as a Tool to Defend Human Rights and the Environment in Guatemala's Genocidal Shadow

J. P. Laplante

Since 2005, almost one million Guatemalans have mobilized to participate in a democratic referenda process called the Consulta Comunitaria de Buena Fe (community consultation in good faith, or simply "*consulta*"). Over the space of three years, the *consultas* transformed into a social movement to assert legally-binding self-determination over local natural resources and territory. The movement helped reinvigorate and reframe efforts to secure legal recognition for the rights of local communities over their lands, especially as they relate to the rights of many Indigenous Maya, Xinca, and Garifuna peoples of Guatemala.

The *consulta* process was and remains immensely important as a clarion call to make known the voices of communities purposely excluded in Guatemala, a wake-up call for a genuine democracy and rule of law in the face of a political and legal system bereft of legitimacy. As important, the movement gave a voice to the many communities who rejected the arguably illegal sale of their lands by the Guatemalan government in the form of the mineral rights to multinational private corporations, many of them based in Canada. In doing so, the *consultas* are part of multiple strategies to reclaim self-determination in the face of an exploitative system that puts the rights of international companies and investors before Guatemala's own citizens (see Figure 13, page 161).

Based on six months of fieldwork in Guatemala's western highlands interviewing *consulta* organizers and supporters, and participant observation of two *consultas*, this piece explores the impact, challenges, and legacy of the movement in Guatemala and internationally.

The *consultas* are also a direct challenge to the political and economic forces that manipulate Guatemalan laws and government to cement an extremely unequal development model, poverty, and discrimination[1] and that benefit from the corruption, violence and vulnerability that keep Guatemala from escaping the shadow of its brutal genocides.[2]

The *consulta* movement's legacy is still felt in the ongoing work of new Indigenous and human rights advocacy organizations in Guatemala and in the organizational capacity of rural Indigenous communities who have since challenged Guatemala's mining laws in court. These communities are transforming the discourse in Guatemala with respect to collective land rights and the extractives sector.

The *Consulta* Movement

The first well-known Guatemalan *consulta* occurred in Sipakapa (aka Sipacapa), San Marcos on January 24, 2005, in response to the complete lack of consultation and serious concerns about the proposed Marlin Mine. At that time the project was owned by US mining company Glamis Gold Ltd., who later merged with Goldcorp Inc., a Canadian gold miner from Vancouver, British Columbia (BC). The *consulta* organizers were met with repression and violence,[3] but the *consulta* proceeded anyway, and the Goldcorp mine was overwhelmingly rejected by the community. Despite the clear lack of consent, the mine went into production and became a focal point for everything that is wrong with extractive projects in Guatemala.

In the context of Guatemala's endemic lack of rule of law and democracy, Goldcorp's mine was embroiled in conflict long before its construction, fuelled by improper and fraudulent consultation,[4] intimidation and assassination of mining critics,[5] disputed or deceitful land acquisition,[6] damaged homes,[7] the depletion and contamination of scarce water resources,[8] adverse human health and other environmental impacts,[9] and serious social conflict in the adjacent communities of San Miguel Ixtahuacán and Sipakapa.[10]

The mine closed on May 31, 2017[11] although the impacts linger and full and proper reclamation remains highly questionable under Guatemala's anemic environmental and mining regulatory regime.[12]

The notoriety of Goldcorp's mine fostered the spread of the *consultas* (see Figure 14). What began with a few communities morphed into a country-wide movement in the space of three years, at the level of the community (municipality, or *municipio*). The *consulta* quickly became the primary process adopted by many communities to inform themselves about the potential impacts of mining, hydroelectric, and other extractive projects, and to affirm widespread community opposition to such projects. More than seventy *municipios* (approximately 22 percent of Guatemala's municipalities) and nearly one million Guatemalans have participated in the process, all of them rejecting the presence of mining, hydroelectric, oil and gas, and cement factories in their lands.[13]

Consultas as Response to Endemic Exploitation,
Exclusion, and Impunity

The *consultas* are more than the rejection of a particular mining company
or project. The movement spread quickly because the *consultas* were a
means of resisting the untenable status quo in Guatemala, made worse by
the country's neoliberalized extractives sector laws that prioritize foreign
multinationals ahead of local communities.

Guatemala's mining system has a long history of provoking community opposition with ensuing government repression against community
members and critics,[14] but the modern mining regime legislated in the
1990s represented a race to the bottom with other Central American countries to attract foreign investment post-conflict and enormous profits for
the country's elite business sector.

Catherine Nolin and Jacqui Stephens describe the gold rush of the
late 1990s and early 2000s as Guatemala's "Fourth Invasion," following
the Spanish Conquest, the liberal land reforms of the nineteenth century,
and the decades of US-backed repression culminating in the genocides of
the late 1970s and early 1980s.[15] One *consulta* organizer from Cabricán,
Quetzaltenango described the *consulta* as "an expression of resistance to
everything about the situation in which we live. The desire to improve the
conditions of life, the desire to have a more democratic country, not only in
word but in substance, so that the people share in the power of decisions of
the state."[16]

In the passing of the 1997 Mining Law, then-President Álvaro Arzú and
his government predictably ignored both the rights of Guatemala's citizens
to determine the future of their lands, and binding commitments set out
in the Peace Accords that land tenure systems would be reformed and
Indigenous rights enshrined in law.[17] Contrary to these commitments, the
new mining law empowered the government to sell mineral rights without
any consultation or consent from affected communities.[18]

The situation was made worse by hungry mineral exploration companies, the World Bank, the Canadian and US governments, and other investors (including public pension funds such as the Canada Pension Plan),
attracted by cheap land, cheap operating costs, and huge returns. The
inevitable fruits of this exclusion and exploitation operating in a culture
of corruption and impunity were violence, repression, and serious harms
that continue today. The *consulta* movement was a response to both the

emerging crisis associated with mining, and the overall climate of exclusion and corruption crippling Guatemala.

Consultas as Exercise in Self-Determination

The *consulta* movement reinvigorated and reframed how communities understand and exercise their human and Indigenous rights through a participatory democratic process at the local level. Figure 15 demonstrates the high degree of popular participation in the process. The *consultas* reclaim power from a corrupt system and help refocus an Indigenous rights movement to pursue self-determination through exercising the right to free, prior, and informed consent over megaprojects.[19] A community leader and *consulta* organizer from Sipakapa described their *consulta* as a "light," and a way to "make known the voice of the people, the voice of the community, the voice of the people who are most remote, excluded, as one of the collective rights that exist."[20]

The *consulta* was also a teaching moment, providing space for Guatemalans, the majority of whom are Indigenous, to organize and educate themselves and their neighbours about the right to participate meaningfully in decisions that affect them, including whether or not a mine could be built on their land. The *consulta* movement helped elevate the debate about participatory rights to the national stage, and thrust into the spotlight international human rights instruments that support self-determination, such as Convention 169 of the International Labour Organization,[21] and the United Nations Declaration on the Rights of Indigenous Peoples.[22]

The movement to resist the mining regime faces enormous challenges: the *consultas* were organized by the country's excluded and most vulnerable, brave fish swimming upstream against an enormous current of entrenched power. Mining critics and communities who stand up for their rights face an almost sociopathic government, paramilitary apparatus, and complicit business partners willing to use extrajudicial violence, disappearance, and assassination against opponents.[23]

Despite the pressures, the *consultas* have succeeded on various fronts. In particular, the movement painted a clear picture of the legal and political reforms needed in Guatemala and internationally. Canada, as the epicentre of worldwide mining companies and investment, is wholly implicated in the need for serious political and legal reform.

Consultas as a Challenge for Guatemala, Canada, and the Mining Sector

The *consulta* movement unmasked some of the laws, structures, and policies that enable and reinforce the extremely unequal, exploitative development and resulting poverty in Guatemala. In this respect, the *consulta* process is a challenge to the Guatemalan government, corporations, and their investors operating in the country.

The challenge is this: *consultas* assert the political and legal authority of a community to decide its own future, and the rejection of an extractive project through the *consulta* process draws a clear line in the sand. For a government or company or investor to proceed despite a community's rejection of that project is to make very stark the violation of the community's collective and individual human rights (that would have happened with or without the *consulta*).

From this perspective, it is not surprising then that the Guatemalan and Canadian governments, mining companies, and other international actors worked to try to undermine the *consulta* movement.[24] When the movement spread anyway, they deployed corporate social responsibility (CSR) public relations campaigns to dismiss and deflect attention from the harms suffered by local communities and to hide the widespread opposition to mining. The movement and the calls to shut down Goldcorp's mine did effect change: Guatemala and Goldcorp made some concessions to stifle some of the more obvious embarrassments. One example is Goldcorp voluntarily agreeing to pay more than Guatemala's incredibly low 1 percent royalty rate.[25] Despite some concessions, the fundamental issues continue to be ignored: the Mining Law itself; the rights of communities to decide their own future; and real justice and compensation for the harms already suffered by affected communities.

Today, CSR campaigns continue, but have not stopped ongoing violence and harms at other mines in Guatemala, such as the Fénix Nickel mine in El Estor, Izabal, formerly owned by Hudbay Minerals, and Tahoe Resources' Escobal silver mine in San Rafael Las Flores, Santa Rosa.[26] Further legal precedents also highlight that CSR campaigns deflect attention from fundamental legal and human rights failures: in 2017, Guatemala's Supreme Court affirmed that the government does not meaningfully consult its citizens and ordered an overhaul of the consultation process for Tahoe Resources' Escobal mine.[27]

Sadly, Canada is implicated in these violations and in Guatemala's endemic corruption and impunity. In Canada, political processes and domestic laws provide safe haven to companies carrying out human rights violations in Guatemala, and Canada's consular services are directly promoting and supporting the expansion of Canadian mining operations while ignoring systemic repression, immunity, and corruption.[28] The continuing lack of respect for human rights or the results of the *consultas* make it clear that the exploitative pro-mining system remains entrenched. The *consultas* are but a step in the process to change that. One *consulta* supporter from the Consejo Mam (Mam Council) in Quetzaltenango described this challenge for the investors:

> I believe the duty is on those who have funds there [in Canada] to be vigilant as well, to be vigilant that their investments don't cause death or violations of human rights in other places. I believe as well that this instance must guarantee that those who invest funds there have sufficient information about what is done with those funds.[29]

Consultas and the Unfinished Business of the Peace Accords

The *consulta* movement has not solved Guatemala's mining or human rights problems, or stopped projects from proceeding. However, the real lesson from sixteen years of asserting self-determination and challenging the status quo in Guatemala is that communities organized and educated themselves, took action, and laid a foundation for future efforts.

The fruits of the *consultas* can be seen in how organizations such as the Consejo de Pueblo Maya (Maya Peoples Council) have emerged to carry the work forward. Communities such as Cabricán, Quetzaltenango, continue post-*consulta* to challenge the country's mining laws and demonstrate how they breach human rights. The community's efforts are realizing small but important gains toward reform of the laws. Further, community organizers learned from their *consultas* and are now advancing other strategies to affirm and empower participatory democracy and community self-determination.

Guatemala is a country still in the shadow of its brutal genocides, with the intellectual authors of the repression not only free but often still in powerful political, military, and economic positions. The international mining industry, with the support of the Canadian government, is doing business directly with many of these people. Within this shadow, the *consultas* shine light on the endemic corruption and impunity that rule

Guatemala, and are an important step in the unfinished business of the 1996 Peace Accords, the work to transform Guatemala to be a more just and equitable country.

Testimonios: Santa Cruz del Quiché, Consejo de los Pueblos del Quiché / Council of the Peoples of the Quiché, voices of Osmundo and Anibel

The Fourth Assembly of the Consejo de los Pueblos del Quiché / Council of the Peoples of the Quiché gathered on August 28, 2010 in Santa Cruz del Quiché to plan and set the date for the *consulta*, their community referendum, when they would pose the question: "Are you in favour of the intervention of transnational corporations / private Guatemalan interests regarding hydroelectric projects and mining?"

Committed community leaders and organizers presented the issues for all attendees to consider. Osmundo said,

> We have the right to development, the right to *consultas*. Our laws and constitution, though, have been hijacked by those in power for their own purposes. . . . What is OUR benefit from mining? We need to defend life, defend our territory. Water is life. If we let Mother Earth get an infection (contaminated), she dies and so will we. It is time to come together to defend Madre Tierra.[30]

Anibel, a true force, encouraged the other leaders: "Here, we are collective; here, we are as communities. We are not here as individuals, we are here as collectives. We ARE Santa Cruz del Quiché!"

Osmundo called this "a triumph" for them all—a collective decision to set October 22 as the date for the *consulta*—which they hope will result in a strong statement: "No to mining and yes to life."

Towards Legal Accountability for the Canadian Mining Industry
Cory Wanless and Murray Klippenstein

The Canadian government frequently likes to boast about Canada's dominance of the international mining industry; and, indeed, the dominance is impressive. Canada is home to approximately half of the world's publicly listed mining and exploration firms[31] which is more than any other nation on earth by a fair margin. As of 2017, a staggering 1,364 Canadian companies had mining assets worth a total of over $260 billion located in 101 countries around the world.[32] According to the Mining Association of Canada, a full 57 percent of the world's public mining companies are listed on Canada's two big stock markets: the TSX and TSX-Venture Exchanges.[33]

There is a dark side to this dominance, however. Canadian mining companies have been accused of involvement in cases of environmental catastrophe and severe human rights abuse, including forced labour, rape, and murder, all over the world. In Latin America alone, Canadian-owned mines have been linked to at least forty-four deaths and four hundred injuries between 2000 and 2015.[34]

To make matters worse, the Canadian legal system has proved itself woefully deficient at ensuring that victims of corporate wrongs have access to courts and access to remedies when things go wrong. The harsh reality is that it remains nearly impossible for individuals harmed by Canadian companies to bring lawsuits in Canadian courts, or anywhere else for that matter.* The problem is described as a "governance gap" by Harvard Professor John Ruggie,[35] former United Nations Special Representative of the Secretary-General on the Issue of Human Rights and Transnational Corporations and other Business Enterprises:

> The root cause of the business and human rights predicament today lies in the governance gaps created by globalization—between the scope and impact of economic forces and actors, and the capacity of societies to manage their adverse consequences. These governance gaps provide the permissive environment for wrongful acts by companies of all kinds without adequate sanctioning or reparation.

---

* There are a number of court cases underway including the three lawsuits against HudBay Minerals Inc. in Ontario and one in BC, *Araya v. Nevsun Resources Ltd.*, that are attempting to use Canadian law as it currently exists in order to achieve some level of justice for victims of corporate wrongdoing. Another BC Case, *García v. Tahoe Resources Inc.*, was recently favourably resolved out of court in what is a rare win for victims of abuses by Canadian companies. Despite these efforts legal reform is sorely needed. *Araya v. Nevsun Resources Ltd.*, BCCA 402 (CanLII), 2017, canlii.ca/t/hnspr; *García v. Tahoe Resources Inc.*, BCCA 39 (CanLII) 2017, canlii.ca/t/gx49k.

CSR: Corporate Impunity and Immunity Reinforced

The Canadian government seems entirely uninterested in doing anything to fill these legal gaps. With the mining industry whispering in its ear, the Canadian government has repeatedly rejected any attempt to introduce true legal accountability for corporate abuses and instead has posed voluntary corporate social responsibility (CSR) as the "solution."

Under the CSR model, Canadian companies can sign up (or not) to various voluntary environmental and human rights standards and then apply those standards within their business (or not). If something goes wrong, and human rights abuses are committed at a Canadian-owned mine, there is no sanction, no liability, and no accountability. It is essentially a model in which companies are supposed to "try" to behave responsibly, and if instead their security forces kill someone, or there is a tailings dam collapse, or the contractor they use employs slave labour at their mine, no problem, simply try to do better next time.

Companies love the voluntary CSR model because it gives them the best of both worlds. Companies can and do reap the public relations benefits of claiming to be responsible companies and good global citizens (simply by stating that they are), but without the burden of actually being responsible or accountable to anyone for their behavior. It is a world where, as we have seen in the context of the lawsuits against Canadian mining company Hudbay Minerals Inc.[36] regarding the killing of Adolfo Ich, the shooting and paralysis of German Chub Choc, and the rape of eleven women during a forced eviction (Figure 16), a company can proudly proclaim in its glossy-paged CSR Report that "part of the reason that we have stayed in business over eight decades is that we take responsibility for our actions," and that "we embrace our responsibilities through our Company-wide commitment to the welfare of neighbouring communities, the safety and health of our employees and the environment"[37] while having their lawyers argue in court that, actually, they do not owe any legal duty to ensure that security personnel at their mine heavily armed with machetes, shotguns, and pistols do not hack, shoot, maim, and kill neighbouring community members. Those commitments that were made? They were voluntary!

A Hypocritical Double Standard

To those who may be swayed by emphasis on voluntary standards, if we

Figure 13. Consultation in Santa Cruz Quiché. Residents of Cantón Pajajxit I, II, and III vote during the community consultation on the exploitation of natural resources. On a historic day, residents from the municipality of Santa Cruz del Quiché—one of Guatemala's most important hubs and the birthplace of the Maya K'iche' people—unanimously rejected the exploitation of natural goods and resources, in particular through mining and hydroelectric activities. Santa Cruz, Quiché, Guatemala, October 22, 2010. Photo: James Rodríguez.

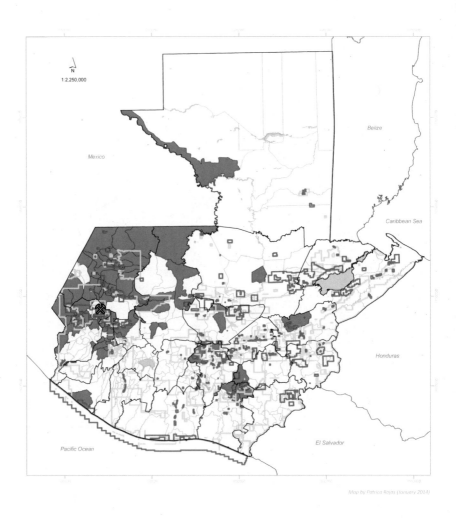

⬜ Authorized Mineral License 2011	**Projection:**
⬜ Application for Mineral License 2011	Universal Transverse Mercator Datum: NAD 1927
◼ Municipality with Consultas 2005-2013	**Source Data:**
⛏ Marlin Mine	Instituto Geográfico Nacional de Guatemala (2011) (National Geographic Institute of Guatemala)
⬜ Department	Ministerio de Energía y Minas (2011) (Ministry of Energy and Mines)
▨ Lake or River	Ministerio de Medio Ambiente y Recursos Naturales (2012) (Ministry of Environment and Natural Resources)

Figure 14. Mineral Interests and *Consultas* in Guatemala, by Patricia Rojas, illustrates the extent of the consultas across Guatemala, and their proximity to communities rejecting particular industrial projects. Source: J. P. Laplante, "'La Voz del Pueblo,'" 205.

Figure 15. Popular Participation in *Consultas* in Guatemala, 2005–2013, by Patricia Rojas, illustrates the extent of the *consultas* across Guatemala, and the percentage of municipal participation in seventy-six *consultas* between 2005 and 2013. Source: Laplante, "'La Voz del Pueblo,'" 203.

Figure 16. Mining Conflictivity: CGN and Lote Ocho. From left to right: Carmelina Caal Ical, Margarita Caal Caal, Rosa Elbira Coc Ich, Amalia Cac Tiul, Lucia Caal Chun, and Olivia Asig Xol, all six women plaintiffs in the *Caal vs. Hudbay* legal case in Canada, here in their community of Lote Ocho. Lote Ocho, El Estor, Izabal, Guatemala, September 29, 2014. Photo: James Rodríguez.

are so convinced that voluntary standards are the answer and can stop bad behaviour, it is worth asking why we do not expand voluntary principles to every other aspect of society. In few other areas of society do we think that "voluntary guidelines" can actually solve real-world problems.

The lives of average Canadians are governed by a myriad of enforceable laws, not voluntary codes; why should it be any different for Canada's corporations? If we honestly believe voluntary guidelines are sufficient to control behaviour, why do we not rely on voluntary principles to prevent bad behaviour in other realms? Why have traffic laws? Tax laws? Criminal laws? Why have laws at all?

The answer is obvious: while most people would follow voluntary codes most of the time, there are some people who would not. We do not "do away" with criminal laws because most Canadians do not kill or steal. The very point of law is to control the "bad actors," not everyone else. And the matter is worse with corporations. Corporations are not moral beings; by definition, they cannot be. Corporations are legal fictions that are legally mandated to follow a profit-maximizing imperative, consequences be damned. The result is that corporations will not (and arguably legally cannot) do anything "voluntarily" that will impact their bottom line. The only way corporations can be reliably made to abide by human rights and environmental standards is through proper regulations with penalties for non-compliance that seriously bite.

We need to call a spade a spade: when corporations say that "voluntary guidelines" are sufficient, they are actually asking to be given a "get-out-of-jail-free" card.

* * *

There is also further hypocrisy in industry's emphasis on voluntary principles. At the same time that industry has repeatedly insisted that unenforceable voluntary principles are good enough to protect the human rights of those impacted by Canadian mining, companies insist on actual hard law when it comes to protecting their financial rights. The Canadian government, again cheered on by industry, has been slowly and steadily negotiating bilateral foreign investment promotion and protection agreements (FIPAs) with dozens of other nations with the explicit goal of giving legally enforceable rights to Canadian companies operating in foreign countries. At last count, such agreements have been negotiated with thirty-six nations from Mongolia to Mali, from Senegal to Serbia, from Costa Rica to the Czech Republic.

FIPAs give corporations actual enforceable legal rights to protect their investments from everything from expropriation to unequal treatment by foreign governments.[38] These agreements not only guarantee that there is a specific court or tribunal where a corporation can go to press its rights and seek a remedy if it believes its investment rights have been infringed, but even allow a parent corporation to bring a claim based on the violation of the rights of its subsidiaries—a right that is particularly galling in light of parent corporations' frequent reliance on the formal legal separation between a parent and subsidiary corporation to avoid liability when facing claims related to wrongdoing committed by their wholly owned subsidiaries.

Curiously, and to make the hypocritical double-standard even more striking, in the very same FIPA agreements that give corporations actual hard enforceable legal rights, the Canadian government doubles down on the "voluntary principles are good enough for victims of human rights abuse" approach. For example, the FIPA negotiated with Cameroon, which came into force on December 16, 2016, states:

> Each Party should encourage enterprises operating within its territory or subject to its jurisdiction to voluntarily incorporate internationally recognized standards of corporate social responsibility in their practices and internal policies, such as statements of principle that have been endorsed or are supported by the Parties. These principles address issues such as labour, the environment, human rights, community relations and anti-corruption.[39]

It is frankly shameful that Canada has a legal regime that absolutely protects the investments of Canadian corporations, but only meekly encourages Canadian corporations to voluntarily agree to merely consider human rights, the environment, labour, and anti-corruption in their practices and internal policies.

CORE

In early 2018, to much fanfare from some people and organizations in civil society, Canada's ruling Liberal Party announced the creation of an independent Canadian Ombudsperson for Responsible Enterprise (CORE). According to the Government of Canada:

> CORE will be mandated to investigate allegations of human rights abuses linked to Canadian corporate activity abroad. The CORE will seek to assist wherever possible in collaboratively resolving disputes or conflicts between impacted communities and Canadian companies. It will be empowered to independently investigate, report, recommend remedy and monitor its implementation.[40]

Initial optimism regarding CORE quickly turned to disappointment. In part, due to an extensive and successful lobbying effort by the mining industry, Canada reneged on its initial assurances that CORE would have the necessary tools to conduct credible independent investigations, including the power to compel documents and summon witnesses. On July 12, 2019, all fourteen civil society and labour union representatives of the government's Multi-Stakeholder Advisory Body on Responsible Business Conduct Abroad resigned *en masse* in frustration and protest, calling CORE "nothing more than a broken promise."[41] As of early 2021, Canada continued to push forward with a toothless ombuds office that lacks the confidence of civil society. In any event, even an effective CORE cannot and should not be thought of as a replacement for civil lawsuits brought against Canadian companies in Canadian courts.*

Civil Law Reform Needed†

There are a number of recent civil legal cases brought in both Ontario

---

* Importantly, the Government of Canada itself recognizes that the CORE is not a replacement for civil lawsuits. As noted by the Supreme Court of Canada in *Nevsun Resources Ltd. v. Araya*: "With respect to the Canadian Ombudsperson for Responsible Enterprise, mandated to review allegations of human rights abuses of Canadian corporations operating abroad, the Canadian government has explicitly noted that '[t]he creation of the Ombudsperson's office does not affect the right of any party to bring a legal action in a court in any jurisdiction in Canada regarding allegations of harms committed by a Canadian company abroad.'" *Nevsun Resources Ltd. v. Araya*, 2020 SCC 5 para. 115, canlii.ca/t/j5k5j.

† While this piece deals only with needed reforms to civil law, reforms to Canadian criminal law to allow for the criminal prosecution of Canadian corporations that abuse

and BC that are attempting to change this legal regime. The civil lawsuits against Hudbay Minerals Inc. regarding rape, killings, and shootings,[42] against Nevsun Resources Ltd. regarding forced labour and slavery in Eretria,[43] and against Tahoe Resources Inc. regarding shootings by security personnel[44] are using the law as it currently exists to hopefully achieve some measure of accountability, and all are making serious headway in court. All three lawsuits have survived various procedural attacks by the defendants, and two have now ended in successful out-of-court settlements, while the third continues to wind its way slowly to trial. In July 2019, the plaintiffs in *García v. Tahoe Resources Inc.* scored the first real breakthrough when they were able to negotiate a favourable resolution of the lawsuit for an undisclosed amount with Tahoe Resources' new owners Pan American Silver Corp. that included an admission that human rights were infringed and an apology to the victims and to the community.[45] Next, after scoring an important preliminary win at the Supreme Court of Canada in February 2020, the plaintiffs manage to secure a successful settlement in *Araya v. Nevsun Resources Ltd.*, also on undisclosed terms.

Despite these successes, law reform is desperately needed if we are to have a legal system that actually and realistically causes corporations to behave responsibly, and provides reasonable access to justice to their victims in civil court when these companies do not. This requires less of a change than you would think. There is no need to invent new regulatory regimes or draft complex legislation—basic tort law in the superior court of each province provides the legal regime and most of the rules that are needed. Instead, only two legislative tweaks are needed.

Jurisdiction and *forum non conveniens*

First, legal reform is needed to make clear that individuals harmed by the actions of Canadian corporations abroad can sue in Canadian courts.* This

---

human rights abroad are desperately needed as well. As is the case with civil law reforms, reforms to the Criminal Code are easier than one might assume; at root, the only thing that is stopping Canada from passing criminal laws that apply to Canadian corporations abroad is a lack of political will.

* There is some debate about whether such law reform should be passed at the federal or provincial level. While a detailed analysis of this issue is beyond the scope of this piece, our view is that it is both a better fit and easier for legal reform at the provincial level, mainly because the Canadian constitution gives provinces power over the "Administration of Justice in the Province, including the Constitution, Maintenance and Organization of is less of a change than it first appears; it is already the case that Canadian courts always have jurisdiction over Canadian corporations, regardless of where they operate. It is also already the case that Canadian courts are comfortable adjudicating cases where part of the events in question happened in a foreign country—Canadian courts do it all the time in areas as diverse as family law, product liability cases, contract cases, and even, in certain situations, criminal law.

The civil law reform would only need to make clear that Canadian courts should exercise the jurisdiction they already have instead of punting the dispute about the actions of a Canadian company to a country where indices of repression, corruption, and impunity are high, and the risks of injustice are high. This can be done by either eliminating or modifying a legal concept known as *forum non conveniens*, which is a "common law" doctrine that allows a court to decline to exercise the jurisdiction it has on the grounds that it is more appropriate for the claim to be heard in another country.

From a real-world perspective, companies accused of causing environmental disasters or human rights abuse do not invoke *forum non conveniens* out of concern that the lawsuit be heard in the most appropriate forum; instead, the doctrine is used by companies in a cynical attempt to deprive victims of their day in court by moving the lawsuit to another jurisdiction where it is unlikely that the claim will be heard at all.

To the majority of the world, *forum non conveniens* is a decidedly odd legal concept. It is unknown to all legal jurisdictions apart from the common law countries which all inherited it from England (which in turn took it from Scotland). Given that the majority of the world does not have the doctrine and seems to get along fine without it, it is hard to see why Canada needs it.

In any event, we need not go so far as eliminating it completely; it would be sufficient to pass a law that simply states that when: a) a foreign plaintiff has chosen to sue a Canadian corporation in a Canadian superior court; and b) the Canadian court has jurisdiction over the defendant, that

Provincial Courts, both of Civil and of Criminal Jurisdiction, and including Procedure in Civil Matters in those Courts," and because provincial-based Superior-level courts have inherent jurisdiction over all criminal and civil matters. Some provinces, specifically BC, already have statutes that deal with the doctrine of *forum non conveniens* that could be easily amended: see e.g. *Court Jurisdiction and Proceedings Transfer Act*, SBC 2003, c 28, canlii.ca/t/kv3s. Similar legislation could be passed in other provinces.

court is required to exercise that jurisdiction unless the defendant can satisfy that court that it would be manifestly unfair for the claim to be heard in Canadian courts.

Curtailing Limited Liability

Next, law reform is needed to ensure that corporations cannot abuse the concept of "limited liability" to avoid legal liability for harms created abroad through the clever use of wholly owned and controlled subsidiaries.

At the moment, there is a real disconnect between how the business or real world sees and treats a corporation, and how the law sees and treats corporations. For example, the business and real world see Barrick Gold as a very large integrated company with a head office that controls its operations all over the world. Barrick Gold sees itself that way too. When it describes itself as "one of the world's leading gold mining companies with annual gold production and gold reserves that are the largest in the industry," it is not describing one of its subsidiaries, it is describing the corporation as a whole.[46]

Investors invest money and are paid dividends based on Barrick's global operations. For all intents and purposes in the real world, Barrick is one company. Yet in the legal world, the picture is much different. Instead of being one company, Barrick Gold's corporate structure looks like a labyrinth of more than one hundred companies.[47] Each one of the boxes in that structure are considered in law to be separate "legal persons" that, for liability purposes, have nothing to do with any of the other legal persons in the chart, no matter if all of the boxes are ultimately owned and controlled by Barrick Gold Corporation (Ontario) at the top of the chart. This is limited liability.

This structure allows parent corporations (i.e., the top corporation that owns subsidiary corporations) to maintain complete control over the operation and management of its subsidiaries' business, and to reap all of the financial rewards of its subsidiaries' business, but if something goes wrong, to claim that the subsidiary is an entirely separate corporation that has nothing to do with it for purposes of liability. Corporations get all of the benefits of law, but without any of the burdens.

We are going to leave untouched and without critique the core principle of limited liability—namely that shareholders who are natural persons (i.e., living, breathing humans) who own shares in a company are treated as separate from that company and, therefore, cannot be held personally liable for the company's debts or liabilities.

Instead, and much more modestly, we are only going to question the notion that limited liability should be extended to situations where there is only one shareholder and that shareholder is itself a corporation. The benefits for corporations are obvious: by simply creating another corporation (which can be created basically out of thin air with just a little paperwork and payment of a filing fee), and by designating the first corporation as the sole shareholder of the second corporation, the corporation has ensured that it fully controls the second corporation and can reap the financial benefits of any business conducted by that second corporation, but the separation it has created between it and the second corporation means that it can avoid any liabilities or debts of the second corporation.

All upside, no downside.

So again, what do we do? What legal reform is necessary? Again, the change is less drastic than you would think. There are various options regarding what the legislation should look like, but perhaps the simplest would be to simply do away with the concept of limited liability as between parent corporations and subsidiaries over which they have the ability to exercise complete control. The reform could be made to the various business corporation acts that exist both federally and in each of the provinces, and need only create an exception to the limited liability that is set out in those acts.

The exception could read something like (this wording, and the definitions therein, are taken from Ontario's Business Corporations Act, RSO 1990, c B.16):

> The shareholders of a corporation are not, as shareholders, liable for any act, default, obligation or liability of the corporation except where the corporation is a subsidiary body corporate as defined by this Act and the claim resulting in liability is brought by an involuntary creditor.

This is just a fancy legalistic way of saying: if a corporation owns a critical mass of shares of another corporation, and has the ability to exercise complete control over that other company, and has the ability to collect all the benefits of that company, it is fully responsible for the harms created by that corporation.

With the good comes the bad.

Neither of these suggested legal reforms are complicated; we also do not believe they should be controversial. The result of these reforms would be essentially to bring to transnational corporations the same level of legal accountability as the rest of us face all the time. These reforms would ensure that individuals who believe that they have been harmed by Canadian corporations have access to a court in which to bring their claims.

Canadian corporations are in no way disadvantaged: they would retain all defences available in law to any civil law defendant. For example, if the claim is frivolous or vexatious, corporations can make use of our legal system's robust safeguards to ensure that the claim is thrown out. If the claim cannot be proved through court admissible evidence, the lawsuit will be dismissed.

Access to justice for victims of corporate wrongdoing does not equal injustice for corporations; on the contrary, access to justice for those who accuse corporations of wrongdoing necessarily implies access to justice for corporations accused of such wrongdoing.

The reality is that communities harmed by the Canadian mining industry will continue to seek access to justice in Canadian court as they already are in the cases against Hudbay, Nevsun, and Tahoe whether or not Parliament gets involved. Instead of resisting these attempts, Canadians, and even the Canadian mining industry, should be welcoming them.

Passing legislation allowing for easier access to Canadian courts would send a clear signal that not only is Canada "open for business," but we are "open for accountability" when things go wrong. Not only is it the right thing to do, but it might actually help restore Canada's reputation on the world stage.

Conclusion
Visions of a Way Forward

Grahame Russell and Catherine Nolin

Mining Violence, Evictions and Harms, Corruption, and Impunity Are Not "Guatemalan" Problems

We reiterate here an underlying conclusion of our work and this book:

In Guatemala, it is not possible to operate a large-scale mine (let alone just about any large-scale economic "development" project in the sectors of hydroelectric dams, garment sweatshops, for-export production of African palm, sugar cane, bananas, and more) without participating in and benefiting from human rights violations and repression, corruption, and impunity.

The *testimonios*, news reports, and overview pieces included in this book demonstrate, we believe quite conclusively, that violating human rights, using repression, and acting with corruption and impunity are how the Canada-dominated mining industry has operated in Guatemala.

Each chapter helps expose and explain why there is no easy fix to the mining-linked violence, evictions, and harms that are, in fact, predictable, logical, and repetitive. We conclude that there will be no end to mining-linked repression, environmental destruction, and human rights violations in Guatemala until there are serious changes in how Guatemala and Canada operate as countries, and how the unjust global economic, political, and military order operates. It is an unjust and sorry state of affairs, profitable for mining companies, shareholders, and investors, harmful and deadly for many Guatemalans.

"Canadian" Problems, "Canadian" Responsibilities

Questions need to be asked about what needs to be done to put an end to these mining-related injustices in Guatemala, and where do these changes need to take place? *The Canada Brand: Violence and Canadian Mining Companies in Latin America*, a significant report by the Justice and Accountability Project (JCAP), based out of two Canadian law schools, found that Canadian mining companies in Latin America contribute to violence and act with impunity. Called the first investigation of its kind,[1] the report "documented 44 deaths, 403 injuries and 709 cases of criminalization against peaceful protesters involving 28 Canadian companies in 13 Latin American countries over a 15-year period."[2]

"Out of sight, out of mind" should not remain the status quo of how many sectors of the global economy work. That the harms, evictions, and violence caused by Canadian companies are occurring in Guatemala and elsewhere does not make these issues any less "Canadian." Once defined as significantly "Canadian" problems, it becomes clearer what needs to be done, and where.

Canadian Public Policy

All recent Canadian governments have promoted "free market" economic policies, pressuring other countries—particularly weaker, poorer countries—to sign "free trade" agreements that more aptly might be called "corporate and investor rights agreements," as they further enshrine enforceable rights for global companies and investors while excluding even minimal enforceable protections for human rights and the environment.

As part of this vision of global economic development, the Canadian Embassy in Guatemala City has often acted as a public relations office for Canadian mining companies.[3] The embassy paid for and hosted "mining is good for development" public events. Embassy officials have appeared with company officials and Guatemalan politicians at ribbon-cutting ceremonies at mine operations.[4] Former ambassador James Lambert even wrote op-eds in Guatemalan newspapers extolling the virtues of how "mining brings development."[5]

At the same time, Canadian government officials—in Ottawa and in the Embassy in Guatemala—have ignored or openly denied reports of repression, harms, and violations linked to Canadian companies.[6] In Rights Action's work related to the community defence struggles highlighted in this book, Rights Action eventually stopped sending mining-linked urgent actions and reports to government officials—there is seemingly no point.

Across Canada, citizens and civil organizations are working hard to challenge politicians and government officials on Canada's relentless advocacy for this "free markets, free trade" model of global economic development, and to hold politicians and government officials accountable for the predictable and repetitive injustices and harms caused by this pro-global corporate and investor model of economic development (see Appendix for a listing of relevant resources and organizations).

Corporate and Investor Decision Making in Canada

As the contributions in this book demonstrate, while the harms, repression, and violations are occurring in Guatemala, the mining operations are owned and controlled by companies in other countries, primarily Canada. All important mining operational and investor decisions are made in Canada. The vast majority of financial profits go to company directors, officers, and shareholders, and to pension fund and private investors in Canada and around the world. These same corporate and investor elites have shown no political will to call for reforms to private and public investment funds (including funds such as the Canada Pension Plan) so that "maximizing profits" is not the only criteria that fund managers need to pay attention to.

It is incidental to Hudbay Minerals, Skye Resources, Goldcorp Inc., Tahoe Resources, Pan American Silver, KCA, and Radius Gold—and to their shareholders and investors—that the minerals they covet are in Guatemala. These are (mainly) Canadian mining operations, supported by Canadian government policies and actions, answering to corporate and investor decision makers.

New research by Jen Moore and Manuel Perez Rocha for MiningWatch Canada demonstrates that to answer to those decision makers, over the past twenty years or so—but particularly during the last ten years—mining companies have filed dozens of claims against Latin American countries before international arbitration panels.[7] At these panels, established through "free trade" agreements, they demand compensation for court decisions, public policies, and other government measures that they claim reduce the value of their investments.[8] In a majority of these cases, the communities most affected by the mining projects have been actively organizing to defend their territories and natural resources.

Additionally, research by Charlotte Connolly for JCAP shows that the Canadian mining industry also lobbied the Canadian government 530 times between January 2018, when investigative powers were given to the newly established Ombudsperson role, and April 2019, when the actual, toothless Ombudsperson was appointed.[9] These 530 lobbying initiatives include thirty-three meetings with the Prime Minister's Office. These reports, among others, illuminate the way in which Canadian mining companies operate in Canada, Guatemala, and beyond.

Media Underreporting

With some recent exceptions, mostly related to the landmark Hudbay Minerals lawsuits, the Canadian mainstream media is not providing proper coverage to the breadth of human rights violations and repression, corruption, and impunity that characterize the operations of Canadian companies in Guatemala, let alone around the world. To get a sense of the extent of mining-linked harms and violations in Canada and around the world, we recommend that folks follow the work of MiningWatch Canada, along with a growing list of Canadian solidarity groups and NGOs (see Appendix). The lack of proper media coverage perpetuates a lack of knowledge amongst the public that in turn reinforces the impunity of the companies and investors.

Impunity and Immunity from Liability

Building on the silence of, or outright denials by, Canadian government officials about corporate and investor harms and violence in Guatemala (let alone around the world), and building on a lack of media reporting, the Canadian companies and investors are further protected by immunity from legal accountability and a lack of political oversight in Canada.[10]

Except for the recent landmark Hudbay Minerals and Tahoe Resources lawsuits, discussed in this book, the Canadian government and Canadian political, economic, and intellectual elites have shown no political will to advocate for or pass criminal and civil law reforms needed to put an end to a manifest double-standard in law whereby if a company commits or contributes to crimes and/or harms in other countries, it is next to impossible to file civil law suits in Canada, let alone have the Attorney General's office consider filing criminal charges.

Importantly, former Supreme Court Justice Ian Binnie, while speaking at a Canadian Bar Association and Department of Justice event, argued that we "cannot have a functioning global economy with a dysfunctional global legal system: there has to be a somewhere, somehow, that people who feel that their rights have been trampled on can attempt redress."[11] Binnie later challenged: "Why shouldn't legal responsibility follow the money up the corporate food chain?"[12]

Long Overdue Debate about the Global Economic Development Model

Underlying all these pending challenges related to a lack of political over-sight and immunity from legal accountability, there is little discussion and debate in Canada about the merits of the global "free trade, free market" economic systems, about why private sector-owned, profit-driven mining companies and investor firms, promoted by the World Bank[13] and other key international "development" organizations are "good for development" in the first place.

The Canadian-dominated global mining industry is very profitable for certain sectors of the Canadian and global economy, and at the very same time violent and unjust for the victims of mining harms and vio-lence around the world, such as the Maya and Ladino communities of Guatemala, as documented in this book. This is the antithesis of how a fair and just global development economic model should operate.

Transnational Sutures: Recommendations for Actions in Guatemala and Canada

As major players in the global mining scene, let alone in Guatemala, we call on the Canadian government to make long-overdue changes to Canada's foreign policy regarding the global mining sector via the adop-tion of a legislative framework that would, at a bare minimum, hold state agencies and companies to legal account, criminally and civilly, for abuses and crimes caused directly or indirectly by Canadian mining companies' overseas operations.

A *Toronto Star* editorial called for "the government [to] make it a pri-ority to re-introduce—and strengthen—a private member's bill that was narrowly defeated in 2010. Bill C-300 was introduced by Liberal MP John McKay to establish corporate accountability for Canadian mining compa-nies in developing countries."[14]

While the *Toronto Star*'s call for legal reform is correct, re-introducing

Bill C-300—and the weak administrative law framework it offers— is not what Canadians should be advocating for. Rather, there must be mandatory, not voluntary, compliance with legal and human rights norms in all corporate and investor operations around the world, and full enforceable criminal and civil law sanctions and remedies, when harms and crimes are found to have been caused or committed.

Furthermore, government financial and diplomatic support must be dependent on full compliance with binding legal and human rights laws and norms.

Corporate social responsibility (CSR) policies are not enough. Actually, they provide a smoke screen to companies that pretend they are paying serious attention to human rights and social/economic community needs of mining-affected communities.[15] CSR policies reinforce a climate of impunity and immunity from accountability. CSR policies enable companies and the Canadian government to step over a community's right to consultation and right to informed consent (i.e., their right to say "yes" or "no" to any given mining project), and become a tool to ignore any community's vocal "no" by recommending dialogue, conflict resolution, and positive outcomes for all.

Finally, and specifically related to Canadian mining operations in Guatemala, we echo the demand of Guatemalan scholar Irma Alicia Velásquez Nimatuj that the Guatemalan Attorney General investigate the corrupt "parallel structures of power" within the State apparatus that have approved hundreds of mining licenses across Guatemala since the Peace Accords were signed in 1996.[16] In addition, Canadian and American parliamentary, congressional, and senate committees should investigate the operations of Canadian and American mining companies within this corrupt Guatemalan state apparatus and mining license process.

Velásquez Nimatuj's opinion piece in the Guatemalan national newspaper *El Periódico* came to our attention the day after we attended the Supreme Court hearing in Guatemala City, discussed in chapter 6, on the requested closure of the El Tambor mine—owned by Kappes, Cassiday & Associates (KCA), previously owned by Canadian-based Radius Gold (which maintains significant financial interests)—on the grounds of lack of free, prior, and informed consultation with Indigenous people in the region before the development of the mine and for their lack of compliance with the Constitutional Court's ruling to cease operations. Velásquez Nimatuj wrote [our translation]:

The country does need employment and investment, but here, mining is not investment for communities or for the country on a financial level. Mining has only given money to the companies that benefit from Article 63 of the Mining Law that literally gives away our resources, by allowing them to return a miserable 1%. On the contrary, mining has brought poverty, the contamination of water sources, illnesses and a deep social division. In Guatemala, the mining business operates in the millionaire corruption that is fomented within and outside the State apparatus, so that licenses are issued for reconnaissance, exploration and exploitation. . . . The Attorney General and CICIG should investigate the parallel structures of power within the State apparatus that approve mining licenses in Indigenous territories, fueling more than one thousand conflicts across the country.[17]

In Guatemala, Canada, and the US, inspiring work and struggle continue to hold Canadian companies and investors politically and legally accountable. These mining-related struggles are part of broader work and struggle around the world to transform the unjust, unequal, and environmentally harmful global economic order. We remain hopeful, as we must.

To be hopeful in bad times is not just foolishly romantic. It is based on the fact that human history is a history not only of cruelty, but also of compassion, sacrifice, courage, kindness.

What we choose to emphasize in this complex history will determine our lives. If we see only the worst, it destroys our capacity to do something. If we remember those times and places—and there are so many—where people have behaved magnificently, this gives us the energy to act, and at least the possibility of sending this spinning top of a world in a different direction.

And if we do act, in however small a way, we don't have to wait for some grand utopian future. The future is an infinite succession of presents, and to live now as we think human beings should live, in defiance of all that is bad around us, is itself a marvelous victory.

—Howard Zinn[18]

Permissions

Chapter 1

"The Genocidal World Bank Project." Cyril Mychalejko.
Excerpted and originally published by Truthout, March
8, 2013. Copyright, Truthout.org. Reprinted with permission. Access: truth-out.org/news/item/14823-profiting-from-genocide-the-world-banks-bloody-history-in-guatemala.

"The Genocidal Chixoy Dam Project." Nathan Einbinder. A version of
this article was published in *NACLA Report on the Americas* 47, no. 2
(Summer 2014) with the title "Rio Negro Survivors Rebuilding Lives
and Community, Thirty-Five Years after World Bank and IDB's
Genocidal Chixoy Hydroelectric Dam Project." Used with permission.

"Genocide's Legacy: Can These Bones Live?" Emilie Smith. A version of
this article originally appeared in the June 2012 issue of *Sojourners*
magazine as "Can These Bones Live?" Used with permission. Access:
sojo.net/magazine/june-2012/can-these-bones-live.

Chapter 2

"When You Benefit from Destruction." Jackie McVicar.
Edited, previously published in 2019 by United for Mining
Justice, May 14, 2019. Reprinted with permission. Access:
unitedforminingjustice.com/single-post/2019/05/14/when-you-benefit-from-destruction-united-church-pension-board-federal-government-put-econ.

Chapter 3

"Is Canada to Blame for Human Rights Abuses in Guatemala?" Annie
Hylton. Edited, previously published in 2018 in *The Walrus* as "Canada
to Blame for Human Rights Abuses in Guatemala? Canadian Mining
Firms Are Not Held Responsible for Horrors Inflicted on Indigenous
Communities by Foreign Subsidiaries. But a Toronto Court Could
Change That." This story was supported by the Stabile Center for
Investigative Journalism at Columbia University. Access: thewalrus.ca/
is-canada-to-blame-for-human-rights-abuses-in-guatemala/.
"Diodora Hernández and Goldcorp Inc.: A Stark Contrast."
Grahame Russell, Catherine Nolin, and James Rodríguez.
Edited, previously published in 2016 as "UNBC Geography
+ Rights Action Emergency Delegation Alert #2: Diodora
Hernandez & Goldcorp Inc.: A Stark Contrast." Access:
unbc.ca/sites/default/files/sections/geography/field-schools/
2016guateemergencydelegationmay16goldcorpdiadorafinal.pdf.
"Goldcorp Inc.'s Marlin Mine—A Family's Pain: Death of Jaime Otero
Pérez López." Catherine Nolin, Grahame Russell, and James
Rodríguez. Edited, previously published in 2016 as "UNBC Geography
+ Rights Action Emergency Delegation Alert #1: Goldcorp Inc.'s
Marlin Mine: A Family's Pain: Death of Jaime Otero Pérez López."
Access: unbc.ca/sites/default/files/sections/geography/field-schools/
2016guateemergencydelegationmay14goldcorpfinal.pdf.
"Something in the Water: The Lasting Violence of a Canadian
Mining Company in Guatemala." Jeff Abbott. A version of this
article originally appeared in the September/October 2018 issue
of *Briarpatch* magazine as "Something in the Water: The Lasting
Violence of a Canadian Mining Company in Guatemala." Used
with permission. Access: briarpatchmagazine.com/articles/view/
something-in-the-water.

Chapter 4

"Formal Human Rights Violation Complaint." Catherine Nolin, Grahame
Russell, and UNBC + Rights Action 2010 Delegation. Edited, original
previously posted in 2010 at: unbc.ca/sites/default/files/sections/
catherine-nolin/guatemala/201010guateunbc-raformalhrcomplaint-
finalwithphotos.pdf.

"Mynor Padilla, Hudbay Mineral's Former Head of Security, Provided with Police 'Security Detail' for Safety." Grahame Russell and Catherine Nolin. Edited, previously published in 2016 as "UNBC Geography + Rights Action Emergency Delegation Alert #4, Mynor Padilla, Hudbay Mineral's Former Head of Security, Provided with Police 'Security Detail' for Safety." Access: unbc.ca/sites/default/files/sections/geography/field-schools/2016guateemergencydelegationmay18puertobarriosfinal-min.pdf.

"Murder of Héctor: Nephew of Maya Land and Rights Activist Beaten to Death in Guatemala" is an edited version of an article by Heather Gies that originally appeared on the website of global environmental news service Mongabay.com on April 27, 2018 as "Nephew of Maya Land and Rights Activist Beaten to Death in Guatemala."

Chapter 5

"Tahoe Resources' Violent Mining Operation." Simon Granovsky-Larsen and Caren Weisbart. Parts of this paper were originally presented by the authors at the 2016 Canadian Association for Latin American and Caribbean Studies (CALACS) conference held in Calgary, Alberta. We would also like to acknowledge the important and ongoing community resistance and solidarity work taking place in Guatemala, Canada, and the United States including, but not limited to, the work of the Center for International Environmental Law (CIEL); Centre for Environmental, Social and Legal Action (CALAS); Diocesan Commission in Defense of Nature (CODIDENA) and other community members and neighbouring supporters in and around the San Rafael Las Flores region and Guatemala; Mining Watch Canada; Maritimes–Guatemala Breaking the Silence Network (BTS); Mining Injustice Solidarity Network (MISN); Network in Solidarity with the People of Guatemala (NISGUA); and United for Mining Justice. This piece could not have been written without their collective and ongoing commitment to bringing to light the environmental and human rights abuses related to the San Rafael mine, and their vigorous on-the-ground research and reporting.

"The Peaceful Encampment at La Puya." A version of Alexandra Pedersen's contribution was initially printed in ReVista: Harvard Review of Latin America, special issue on mining, in 2014 as "Power,

Violence, and Mining in Guatemala: Non-Violent Resistance to
Canada's Northern Shadow." Used with permission.

"Guatemalan Supreme Court of Justice: KCA (& Radius Gold) vs. 'La
Puya' Land and Environmental Defenders." Catherine Nolin,
Grahame Russell, and James Rodríguez. Edited, previously published
in 2016 as "UNBC Geography + Rights Action Emergency Delegation
Alert #3: At the Guatemalan Supreme Court of Justice: KCA (&
Radius Gold) vs. 'La Puya' Land & Environmental Defenders."
Access: unbc.ca/sites/default/files/sections/catherine-nolin/
2016guateemergencydelegationmay18lapuyafinal.pdf.

List of Resources

Organizations

Breaking the Silence Network (BTS) — breakingthesilenceblog.com

Choc vs. HudBay. Summary of lawsuits against HudBay Minerals Inc. over human rights abuse in Guatemala, compiled by Klippensteins Barristers & Solicitors — chocversushudbay.com

Colectivo MadreSelva — madreselva.org.gt

Comisión Pastoral Paz y Ecología (COPAE) — copaeguatemala.org/2021

Consejo de los Pueblos Maya de Occidente (CPO) — consejodepueblosdeoccidente.blogspot.com

Fundación de Antropología Forense de Guatemala (FAFG) — fafg.org

Facultad Latinoamericano de Ciencias Sociales Guatemala (FLACSO Guatemala) — flacso.edu.gt

Guatemala Human Rights Commission (GHRC) — ghrc-usa.org

Human Rights Defenders Project — defendersproject.org

KAIROS MERE Hub. Mother Earth and Resource Extraction: Women Defending Land and Water — scalar.usc.edu/works/mere-hub/

MiMundo — mimundo.org

Mining Injustice Solidarity Network (MISN) — mininginjustice.org

Mining Justice Alliance — miningjusticealliance.wordpress.com

MiningWatch Canada — miningwatch.ca

Network in Solidarity with the People of Guatemala (NISGUA) — nisgua.org

Resistencia de los Pueblos — resistenciadelospueblos.blogspot.com

Rights Action — rightsaction.org; rightsaction.org/archives; rightsaction.org/hudbay-minerals-archives

Unidad de Protección a Defensoras y Defensores de Derechos Humanos Guatemala (UDEFEGUA) — udefegua.org

United for Mining Justice — unitedforminingjustice.com

Books

Camus, Manuela, Santiago Bastos, and Julián López García. *Dinosaurio reloaded: violencias actuales en Guatemala*. Guatemala City: FLACSO y Fundación Constelación, 2015.

Copeland, Nicholas. *The Democracy Development Machine: Neoliberalism, Radical Pessimism, and Authoritarian Populism in Mayan Guatemala*. Ithaca, NY: Cornell University Press, 2019.

Deonandan, Kalowatie, and Michael Dougherty. *Mining in Latin America: Critical Approaches to the New Extraction*. Oxon, UK: Routledge, 2016.

Galeano, Eduardo. *The Open Veins of Latin America: Five Centuries of the Pillage of a Continent*, Cedric Belfrage. New York: Monthly Review Press, 1997 [1973].

Gordon, Todd, and Jeffery Webber. *Blood of Extraction: Canadian Imperialism in Latin America*. Halifax, NS: Fernwood Publishing, 2016.

Granovsky-Larsen, Simon. *Dealing with Peace: The Guatemalan Campesino Movement and the Post-conflict Neoliberal State*. Toronto: University of Toronto Press, 2019.

Henighan, Stephen, and Candace Johnson. *Human and Environmental Justice in Guatemala*. Toronto: University of Toronto Press, 2018.

Instituto Centroamericano de Estudios Fiscales (ICEFI). *La minería en Guatemala: realidad y desafíos frente a la democracia y el desarrollo*. Guatemala: ICEFI, 2014.

Lovell, W. George. *A Beauty That Hurts: Life and Death in Guatemala*. 4th ed. Toronto: Between the Lines, 2019.

McFarlane, Peter. *Northern Shadows: Canadians and Central America*. Toronto: Between the Lines, 1989.

North, Liisa, Timothy D. Clark, and Viviana Patroni. *Community Rights and Corporate Responsibility: Canadian Mining and Oil Companies in Latin America*. Toronto: Between the Lines, 2006.

Russell, Grahame. *Code Z59.5 There Is Only One People*. Toronto: Rights Action, 2010.

Solano, Luís. *Guatemala: Petróleo y minería en las entrañas del poder*. Guatemala City: Infopress Centroamericano, 2005.

Guatemala-Based News

Centro de Medios Independientes (CMI) — cmiguate.org; @cmiguate

Festivales Solidarios: Artistas/gestores, investigadores y diseñadores que trabajamos: memoria histórica, defensa del territorio y prisión política [Solidarity Festivals: Artists / managers, researchers, and designers we work with: historical memory, defence of the territory and political prison] — panal.gt; @festivalesgt

Nómada: Independiente, feminista, investigativo, nómada—Periodismo transparente [Nomad: Independent, Feminist, Investigative, Nomad—Transparent Journalism] — nomada.gt; @nomadagt

Prensa Comunitaria: Agencia de noticias desde las ciencias sociales, periodismo comunitario e indígena, arte y feminismos [Community Press: News agency coming from the social sciences, community and Indigenous journalism, art and feminisms] — prensacomunitaria.org; @prensacomunitar

Ruda: Revista digital—mujeres + territorio [Ruda: Digital magazine—women + territory] — rudagt.org; @ruda_gt

Reports

Amnesty International. *Creating a Paradigm Shift: Legal Solutions to Improve Access to Remedy for Corporate Human Rights Abuse.* London, UK: Business and Human Rights Resource Centre, 2017. https://www.amnesty.org/en/documents/pol30/7037/2017/en/.

Amnesty International. *Mining in Guatemala: Rights at Risk.* London, UK: Amnesty International Secretariat, 2014. https://www.amnesty.org/en/documents/amr34/002/2014/en/.

Global Affairs Canada. *Building the Canadian Advantage: A Corporate Social Responsibility (CSR) Strategy for the Canadian International Extractive Sector.* Ottawa, ON: Government of Canada, 2009. international.gc.ca/trade-agreements-accords-commerciaux/topics-domaines/other-autre/csr-strat-rse-2009.aspx.

Global Affairs Canada. *Doing Business the Canadian Way: A Strategy to Advance Corporate Social Responsibility in Canada's Extractive Sector Abroad.* Ottawa, ON: Government of Canada, 2014. international.gc.ca/trade-agreements-accords-commerciaux/topics-domaines/other-autre/csr-strat-rse.aspx.

Russell, Grahame. *Canadian Companies Mining with the Genocidal Generals in Guatemala.* Toronto, ON: Rights Action, 2020. rightsaction.org/articles/canadian-companies-mining-with-the-genocidal-generals-in-guatemala.

Standing Committee on Foreign Affairs and International Trade. *Mining in Developing Countries: Corporate Social Responsibility.* Ottawa, ON: Government of Canada, 2005. ourcommons.ca/DocumentViewer/en/38-1/FAAE/report-14/.

Films

Schmidt, Rachel, dir. *Defensora.* 2013. 6kidsProductions. vimeo.com/329494479.

Sherburne, Andrew, J. T. Haines, and Tommy Haines, dirs. *Gold Fever.* 2013. Northland Productions.

Becker, Manfred, and Angela Andersen, dirs. *In Search of a Perfect World.* 2018. Canadian Broadcasting Company (CBC). gem.cbc.ca/media/media/docs-special-presentation/episode-20/38e815a-00fea780d27.

"Paradise Lost." *W5.* CTV, 2010. ctvnews.ca/w5-searching-for-gold-at-the-end-of-the-guatemalan-rainbow-1.502718.

Schnoor, Steven, filmographer, and James Rodríguez, photographer. *Violent Evictions at El Estor, Guatemala—updated*. Video file, Youtube. 2010 [2007]. youtube.com/watch?v=JgwtLuISE1Y&t=10s.

Dissertations and Theses

Caxaj, C. Susana. "Gold Mining in Guatemala: Community Health and Resistance amidst Violence." PhD diss. in Nursing, University of Western Ontario, 2013, ir.lib.uwo.ca/etd/1563.

Connolly, Charlotte. "Exporting Canada's Extractives Approach to Development: The Nexus of Law, Violence and Development in the Case of Tahoe Resources Inc. in Guatemala." Master's thesis in Natural Resources and Environmental Studies (NRES-Geography), University of Northern British Columbia, 2019, core.ac.uk/download/pdf/236972598.pdf.

Davis Matthews, Merle. "Researching Extraction, Refusing Extractive Research." Master's thesis in Science and Technology Studies, York University, 2018.

Laplante, J. P. "La Voz del Pueblo: Maya Consultas and the Challenge of Self-Determination for Socially Responsible Investment in the Mining Sector." Master's thesis in Natural Resources and Environmental Studies (NRES-Geography), University of Northern British Columbia, 2014, wizard.unbc.ca/record=b2050760~S3.

McNabb, Chase. "Valuing Vigilance: Confronting the Role of Canadian Mining Companies in Resource Colonialism in Guatemala." Master's thesis in Human Rights Studies, Columbia University, 2018, doi.org/10.7916/D8SF4D4X.

Pedersen, Alexandra. "¡Somos La Puya! (We Are La Puya!): Community Resistance to Canadian Mining Company Operations in Guatemala." PhD diss. in Geography, Queen's University, 2018, CN: https://qspace.library.queensu.ca/handle/1974/24499.

Schnoor, Steven. "Governmentality and the New Spirit of Exploitation: The Politics of Legitimacy and Resistance to Canadian Mining in Guatemala and Honduras." PhD diss. in Communication and Culture (Joint Program), Ryerson and York Universities, 2013, digital.library.ryerson.ca/islandora/object/RULA%3A2696.

Small, Rachel. "'¡Agua, Vida, y Maíz! ¡Minería Fuera del País!': A Praxis Project in Solidarity with Communities Resisting Canadian Mining in Guatemala." Master's thesis in Environmental Studies, York University, 2015, hdl.handle.net/10315/30212.

Stephens, Jacqueline. "Conflicting Perspectives: Neoliberal Resource Development, Indigenous Communities, and Modern Canadian Imperialism in Guatemala." Master's thesis in Interdisciplinary Studies, University of Northern British Columbia, 2006, doi.org/10.24124/2006/bpgub376.

Sveinsdóttir, Anna. "Corporate-Community Mining Conflicts in Guatemala: Unsettling Hegemonic Power Relations in Environmental Struggles." PhD diss. in Geography, University of Denver, 2019, digitalcommons.du.edu/etd/1626.

For more information about the particular struggles and broader issues addressed in this book, contact Grahame Russell at Rights Action: grahame@rightsaction.org, rightsaction.org.

Notes

Foreword

1. Eduardo Galeano, *The Book of Embraces*, transl. Cedric Belfrage (New York: W. W. Norton & Company [1989] 1991), 73.

2. Peter McFarlane, *Northern Shadows: Canadians and Central Americans* (Toronto: Between the Lines, 1989), 9.

3. W. George Lovell, "Surviving Conquest: The Maya of Guatemala in Historical Perspective," *Latin American Research Review* 23, no. 2 (1988): 25-57.

Introduction: Canadian Mining in a Time of Violence, Corruption, and Impunity in the Aftermath of Genocides in Guatemala

1. Recuperación de la Memoria Histórica—Informe Proyecto Interdiocesano (REMHI), *Guatemala: Nunca Más*, Guatemala: Oficina de Derechos Humanos del Arzobispado de Guatemala (ODHAG), 1998.

2. Comisión para el Esclarecimiento Histórico (CEH), *Guatemala: Memoria del silencio* —*Informe de la Comisión para el Esclarecimiento Histórico* (Guatemala: Comisión para el Esclarecimiento Histórico, 1999), ProQuest. Publicly accessible excerpts from the report in English and Spanish can be found in links in Doc M. Billingsley's blog post "Informe de la comisión de esclarecimiento histórico: Memoria del silencio (full document)," March 11, 2014, blog.anthropo.org/category/guatemala.

3. Giovanni B'atz', "Ixil Maya Resistance against Megaprojects in Cotzal, Guatemala," *Theory & Event* 23, no. 4 (October 2020): 1016-36.

4. W. George Lovell, "Surviving Conquest: The Maya of Guatemala in Historical Perspective," *Latin American Research Review* 23, no. 2 (1988): 25-57.

5. J. P. Laplante, "La Voz del Pueblo: Maya Consultas and the Challenge of Self-Determination for Socially Responsible Investment in the Mining Sector" (master's thesis, University of Northern British Columbia, 2014).

6. José De Echave, "La minería peruana y los escenarios de transición," in *Transiciones, Post Ex Extractivismo y alternativas al extractivism en Perú*, eds. Alejandro Alayza and Eduardo Gudynas (Lima: RedGe/CEPES, 2011), 82.

7. Fundación de Antropología Forense de Guatemala / Guatemalan Forensic Anthropology Foundation (FAFG), "Comunicado de Prensa: Cementerio la Verbena," January 5, 2015; Catherine Nolin, "Memory, Truth, Justice: The Crisis of the Living in the Search for Guatemala's Dead and Disappeared," in *Human and Environmental Justice in Guatemala*, eds. Stephen Henighan and Candace Johnson (Toronto: University of Toronto Press, 2018): 34–55.

8. Catherine Nolin, *Transnational Ruptures: Gender and Forced Migration*, Gender in a Global/Local World (Aldershot, UK: Ashgate, 2006).

9. Comisión para el Esclarecimiento Histórico (CEH), *Guatemala: Memoria*; Elizabeth Oglesby and Amy Ross, "Guatemala's Genocide Determination and the Spatial Politics of Justice," *Space and Polity* 13, no. 1 (2009): 21–39.

10. Erica Henderson, "Seeking Justice in Guatemala: Dignifying the 'Disappeared' in a Context of Impunity" (master's thesis, University of Northern British Columbia, 2016).

11. Paul Farmer, "An Anthropology of Structural Violence," *Cultural Anthropology* 45, no. 3 (June 2004): 305–25.

12. James Tyner, *Genocide and the Geographical Imagination: Life and Death in Germany, China, and Cambodia* (New York: Rowman & Littlefield, 2012), 10.

13. Tyner, *Genocide*, 2012.

14. J. P. Laplante and Catherine Nolin, "Consultas and Socially Responsible Investing in Guatemala: A Case Study Examining Maya Perspectives on the Indigenous Right to Free, Prior and Informed Consent," *Society & Natural Resources: An International Journal* 27, no. 3 (2014): 231–48.

15. Simon Granovsky-Larsen, "Between the Bullet and the Bank: Agrarian Conflict and Access to Land in Neoliberal Guatemala," *Journal of Peasant Studies* 40, no. 2 (2013), 361.

16. Recuperación, *Guatemala: Nunca Más*; Comisión para el Esclarecimiento Histórico (CEH), *Guatemala: Memoria*; Marc Drouin, "Understanding the 1982 Guatemalan Genocide," in *State Violence and Genocide in Latin America: The Cold War Years*, eds. Marcia Esparza, Henry R. Huttenbach, and Daniel Feierstein (New York: Routledge, 2009): 81–104.

17. Grahame Russell, "Canadian Companies Mining with the Genocidal Generals in Guatemala," Rights Action, 2020, rightsaction.org/articles/canadian-companies-mining-with-the-genocidal-generals-in-guatemala.

18. Simon Granovsky-Larsen, *Dealing with Peace: The Guatemalan Campesino Movement and the Post-Conflict Neoliberal State* (Toronto: University of Toronto Press, 2019).

19. Victoria Lawson, *Making Development Geography* (New York: Routledge, 2007).

20. Marcus Power, *Rethinking Development Geographies* (London: Routledge, 2003), 65.

21. De Echave, "La minería," 82.

22. Kay B. Warren, "Conclusion: Death Squads and Wider Complicities: Dilemmas for the Anthropology of Violence," in *Death Squad: The Anthropology of State Terror*, ed. Jeffrey A. Sluka (Philadelphia, PA: University of Pennsylvania Press, 1999), 241.

23. Farmer, "Anthropology," 309.

24. Adam J. P. Gaudry, "Insurgent Research," *Wicazo Sa Review* 26, no. 1 (2011): 113–36.

25. Catherine Nolin Hanlon and Finola Shankar, "Gendered Spaces of Terror and Assault: The Testimonio of REMHI and the Commission for Historical Clarification in Guatemala," *Gender, Place & Culture: Journal of Feminist Geography* 7, no. 3 (2000): 265–86.

26. "Canadian Mining Assets," Natural Resources Canada (NRCan), updated February 2019, nrcan.gc.ca/mining-materials/publications/19323.

27. Angela Bunch and Carlos Loarca, "Mining Conflict and Indigenous Consultation in Guatemala," *Americas Quarterly*, March 25, 2013, americasquarterly.org/article/mining-conflict-and-indigenous-consultation-in-guatemala; EarthWorks and Institute for Policy Studies, "Guatemalan Government Discriminates against Xinka, Puts Escobal Mine Consultation at Risk," 2019, earthworks.org/publications/report-guatemalan-government-discriminates-against-xinka-puts-escobal-mine-consultation-at-risk; Laplante and Nolin, "Consultas."

28. Berta Cáceres, Goldman Environmental Prize Acceptance Speech, April 22, 2015, youtube.com/watch?v=AR1kwx8boms.

Chapter 1.
Genocide's Legacy on the Land and Dominant Economic Model

1. J. T. Haines and Tommy Haines, *Gold Fever*, 2013; US; G Project Films and Northland Films, minute 14:30.

2. Jubilee International, *Generating Terror*, Jubilee Debt Campaign, December 2012, jubileedebt.org.uk/reports-briefings/report/generating-terror.

3. Jubilee, *Generating Terror*.

4. Comisión para el Esclarecimiento Histórico (CEH), *Guatemala: Memoria del silencio—Informe de la Comisión para el Esclarecimiento Histórico* (Guatemala: Comisión para el Esclarecimiento Histórico, 1999), ProQuest. Publicly accessible excerpts from the report in English and Spanish can be found in links in Doc M. Billingsley's blog post "Informe de la comisión de esclarecimiento histórico: Memoria del silencio (full document)," March 11, 2014, blog.anthropo.org/category/guatemala.

5. Barbara Rose Johnston, *Chixoy Dam Legacy Issues Study* (Santa Cruz, CA: Center for Political Ecology, 2005), archive.internationalrivers.org/resources/chixoy-dam-legacy-issues-overview-4050.

6. Jubilee, *Generating Terror*.

7. Jubilee, *Generating Terror*.

8. Susanne Jonas, *The Battle for Guatemala: Rebels, Death Squads, and U.S. Power* (Boulder, CO: Westview Press, 1991), 6.

9. Jonas, *Battle*, 88.

10. Fundación de Antropología Forense de Guatemala / Guatemalan Forensic Anthropology Foundation (FAFG), "Comunicado de Prensa: Cementerio la Verbena," January 5, 2015.

11. Comisión para el Esclarecimiento Histórico (CEH), *Guatemala: Memoria*.

12. Fundación de Antropología Forense de Guatemala / Guatemalan Forensic Anthropology Foundation (FAFG), personal communication, February 18, 2020.

13. Greg Grandin, *The Last Colonial Massacre: Latin America in the Cold War* (Chicago, IL: University of Chicago Press, 2004).

Chapter 2. Mining in the Wake of Genocides

1. Center for International Environmental Law (CIEL), MiningWatch Canada, and Breaking the Silence (BTS), "OAS Human Rights Commission Urges Suspension of Mining Activity at Goldcorp's Marlin Mine in Guatemala," May 24, 2010, miningwatch. ca/news/2010/5/24/oas-human-rights-commission-urges-suspension-mining-activity-goldcorps-marlin-mine; Shin Imai, Leah Gardner, and Sarah Weinberger, "The 'Canada Brand': Violence and Canadian Mining Companies in Latin America," Osgoode Legal Studies Research Paper 17/2017, dx.doi.org/10.2139/ssrn.2886584; Shin Imai, Ladan Mehranvar, and Jennifer Sander, "Breaching Indigenous Law: Canadian Mining in Guatemala," *Indigenous Law Journal* 6, vol. 1 (2007): 101–39, ssrn.com/abstract=1267902.

2. Karen Hudlet and Ana Zbona, "Entrevista con Pedro Rafael Maldonado Flores (CALAS, Guatemala): 'Lo que realmente está en contra del desarrollo es la corrupción y la cooptación del Estado,'" Centro de Información sobre Empresas y Derechos Humanos / Business and Human Rights Centre, May 2, 2017, business-humanrights.org/en/blog/entrevista-con-pedro-rafael-maldonado-flores-calas-guatemala-lo-que-realmente-está-en-contra-del-desarrollo-es-la-corrupción-y-la-cooptación-del-estado/.

3. Luís Solano, *Guatemala petróleo y minería en las entrañas del poder* (Guatemala City: Inforpress Centroamérica, 2005); Luís Solano, *Under Siege: Peaceful Resistance to Tahoe Resources and Militarization in Guatemala*, International Platform against Impunity in Central America and MiningWatch Canada, November 10, 2015, miningwatch.ca/sites/default/files/solano-underseigereport2015-11-10.pdf.

4. Francisca Gómez Grijalva, "Un repaso a los principales proyectos mineros en Guatemala: política gubernamental y conflictividad social [A Review of the Principal Mining Projects in Guatemala: Government Policy and Social Conflict]," *El Observador: Análisis Alternativo sobre Política y Economía* 8, nos 40–41 (May–September 2013): 42–77.

5. Sandra Cuffe, "Maya Q'eqchi' Demand Justice for Fisherman Killed During Police Crackdown on Mining Protest in Guatemala," Intercontinental Cry, Center for World Indigenous Studies, July 11, 2017, intercontinentalcry.org/maya-qeqchi-demand-justice-fisherman-killed-police-crackdown-mining-protest-guatemala/.

6. Comisión para el Esclarecimiento Histórico (CEH), *Guatemala: Memoria del*

silencio—Informe de la Comisión para el Esclarecimiento Histórico, vol. 5 of 12, *Conclusiones y Recomendaciones* (Guatemala: Comisión para el Esclarecimiento Histórico, 1999), 51, ProQuest. Publicly accessible excerpts from the report in English and Spanish can be found in links in Doc M. Billingsley's blog post "Informe de la comisión de esclarecimiento histórico: Memoria del silencio (full document)," March 11, 2014, blog.anthropo.org/category/guatemala.

7. Comisión para el Esclarecimiento Histórico (CEH), *Guatemala: Memoria*, vol. 6 of 12, *Casos ilustrativos, Anexo I*, 100.

8. Comisión para el Esclarecimiento Histórico (CEH), *Guatemala: Memoria*, vol. 8 of 12, *Casos presentados, Anexo II*, 679.

9. Comisión para el Esclarecimiento Histórico (CEH), *Guatemala: Memoria*, vol. 8 of 12, *Casos presentados, Anexo II*, 679.

10. Betsy Rakosy, "Victimization—The EXMIBAL Story," MAC: Mines and Communities, May 23, 2002, minesandcommunities.org/article.php?a=7057.

11. Comisión para el Esclarecimiento Histórico (CEH), *Guatemala: Memoria*, vol. 8 of 12, *Casos presentados, Anexo II*, 105.

12. Comisión para el Esclarecimiento Histórico (CEH), *Guatemala: Memoria*, vol. 8 of 12, *Casos presentados, Anexo II*, 674.

13. United Nations (UN), "Definitions: War Crimes," United Nations Office on Genocide Prevention and the Responsibility to Protect, 2018, un.org/en/genocideprevention/war-crimes.shtml.

14. United Nations (UN), "Definitions: Crimes against Humanity," United Nations Office on Genocide Prevention and the Responsibility to Protect, 2018, un.org/en/genocideprevention/crimes-against-humanity.shtml.

15. Guatemala Human Rights Commission (GHRC), "Allegation Letter," July 6, 2011, ghrc-usa.org/Resources/2011/War_Crimes/UN_letter_PerezMolina.htm.

16. Simon Granovsky-Larsen, "The Guatemalan Campesino Movement and the Postconflict Neoliberal State," *Latin American Perspectives* 44, no. 5 (2017): 53-73.

17. Instituto Centroamericano de Estudios Fiscales (ICEFI), *La minería en Guatemala: realidad y desafíos frente a la democracia y el desarrollo*, 2nd ed., Guatemala: Instituto Centroamericano de Estudios Fiscales, 2014, icefi.org/sites/default/files/la_mineria_en_guatemala_-_2da_edicion.pdf.

18. Solano, *Guatemala petróleo y minería*.

19. Solano, *Guatemala petróleo y minería*, 124.

20. Solano, *Guatemala petróleo y minería*, 124.

21. Yuri Melini, personal interview, Guatemala City, May 2017.

22. Melini, personal interview.

23. On Common Ground Consultants Inc., *Human Rights Assessment of Marlin Mine* (Vancouver, BC: On Common Ground Consultants Inc., 2010), 34, https://s24.q4cdn.com/382246808/files/doc_downloads/2020/09/OCG_HRA_Marlin_Mine_June_7.pdf.

24. Recuperación de la Memoria Histórica—Informe Proyecto Interdiocesano (REMHI), *Guatemala: Nunca Más* (Guatemala: Oficina de Derechos Humanos del Arzobispado de Guatemala [ODHAG], 1998).

25. Francisco Goldman, *The Art of Political Murder: Who Killed the Bishop* (New York: Grove Press, 2008).

26. Néstor Galicia, "Dos involucrados en Caso Gerardi murieron de forma similar," *Prensa Libre*, July 18, 2016, prensalibre.com/hemeroteca/muerte-de-byron-lima-oliva-y-obdulio-villanueva.

27. Comisión Internacional contra la Impunidad en Guatemala (CICIG), *Caso Caja de Pandora*, Guatemala City: CICIG, 2017, cicig.org/casos/caso-caja-de-pandora/.

28. CICIG, *Caso Caja.*

29. Inter-American Commission on Human Rights (IACHR), *PM 260-07—IACHR Precautionary Measures: Communities of the Maya People (Sipakepense and Mam) of the Sipacapa and San Miguel Ixtahuacán Municipalities in the Department of San Marcos, Guatemala* (Organization of American States, 2010), oas.org/en/iachr/indigenous/protection/precautionary.asp.

30. Coalition against Unjust Mining in Guatemala (CAMIGUA), "Violence Near Goldcorp Mine in Guatemala Underscores Need for Mine Suspension," March 9, 2011, miningwatch.ca/blog/2011/3/9/violence-near-goldcorp-mine-guatemala-underscores-need-mine-suspension.

31. Roni Pocón, "Álvaro Colom y varios exministros son capturados por caso Transurbano," *Prensa Libre*, February 13, 2018, prensalibre.com/guatemala/justicia/Alvaro-Colom-capturado-caso-corrupcion-transurbano-exministros-une.

32. Oswaldo J. Hernández, "De Presidente a perseguido, retirado, y a prisión en 24 horas," *Plaza Pública*, September 4, 2015, plazapublica.com.gt/content/de-presidente-perseguido-retirado-y-prision-en-24-horas.

33. See Comisión Internacional contra la Impunidad en Guatemala (CICIG), La Línea archivos (Guatemala City: CICIG, 2018), cicig.org/casos/caso-la-linea.

34. Martín Rodríguez Pellecer, "El PP era un cártel y estos empresarios, sus socios," *Nómada*, June 3, 2016, tiempo.hn/guatemala-pp-cartel-empresarios-socios.

35. Extractive Industries Transparency Initiative (EITI), home page, 2018, eiti.org.

36. Sandra Cuffe, "State of Siege: Mining Conflict Escalates in Guatemala," MAC: Mines and Communities, May 2, 2013, minesandcommunities.org/article.php?a=12272.

37. Plurijur, "CICIG: Caso cooptación del Estado de Guatemala y la empresa Goldcorp de la mina Marlin," June 21, 2016, plurijur.blogspot.com/2016/06/cicig-caso-cooptacion-del-estado-de.html.

38. Melini, personal interview.

39. Comisión Internacional contra la Impunidad en Guatemala (CICIG), *Presentan informe Guatemala un Estado capturado* (Guatemala City: CICIG, August 28, 2019), cicig.org/comunicados-2019-c/informe-guatemala-un-estado-capturado/.

40. CICIG, *Presentan*, para. 3.

41. Sandra Cuffe, "Guatemala's New President Is More of the Same, Experts Say," *The World*, Public Radio International (PRI), January 20, 2020, pri.org/stories/2020-01-20/guatemalas-new-president-more-same-experts-say.

42. Restitution Project, Webinar: A Project of Mining the Connections Working Group of the Church in Action Committee of the Maritime Conference of the United Church of Canada and United for Mining Justice, 2018, unitedforminingjustice.com/divestment.

43. EarthWorks, "Over 50 Organizations Urge World Bank to Boost Recycling, Circular Economy & Non-Mining Solutions for a Truly Climate Smart Agenda," EarthWorks, May 1, 2019, earthworks.org/media-releases/over-50-organizations-urge-world-bank-to-boost-recycling-circular-economy-non-mining-solutions-for-a-truly-climate-smart-agenda/.

44. EarthWorks, "NGO Letter to the World Bank re Mining & Renewables," EarthWorks, April 30, 2019, earthworks.org/publications/ngo-letter-to-the-world-bank-re-mining-renewables/.

45. Berta Cáceres, Goldman Environmental Prize Acceptance Speech, translated by Jackie McVicar, April 22, 2015, youtube.com/watch?v=AR1kwx8boms.

46. Greta Thunberg, prepared speech, World Economic Forum at Davos, 2019, youtube.com/watch?v=51u4JECraLQ.

47. Sherri Mitchell, *Sacred Instructions: Indigenous Wisdom for Living Spirit-Based Change* (Berkeley, CA: North Atlantic Books, 2018).

Chapter 3. Confronting Goldcorp at Every Step of the Destruction and Repression

1. Catherine Nolin and Jacqui Stephens, "'We Have to Protect the Investors': 'Development' & Canadian Mining Companies in Guatemala," *Journal of Rural and Community Development* 5, vol. 2 (2010): 37–70, journals.brandonu.ca/jrcd.

2. Emily Willard, "Otto Pérez Molina, Guatemalan President-Elect, with 'Blood on His Hands,'" *Unredacted: The National Security Archive Blog*, November 14, 2011, unredacted.com/2011/11/14/otto-perez-molina-guatemalan-president-elect-with-"blood-on-his-hands"/.

3. Shin Imai, Director of the Justice and Corporate Accountability Project, personal communication, 2018, Osgoode Law School, Toronto, Ontario.

4. Klippensteins Barristers & Solicitors, "Statement of Civil Claim: *Caal v. HudBay Minerals, Inc.*," 2010, chocversushudbay.com/wp-content/Uploads/2010/11/Amended-Statement-of-Claim-Caal-v.-HudBay-FILED.pdf.

5. Comisión para el Esclarecimiento Histórico (CEH), *Guatemala: Memoria del silencio—Informe de la Comisión para el Esclarecimiento Histórico* (Guatemala: Comisión para el Esclarecimiento Histórico, 1999), ProQuest. Publicly accessible excerpts from the report in English and Spanish can be found in links in Doc M. Billingsley's blog post "Informe de la comisión de esclarecimiento histórico: Memoria del silencio (full document)," March 11, 2014, blog.anthropo.org/category/guatemala.

6. "Countering the Spin: Hudbay's 'Facts' about Its Operations in Guatemala," chocversushudbay.com, chocversushudbay.com/wp-content/uploads/2010/10/Countering-the-spin-no-video.pdf.

7. Human Rights Watch, *World Report 2013: Guatemala,* Human Rights Watch, 2013, para. 4, hrw.org/world-report/2013/country-chapters/guatemala.

8. Human Rights Watch, *World Report 2017: Guatemala: Events of 2016,* Human Rights Watch, 2017, para. 11, hrw.org/world-report/2017/country-chapters/guatemala.

9. Malavika Krishnan, "Canadian Mining in Latin America: Exploitation, Inconsistency, and Neglect," Council on Hemispheric Affairs, June 11, 2014, para. 10, coha.org/canadian-mining-in-latin-america-exploitation-inconsistency-and-neglect.

10. Gabriel Friedman, "Big Win for Foreign Plaintiffs as Pan American Settles Guatemala Mine Case," *Financial Post,* July 31, 2019, business.financialpost.com/commodities/mining/big-win-for-foreign-plaintiffs-as-pan-american-settles-guatemala-mine-case.

11. See Wanless and Klippenstein's contribution in chapter 6; see also Klippensteins Barristers & Solicitors, *Choc v. HudBay Minerals Inc. & Caal v. HudBay Minerals Inc.* 2017, chocversushudbay.com.

12. Klippensteins Barristers & Solicitors, "Breakthrough in Legal Liability of Canadian Mining Corporations for Abuses Overseas: Mayans' Lawsuit against HudBay over Shootings and Rapes at Mine in Guatemala to Proceed in Canadian Courts," February 25, 2013, para. 3, marketwired.com/press-release/breakthrough-in-legal-liability-of-canadian-mining-corporations-for-abuses-overseas-1760975.htm.

13. Comisión para el Esclarecimiento Histórico (CEH), *Guatemala: Memoria.*

14. Amnesty International, *Amnesty International Report 1998—Guatemala,* January 1, 1998, refworld.org/docid/3ae6aa0168.html.

15. Amnesty International, *Amnesty International Report 1998.*

16. Grahame Russell, personal communication, March 2017.

17. Comisión para el Esclarecimiento Histórico (CEH), *Guatemala: Memoria.*

18. Comisión para el Esclarecimiento Histórico (CEH), *Guatemala: Memoria,* 23.

19. Comisión para el Esclarecimiento Histórico (CEH), *Guatemala, Memory of Silence: Tz'inil na 'tab'al – Report of the Commission for Historical Clarification: Conclusions and Recommendations* (Guatemala: Comisión para el Esclarecimiento Histórico, 1999), 41, ProQuest. A publicly accessible version can be found in links in Doc M. Billingsley's blog post "Informe de la comisión de esclarecimiento histórico: Memoria del silencio (full document)," March 11, 2014, blog.anthropo.org/category/guatemala.

20. Otto Argueta, *Private Security in Guatemala: Pathway to Its Proliferation* (Switzerland: Nomos Verlagsgesellschaft, 2013).

21. Klippensteins, "Statement."

22. Klippensteins, "Statement."

23. *Voluntary Principles on Security and Human Rights,* 2000, para. 9, voluntaryprinciples.org/the-principles.

24. Cited in Department of Foreign Affairs and International Trade (2014) Access to Information Act request: A-2014-01660.

25. Dominique Ramirez, personal communication, March 2017.

26. On Common Ground Consultants Inc., *Human Rights Assessment of Marlin Mine* (Vancouver, BC: On Common Ground Consultants Inc., 2010), s24.q4cdn.com/382246808/ files/doc_downloads/2020/09/OCG_HRA_Marlin_Mine_June_7.pdf.

27. These comments were recorded by the author in field notes from a meeting with FREDEMI in San Miguel Ixtahuacán in January 2015.

28. Canadian Centre for International Justice (CCIJ), *Statement of Civil Claim: García v. Tahoe Resources, Inc.*, 2014, business-humanrights.org/en/latest-news/ pdf-adolfo-agustin-garcia-et-al-v-tahoe-resources-inc.

29. Canadian Centre for International Justice (CCIJ), *Court of Appeal for British Columbia / Judgement on Forum Non Conveniens: García v. Tahoe Resources, Inc.*, 2017, BCCA 39, 2017, canlii.ca/t/gx49k.

30. Tom Fudge, personal communication, no date.

31. *Voluntary Principles*.

32. Fudge, personal communication.

33. Network in Solidarity with the People of Guatemala (NISGUA), Letter to U.S. Embassy in Guatemala, June 1, 2018, 4, nisgua.org/wp-content/uploads/ Letter-to-US-Embassy-May2018.pdf.

34. Pedro Rafael Maldonado Flores, personal communication, January 2015.

35. J. P. Laplante, "La Voz del Pueblo: Maya Consultas and the Challenge of Self-Determination for Socially Responsible Investment in the Mining Sector" (master's thesis, University of Northern British Columbia, 2014).

36. Guatevisión, "Pobladores bloquean ingreso y retienen avioneta de la Mina Marlín como medida de presión," July 11, 2017, guatevision.com/historico/ bloquear-ingreso-retienen-avioneta-mina-marlin.

37. Rights Action, "Goldcorp Trying to Leave Guatemala Without Paying for Harms and Destruction Left Behind," *Rights Action*, July 17, 2017, mailchi.mp/rightsaction/ goldcorp-trying-to-leave-guatemala-without-paying-for-harms-and-destruction-left-behind; Luís Solano, "Movimiento de resistencia en la mina Marlin pide resarcir daños ambientales," Centro de Medios Independientes, July 11, 2017, cmiguate.org/ movimiento-de-resistencia-en-la-mina-marlin-pide-resarcir-danos-ambientales.

38. Dave Dean, "75% of the World's Mining Companies Are Based in Canada," *VICE News*, July 9, 2013, vice.com/en_ca/article/wdb4j5/75-of-the-worlds-mining-companies-are -based-in-canada.

39. Hayley Woodin, "Goldcorp's Marlin Mine: A Decade of Operations and Controversy in Guatemala," *Business in Vancouver*, May 4, 2015, biv.com/article/2015/05/ goldcorps-marlin-mine-decade-operations-and-contro.

40. Lyuba Zarsky and Leonardo Stanley, *Searching for Gold in the Highlands of Guatemala: Economic Benefits and Environmental Risks of the Marlin Mine* (Medford,

MA: Tufts University, September 2011), business-humanrights.org/en/latest-news/tufts-university-report-on-goldcorps-marlin-mine-in-guatemala.

41. Comisión Pastoral Paz y Ecología (COPAE) and Unitarian Universalist Service Committee (UUSC), *Reclamation Issues and Estimated Cost of Reclamation, Marlin Mine* (San Marcos, Guatemala and Cambridge, MA: COPAE and UUSC, 2011).

42. Comisión Pastoral, *Reclamation*, 1.

43. Rory Carroll, "Gold Giant Faces Honduras Inquiry into Alleged Heavy Metal Pollution," *Guardian*, December 31, 2009, theguardian.com/environment/2009/dec/31/goldcorp-honduras-pollution-allegations; Adam Jarvis and Jaime Amezaga, *Technical Review of Mine Closure Plan and Mine Closure Implementation at Minerales Entres Mares San Martín Mine, Honduras* (UK: Newcastle University, 2009).

44. Karen Spring and Grahame Russell, "The Real Cost of Gold in Honduras: Goldcorp & Honduran Regime Cover-up Blood & Urine Testing & Poisoning at 'San Martín' Mine," *Mines and Communities*, April 27, 2011, minesandcommunities.org/article.php?a=10901.

45. David Hill, "Welcome to Guatemala: Gold Mine Protester Beaten and Burnt Alive," *Guardian*, August 12, 2014, theguardian.com/environment/andes-to-the-amazon/2014/aug/12/guatemala-gold-mine-protester-beaten-burnt-alive.

46. James Rodríguez, "Confronting Goldcorp: An Interview with a Guatemalan Activist," *NACLA Report on the Americas*, September 1, 2009, nacla.org/article/confronting-goldcorp-interview-guatemalan-activist.

47. Jeff Abbott, "Across Latin America, Governments Criminalize Social Movements to Silence Dissent," *Waging Nonviolence*, March 10, 2016, wagingnonviolence.org/2016/03/across-latin-american-governments-criminalize-social-movements-to-silence-dissent/.

48. Carlos Arrazola and Enrique Naveda, "Prófugo por Cooptación del Estado aparece becado en un prestigioso programa internacional de liderazgo," *Plaza Pública*, July 6, 2017, plazapublica.com.gt/content/profugo-por-cooptacion-del-estado-aparece-becado-en-un-prestigioso-programa-internacional-de-.

49. Amilcar Ávila, "TSE hace oficial la cancelación del PP y de Líder," *Publinews*, February 6, 2017, publinews.gt/gt/noticias/2017/02/06/tse-oficial-cancelacion-pp-lider.html.

50. Guatemala Human Rights Commission (GHRC), *Goldcorp's Mining in San Miguel Ixtahuacán* (Washington, DC: GHRC, 2008), para. 8, ghrc-usa.org/AboutGuatemala/Goldcorp.htm.

51. Newmont Goldcorp. *Safe. Productive. Responsible: Goldcorp 2018 Sustainability Report* (Goldcorp, 2018), newmont.com/sustainability/goldcorps-archive-sustainability-reports.

52. Inter-American Commission on Human Rights (IACHR), *PM 260-07—IACHR Precautionary Measures: Communities of the Maya People (Sipakepense and Mam) of the Sipacapa and San Miguel Ixtahuacán Municipalities in the Department of San Marcos, Guatemala*, IACHR, 2010, oas.org/en/iachr/indigenous/protection/precautionary.asp.

53. Comisión Pastoral Paz y Ecología (COPAE), *Informe Final: Elaboración del Monitoreo de Aguas Superficiales Alrededor del la Mina Marlín, San Miguel, Ixtahuacán y*

Sipacapa, San Marcos a través de Análisis Físico Químicos por Espectrofotometría, COPAE, 2018, drive.google.com/file/d/1gdjNbaLz035pObBPTu247tCiYju_IJzm/view.

Chapter 4. Q'eqchi' People Fight Back against Hudbay Minerals, in Their Own Words

1. Eduardo Galeano, *Días y noches de amor y de guerra* (Barcelona, Spain: Siglo XXI de España Editores, 1985), 303.

2. Klippensteins Barristers & Solicitors, "Lawsuits in Ontario against HudBay and HMI Nickel Regarding Murder and Gang-rapes Will Continue," Mines and Communities, August 9, 2011, minesandcommunities.org/article.php?a=11122.

3. Comisión para el Esclarecimiento Histórico (CEH), *Guatemala: Memoria del silencio —Informe de la Comisión para el Esclarecimiento Histórico* (Guatemala: Comisión para el Esclarecimiento Histórico, 1999), ProQuest. Publicly accessible excerpts from the report in English and Spanish can be found in links in Doc M. Billingsley's blog post "Informe de la comisión de esclarecimiento histórico: Memoria del silencio (full document)," March 11, 2014, blog.anthropo.org/category/guatemala.

4. Comisión para el Esclarecimiento Histórico (CEH), *Guatemala: Memoria*.

5. Catherine Nolin and Grahame Russell, "Press Release: Urgent Need to End Impunity of Canadian & U.S. Mining Companies in Guatemala," *UNBC*, May 13, 2016, unbc.ca/sites/default/files/sections/catherine-nolin/2016guateemergencydelegation.pdf.

6. Rights Action, "Mynor Padilla's Day in Court, Puerto Barrios, Guatemala," video file, YouTube, filmed by Steven Schnoor, posted by Rights Action, May 17, 2016, youtube.com/watch?v=rlIt5geTIJc.

7. Sandra Cuffe, "Nickel Mine, Lead Bullets: Maya Q'eqchi' Seek Justice in Guatemala and Canada," *Mongabay News*, May 19, 2015, news.mongabay.com/2015/05/nickel-mine-lead-bullets-maya-qeqchi-seek-justice-in-guatemala-and-canada.

8. Sandra Cuffe, "The Land Is Forever: Rodrigo Tot Wins Goldman Prize for Land-title Quest," *Mongabay News*, April 24, 2017, news.mongabay.com/2017/04/the-land-is-forever-rodrigo-tot-wins-goldman-prize-for-land-title-quest.

9. Cuffe, "Nickel Mine."

10. Rights Action, "Assassination of Héctor Manuel Choc Cuz, Nephew of Angélica Choc," *Rights Action*, April 11, 2018, para. 2, us9.campaign-archive.com/?u=ea011209a2430 50dfb66dff59&id=69b439e638.

11. *Choc v. HudBay Minerals Inc.*, 2013, ONSC 1414 (CanLII), canlii.ca/t/glron.

12. Sandra Cuffe, "Ex-Mine Security Head Cleared of Murder, Assault against Indigenous Guatemalans," Mongabay News, April 10, 2017, news.mongabay.com/2017/04/ex-mine-security-head-cleared-of-murder-assault-against-indigenous-guatemalans.

13. Human Rights Watch, *Guatemala Country Report 2017* (New York: Human Rights Watch, 2018), hrw.org/world-report/2018/country-chapters/guatemala.

14. El Puerto Informa, "Muere joven Hector Choc luego de aparentemente accidentarse en El Estor, Izabal," *El Puerto Informa*, March 31, 2018, elpuertoinforma.com.

Chapter 5. Facing and Resisting KCA / Radius Gold and Tahoe Resources on the Ground

1. Mariel Aguilar-Støen, "Staying the Same: Transnational Elites, Mining and Environmental Governance in Guatemala," in *Environmental Politics in Latin America: Elite Dynamics, the Left Tide and Sustainable Development*, ed. Benedicte Bull and Mariel Aguilar-Støen (London: Routledge, 2015), 132.

2. Tahoe on Trial, "Security Footage Outside Escobal Mine—April 27, 2013," November 19, 2015, perma.cc/QGL4-2LZV.

3. Mariel Aguilar-Støen and Benedicte Bull, "Protestas contra la minería en Guatemala: ¿Qué papel juegan las elites en los conflictos?" *Anuario de Estudios Centroamericanos* 42 (2016): 14-44.

4. Oswaldo J. Hernández, "La oposición a la minería, la nueva amenaza a la seguridad nacional," *Plaza Pública*, July 16, 2014, plazapublica.com.gt/content/la-oposicion-la-mineria-la-nueva-amenaza-la-seguridad-nacional; Caren Weisbart, "Diplomacy at a Canadian Mine Site in Guatemala," *Critical Criminology* 26, no. 4 (2018): 473-89.

5. Aguilar-Støen, "Staying the Same," 131-49.

6. Centre for International Environmental Law, Maritimes–Guatemala Breaking the Silence Network, Mining Injustice Solidarity Network, Mining Watch Canada, and Network in Solidarity with the People of Guatemala, "Investor Alert: Tahoe Resources' Escobal Project in Guatemala," June 12, 2017, miningwatch.ca/sites/default/files/investor_alert_tahoe_resources_june_12_17_0.pdf; Network in Solidarity with the People of Guatemala (NISGUA), "Xinka People's Parliament Denounces the Murder of Environmental Activist Ángel Estuardo Quevedo," Voice of the Xinca Nation of Guatemala, July 12, 2018, nisgua.org/xinka-peoples-parliament-denounces-murder-environmental-activist-angel-estuardo-quevedo/.

7. Parlamento del Pueblo Xinka Guatemala, "Parlamento Xinka denuncia la provocación de Pan American Silver," *Fuera Mina Escobal*, December 29, 2020, fueraminaescobal.com/parlamento-xinka-denuncia-la-provocacion-de-pan-american-silver/; Resist Escobal, "Xinka Parliament Announces Breakthrough in Escobal Mine Consultation Process, Rejects Pan American Silver's Bad Faith," October 26, 2020, resistescobal.com/xinka-parliament-announces-breakthrough-in-escobal-mine-consultation-process-rejects-pan-american-silvers-bad-faith/.

8. Matt Eisenbrandt, "Transnational Justice for Guatemalan Victims of Human Rights Violations at a Canadian-Owned Mine in a Dispute about Lack of Local Consultation," *Global Justice Journal*, October 24, 2019, globaljustice.queenslaw.ca/news/transnational-justice-for-guatemalan-victims-of-human-rights-violations-at-a-canadian-owned-mine-in-a-dispute-about-lack-of-local-consultation.

9. Tahoe on Trial, "The Context," n.d., tahoeontrial.wordpress.com.

10. Amnesty International Canada, "Wiretap Transcripts Raise Troubling

Questions about Tahoe Resources' Militarized Security Detail," April 7, 2015, amnesty.ca/news/public-statements/joint-press-release/wiretap-transcripts-raise-troubling-questions-about-tahoe.

11. Resist Escobal, "The Civil Lawsuit in Canada," 2021, resistescobal.com/the-civil-lawsuit-in-canada.

12. Roger Barany, *Affidavit*, Supreme Court of British Columbia, Vancouver Registry No. S-144726, January 21, 2015, resistescobal.com/wp-content/uploads/2020/03/affadavit-wiretap-transcripts-filed-23jan15-1.pdf, 9.

13. Redacción La Hora, "Capturan a Alberto Rotondo," *La Hora*, January 22, 2016, lahora.gt/capturan-a-alberto-rotondo; MiningWatch Canada, "The Uphill Battle over Violence at Tahoe Resources Escobal Mine in Guatemala," November 5, 2016, miningwatch.ca/blog/2016/11/5/uphill-battle-justice-over-violence-tahoe-resources-escobal-mine-guatemala.

14. Eisenbrandt, "Transnational," para. 8.

15. Network in Solidarity with the People of Guatemala (NISGUA), "Six Police Officers on Duty when Former Head of Security for Escobal Mine Fled House Arrest Sentenced to Multiple Years in Prison," June 8, 2017, para. 5, nisgua.org/six-police-officers-on-duty-when-former-head-of-security-for-escobal-mine-fled-house-arrest-sentenced-to-multiple-years-in-prison/.

16. D. P. Gray, *Affidavit*, Vancouver Registry No. S-144726, Supreme Court of British Columbia, November 24, 2014, 17, resistescobal.com/wp-content/uploads/2021/01/affadavit-donald-paul-gray-24nov14.pdf.

17. Gray, *Affidavit*, 16.

18. Gray, *Affidavit*, 17.

19. Tahoe Resources, "Tahoe Resources Human Rights Policy," 2015, previously posted at tahoeresources.com; Gray, *Affidavit*, 14.

20. Office of the High Commissioner for Human Rights (OHCHR), "Panel on Private Military and Security Companies: Regulations and National Experience. Working Group on the Use of Mercenaries as a Means of Violating Human Rights and Impeding the Exercise of the Rights of Peoples to Self-Determination," *Concept Note*, 2015, ohchr.org/Documents/Issues/Mercenaries/WG/Event2015/ConceptNote.pdf.

21. Otto Argueta, "Private Security in Guatemala: The Pathway to Its Proliferation," GIGA Working Papers no. 144, September 2010, GIGA German Institute of Global and Area Studies / Leibniz-Institut für Globale und Regionale Studien, giga-hamburg.de/en/publications/11576073-private-security-guatemala-pathway-proliferation.

22. Luís Solano, *Under Siege: Peaceful Resistance to Tahoe Resources and Militarization in Guatemala*, International Platform against Impunity in Central America and MiningWatch Canada, November 10, 2015, miningwatch.ca/sites/default/files/solano-underseigereport2015-11-10.pdf, 21.

23. Comisión Internacional Contra la Impunidad en Guatemala (CICIG), "Caso Patrullas: Capturan a 17 Sindicados de Sustraer Fondos de la PNC," *CICIG*, 2017, cicig.org/cicig.org/casos/caso-patrullas; Oscar García, "Exministro Mauricio López Bonilla es

condenado a 13 años de prisión," *Prensa Libre*, May 17, 2019, prensalibre.com/guatemala/justicia/exministro-mauricio-lopez-bonilla-es-condenado-a-13-anos-de-prision/.

24. Global Affairs Canada, Access to Information A-2017-00649, 2017, "Recommended One-on-One Meetings," September 10–November 30, 2014, 5.

25. MiningWatch Canada, "Backgrounder: A Dozen Examples of Canadian Mining Diplomacy," October 8, 2013, miningwatch.ca/blog/2013/10/8/backgrounder-dozen-examples-canadian-mining-diplomacy.

26. Network in Solidarity with the People of Guatemala (NISGUA), "In Wake of Guatemala Corruption Scandals, Tahoe Resources' Escobal License Faces Legal Challenge," July 13, 2015, nisgua.blogspot.ca/2015/07/in-wake-of-guatemala-corruption.html.

27. Sofia Menchu, "Guatemala Court Confirms Suspension of Tahoe Mining Licenses," *Reuters*, July 3, 2017, ca.reuters.com/article/topNews/idCAKBN19R3AF-OCATP.

28. Jennifer Schirmer, *The Guatemalan Military Project: A Violence Called Democracy* (Philadelphia, PA: University of Pennsylvania Press, 1998).

29. República, "¿Terrorismo, y terroristas en Guatemala?" March 30, 2017, republica.gt/2017/03/30/terrorismo-y-terroristas-en-guatemala/; Amnesty International, *We Are Defending the Land with Our Blood: Defenders of the Land, Territory, and Environment in Honduras and Guatemala*, AMR 01/4562/2016, September 1, 2016, amnesty.org/download/Documents/AMR0145622016ENGLISH.PDF.

30. Unidad de Protección a Defensoras y Defensores de Derechos Humanos de Guatemala (hereafter referred to as UDEFEGUA), "Informe 2013: El silencio es historia," 2014; UDEFEGUA, "Informe 2014: Soy defensora, soy defensor, promuevo derechos humanos: Informe sobre situación de defensoras y defensores de derechos humanos, enero a diciembre de 2014," 2015, udefegua.org/informes/informe-sobre-situaci%c3%b3n-de-defensoras-y-defensores-de-derechos-humanos-enero-diciembre-de-0; UDEFEGUA, "Informe 2015: Mi esencia es la resistencia pacífica," 2016, udefegua.org/informes/informe-sobre-situaci%C3%B3n-de-defensoras-y-defensores-de-derechos-humanos-enero-diciembre-de; UDEFEGUA, "Informe 2016: Exprésate con otro rollo sin odio," 2017, udefegua.org/multimedia/expr%C3%A9sate-con-otro-rollo-sin-odio; Network in Solidarity with the People of Guatemala (NISGUA), "Six Police Officers on Duty."

31. United States Government, Bureau of Political-Military Affairs, *US Government Counterinsurgency Guide*, 2009, publicintelligence.net/u-s-government-counterinsurgency-guide, 18; Markus Hochmüller and Markus-Michael Müller, "Locating Guatemala in Global Counterinsurgency," *Globalizations* 13, no. 1 (2016): 94–109.

32. Solano, *Under Siege*.

33. Tahoe Resources, "Annual Information Form for the Year Ended December 31, 2013," March 12, 2014, 14, sec.gov/Archives/edgar/data/1510400/000106299314001363/exhibit99-1.htm; Ministerio de Minas y Energía (MEM), untitled meeting minutes, January 24, 2014.

34. Consejo Nacional de Seguridad, "Oficina Interinstitucional para el Desarrollo Integral San Rafael Las Flores," 2017.

35. Oficina Interinstitucional para el Desarrollo Integral, "Informe de reunión," December 13, 2013.

36. Ministerio de Minas y Energía (MEM), "Minuta de reunión," *Oficina Interinstitucional para el Desarrollo Integral*, San Rafael las Flores, Santa Rosa, March 28, 2014.

37. Oficina Interinstitucional para el Desarrollo Integral, untitled meeting minutes, January 24, 2014.

38. Kirsten Weld, *Paper Cadavers: The Archives of Dictatorship in Guatemala* (Durham, NC: Duke University Press, 2014).

39. Aguilar-Støen, "Staying the Same," 140.

40. Guatemala Human Rights Commission (GHRC), "'La Puya' Environmental Movement," 2016, para. 12, ghrc-usa.org/our-work/current-cases/lapuya/.

41. Alexandra Pedersen, "¡Somos La Puya! (We Are La Puya!): Community Resistance to Canadian Mining Company Operations in Guatemala" (PhD diss., Queen's University, 2018), qspace.library.queensu.ca/handle/1974/24499; Alexandra Pedersen, "Landscapes of Resistance: Community Opposition to Canadian Mining Operations in Guatemala," *Journal of Latin American Geography* 13, no. 1 (2014): 187–214.

42. Anthony Bebbington, "Crossing Boundaries," *Americas Quarterly* 7, no. 1 (2013): 112–18; Todd Gordon and Jeffery R. Webber, *Blood of Extraction: Canadian Imperialism in Latin America* (Winnipeg: Fernwood Publishing, 2016).

43. Arturo Escobar, *Encountering Development: The Making and Unmaking of the Third World* (Princeton, NJ: Princeton University Press, 2012).

44. Radius Gold, "News Release: Radius Gold Sells Interest in Guatemala Gold Property," August 31, 2012, para. 4, goldcorpoutnews.wordpress.com/2012/08/31/radius-gold-sells-interest-in-guatemala-gold-property; Radius Gold, "Radius Gold Comments on Media Reports of Temporary Suspension of Mining Operations at KCA's Tambor Mine in Guatemala," May 11, 2016, radiusgold.com/news/radius-gold-comments-on-media-reports-of-temporary-suspension-of-mining-operations-at-kcas-tambor-mine-in-guatemala.

45. Guatemala Human Rights Commission (GHRC), "'La Puya' Environmental Movement."

46. UDEFEGUA, "Informe 2016: Exprésate."

47. Unidad de Protección a Defensoras y Defensores de Derechos Humanos de Guatemala (UDEFEGUA), "Guatemala: UDEFEGUA Annual Report 2018 Documents 392 Attacks On HRDs Including 26 Killings," *HRD Memorial*, June 25, 2019, hrdmemorial.org/guatemalaudefegua-annual-report-2018-documents-392-attacks-on-hrds-including-26-killings/.

48. UDEFEGUA, "Informe 2014: Soy defensora," 10.

49. Unidad de Protección a Defensoras y Defensores de Derechos Humanos de Guatemala (UDEFEGUA), "Criminalización en Contra de Defensores y Defensoras de Derechos Humanos: Reflexión Sobre Mecanismos de Protección," Protection

International, December 2009, protectioninternational.org/wp-content/uploads/2012/04/criminalizacion_en_contra_de_dddhh.pdf.

50. Amnesty International, *Guatemala: Mining in Guatemala: Rights at Risk*, AMR 34/002/2014, September 2014, 18, amnesty.ca/sites/amnesty/files/mining-in-guatemala-rights-at-risk-eng.pdf; Madre Selva, *Dar la Vida por Nuestra Madre Tierra: Experiencias, memorias y reflexiones de mujeres en la defensa del territorio de La Puya y San Rafael las Flores en los departamentos de Guatemala y Santa Rosa* (Ciudad de Guatemala: Colectivo Madre Selva, November 2014); Simona Violetta Yagenova, *La Mina El Tambor Progreso VII Derivada y la Resistencia de La Puya: Un Análisis de los Antecedentes, Implicaciones e Impactos de este Proyecto Minero* (Guatemala: Madre Selva Colectivo Ecologista, 2014).

51. Rafael Maldonado, "Empresas y violación de derechos humanos en Guatemala," *Por la Paz: Empresas y Derechos Humanos* 30 (2017): 23–26, para. 1.

52. Observatory for the Protection of Human Rights Defenders (OBS), *"We Are Not Afraid": Land Rights Defenders: Attacked for Confronting Unbridled Development*, International Federation for Human Rights Annual Report, December 2, 2014, fidh.org/en/issues/human-rights-defenders/archives-human-rights-defenders/annual-reports/16546-we-are-not-afraid.

53. Guatemala Human Rights Commission (GHRC), "GHRC Condemns Expulsion of Two Human Rights Volunteers from Guatemala," July 7, 2014, ghrcusa.wordpress.com/2014/07/07/ghrc-condemns-expulsion-of-two-human-rights-volunteers-from-guatemala/; Peace Brigades International (PBI), "Decision to Cancel Temporary Residence Permits of Two Volunteers of PBI Guatemala Reversed," July 2, 2014, peacebrigades.org.uk/content/decision-cancel-temporary-residence-permits-two-volunteers-pbi-guatemala-reversed; UDEFEGUA, "Informe 2014: Soy defensora."

54. Yagenova, *La Mina El Tambor*.

55. Amnesty International, *Guatemala: Mining in Guatemala*.

56. Amnesty International, *Guatemala: Mining in Guatemala*; UDEFEGUA, "Informe 2014: Soy defensora."

57. Yagenova, *La Mina El Tambor*.

58. Madre Selva, *Dar la Vida*; Guatemala Human Rights Commission (GHRC), "'La Puya' Environmental Movement."

59. Inter-American Commission on Human Rights (IACHR), "Inter-American Commission on Human Rights: Strategic Plan 2011–2015," *Organization of American States*, 2016, oas.org/en/iachr/docs/pdf/iachrstrategicplan20112015.pdf; UDEFEGUA, "Informe 2015: Mi esencia."

60. IM-Defensoras, *Violence against Women Human Rights Defenders in Mesoamerica 2012–2014 Report*, Mesoamerican Initiative of Women Human Rights Defenders, 2014, 30, im-defensoras.org/wp-content/uploads/2016/04/286224690-Violence-Against-WHRDs-in-Mesoamerica-2012-2014-Report.pdf.

61. IM-Defensoras, *Violence against Women*, 38.

62. Natural Resources Canada (NRCan), "Canadian Mining Assets," January 2021, nrcan.gc.ca/maps-tools-and-publications/publications/minerals-mining-publications/canadian-mining-assets/19323.

63. Canadian Centre for the Study of Resource Conflict (CCSRC), *Corporate Social Responsibility: Movements and Footprints of Canadian Mining Exploration Firms in the Developing World*, CCSRC, October 2009, 7, miningwatch.ca/sites/default/files/CSR_Movements_and_Footprints.pdf.

64. Catherine Nolin and Jacqui Stephens, "'We Have To Protect the Investors': 'Development' and Canadian Mining Companies in Guatemala," *Journal of Rural and Community Development* 5, no. 3 (2010): 37-70.

65. Money Thread, "Call to Divest from the Canadian Companies Goldcorp Inc. and Tahoe Resources Inc.," Blue Planet Project, 2014, para. 1, blueplanetproject.net/lefildelargent/index.php/campagne/appel-au-desinvestissement.

66. Martin Mowforth, *The Violence of Development: Resource Depletion, Environmental Crises, and Human Rights Abuses in Central America* (London: Pluto Press, 2014).

67. Raquel Aldana and Randall S. Abate, "Banning Metal Mining in Guatemala," *Vermont Law Review* 40, no. 3 (2016): 597-671.

68. Silvel Elías and Geisselle Sánchez, "Case Study: Guatemala," *Americas Quarterly* 8, no. 2 (2014): 70-75.

69. Amnesty International, *Guatemala*; Madre Selva, *Dar la Vida*; Yagenova, *La Mina El Tambor*.

70. J. P. Laplante and Catherine Nolin, "Consultas and Socially Responsible Investing in Guatemala: A Case Study Examining Maya Perspectives on the Indigenous Right to Free, Prior and Informed Consent," *Society & Natural Resources: An International Journal* 27, no. 3 (2014): 231-48; United Nations (UN), *Report of the Special Rapporteur on the Rights of Indigenous Peoples, James Anaya*, A/HRC/24/41/Add.4, September 2, 2013, ohchr.org/EN/HRBodies/HRC/RegularSessions/Session24/Documents/A_HRC_24_41_Add.4_ENG.doc.

71. Yagenova, *La Mina El Tambor*.

72. Rights Action, "Amalia Sandoval Palencia: Resistance against El Tambor Mine—San José del Golfo, Guatemala" (video file. YouTube, May 17, 2016), youtube.com/watch?v=o4gvXk2Po9A.

73. Ellen Moore, "International Organizations Speak Out on Multimillion-Dollar Claim against Guatemala over Failed Mine at La Puya," *Earthworks*, January 31, 2019, earthworks.org/blog/international-organizations-speak-out-on-multimillion-dollar-claim-against-guatemala-over-failed-mine-at-la-puya/.

Chapter 6. Using Law and Democracy to Resist Predatory Mining

1. Arturo Escobar, *Encountering Development: The Making and Unmaking of the Third World* (Princeton, NJ: Princeton University Press, 1995); Eduardo Galeano, *Open Veins of Latin America: Five Centuries of the Pillage of a Continent*, 25th Anniversary Edition (New York, NY: Monthly Review Press, 1997 [1973]); Susanne Jonas, *The Battle for Guatemala:*

Rebels, Death Squads, and U.S. Power (Boulder, CO: Westview Press, 1991); W. George Lovell, "Surviving Conquest: The Maya of Guatemala in Historical Perspective," *Latin American Research Review* 23, no. 2 (1988): 25–57; Neil Smith, *Uneven Development: Nature, Capital and the Production of Space*, 3rd ed. (Athens, GA: University of Georgia Press, 2008).

2. Comisión Internacional contra la Impunidad en Guatemala (CICIG), *Noveno Informe de Labores de la Comisión Internacional Contra la Impunidad en Guatemala (CICIG)*, 2017, cicig.org/uploads/img/2016/others/COM_087_20161124_INFORME_ANUAL_2016.pdf; Greg Grandin, *The Blood of Guatemala: A History of Race and Nation* (Durham, NC: Duke University Press, 2000); International Crisis Group (ICG), *Guatemala: Squeezed between Crime and Impunity*, Latin America Report 33, 2010, d2071andvipowj. cloudfront.net/33-guatemala-squeezed-between-crime-and-impunity.pdf; Rachel Sieder, "The Judiciary and Indigenous Rights in Guatemala," *International Journal of Constitutional Law* 5, no. 2 (2007): 211–41; United States Department of State, *Guatemala 2017 Human Rights Report*, 2018, gt.usembassy.gov/wp-content/uploads/sites/253/Human-Rights-2017.pdf.

3. Shin Imai, Ladan Mehranvar, and Jennifer Sander, "Breaching Indigenous Law: Canadian Mining in Guatemala," *Indigenous Law Journal* 6, no. 1 (2007): 101–39; Per Ernesto Øveraas, "The Community Consultation as a Strategy against Mining: A Study of Repertoire Change in Anti-mining Resistance in Guatemala" (unpublished thesis, University of Oslo, 2013); Joris J. van de Sandt, *Mining Conflicts and Indigenous Peoples in Guatemala*, The Hague: Amsterdam University Law Faculty and Cordaid, 2009, cordaid.org/en/wp-content/uploads/sites/3/2013/01/Mining_Conflicts_and_Indigenous_Peoples_in_Guatemala_1.pdf.

4. Compliance Advisor Ombudsman (CAO), *Assessment of a Complaint Submitted to CAO in Relation to the Marlin Mining Project in Guatemala*, September 7, 2005, 32, cao-ombudsman.org/cases/document-links/documents/CAO-Marlin-assessment-English-7Sep05.pdf; On Common Ground, *Human Rights Assessment of Goldcorp's Marlin Mine*, 2010, 54, s24.q4cdn.com/382246808/files/doc_downloads/2020/09/OCG_HRA_Marlin_Mine_June_7.pdf; Procurador de los Derechos Humanos (PDH), *La Minería y los Derechos Humanos en Guatemala*, Guatemala City: PDH, 2005, 23, corteidh.or.cr/tablas/23700.pdf.

5. Amnesty International, "Urgent Action: One Mining Activist Shot, Another Threatened," July 21, 2010, amnesty.org/download/Documents/36000/amr340082010en.pdf; Amnesty International, "Urgent Action: Mine Activists Beaten and Threatened," March 3, 2011, amnesty.org/download/Documents/28000/amr340022011en.pdf; Frente de Defensa San Miguelense (FREDEMI), *Specific Instance Complaint Submitted to the Canadian National Contact Point pursuant to the OECD Guidelines for Multinational Enterprises, Concerning: The Operations of Goldcorp Inc. at the Marlin Mine in the Indigenous Community of San Miguel Ixtahuacán, Guatemala*, December 9, 2009, 12, ciel.org/Publications/FREDEMI_SpecificInstanceComplaint_December%202009.pdf; Imai, Mehranvar, and Sander, "Breaching Indigenous Law," 112; On Common Ground, *Human Rights Assessment*, 173–74; van de Sandt, *Mining Conflicts*.

6. On Common Ground, *Human Rights Assessment*, 133; Sandra Váldez, "Pobladores interponen querella contra Álvarez," *Prensa Libre*, July 29, 2010, prensalibre.com/guatemala/pobladores-interponen-querella-alvarez_0_307169304-html/; van de Sandt, *Mining Conflicts*.

7. Comisión Pastoral Paz y Ecología (COPAE) and Unitarian Universalist Service Committee (UUSC), *Preliminary Investigation and Analysis of Building Damage in the Villages of Agel, El Salitre, San José Ixcaniche, and San José Nueva Esperanza*. San Marcos, Guatemala: COPAE and UUSC, 2009, 9, 48, giscorps.org/wp-content/uploads/2017/01/ Report_and_Figures.pdf; Frente de Defensa San Miguelense (FREDEMI), *Specific Instance*.

8. Niladri Basu, Marce Abare, Susan Buchanan, Diana Cryderman, Dong Ha Nam, Susannah Sirkin, Stefan Schmitt, and Howard Hu, "A Combined Ecological and Epidemiologic Investigation of Metal Exposures amongst Indigenous Peoples near the Marlin Mine in Western Guatemala," *Science of the Total Environment* 409, no. 1 (2010): 70; Flaviano Bianchini, *Estudio Técnico: Calidad de Agua del Río Tzalá (Municipio de Sipakapa; Departamento de San Marcos) [Technical Study: Water Quality of the Tzalá River (Municipality of Sipakapa; Department of San Marcos)]*, 2006, 4, blog.reportero.org/wp-content/estudio_ de_agua_del_rio_tzal.pdf; E-TECH International, *Evaluation of Predicted and Actual Water Quality Conditions at the Marlin Mine, Guatemala*, August 2010, 68, https://bit.ly/3g0cLJ5; Frente de Defensa San Miguelense (FREDEMI), *Specific Instance*, 10.

9. Basu et al., "A Combined Ecological," 70; Nathan Einbinder, "Guatemala: The Hope for an Endless Mine," *Upside Down World*, August 12, 2008, upsidedownworld.org/ archives/guatemala/guatemala-the-hope-for-an-endless-mine.

10. On Common Ground, *Human Rights Assessment*.

11. BSR, *Marlin Mine at Closure: A Review of Goldcorp Commitments to the 2010 Human Rights Assessment*, 2017, 17, ilas.sas.ac.uk/research-projects/ legal-cultures-subsoil/subsoil-reports/2017-marlin-mine-closure-review-goldcorp; Goldcorp, *Goldcorp 2017 Sustainability Report*, 2017, newmont.com/sustainability/ goldcorps-archive-sustainability-reports.

12. Rosa María Bolaños, "Hay vacío en la legislación por el cierre o abandono de minas," *Prensa Libre*, February 22, 2017, prensalibre.com/economia/economia/ hay-vacio-en-la-legislacion; BSR, *Marlin Mine*.

13. Acompañamiento Internacional en Guatemala (ACOGUATE), *Territorios Indígenas y Democracia Guatemalteca bajo Presiones / Guatemalan Indigenous Territories and Democracy under Pressure*, 2009, albedrio.org/htm/documentos/ InformeSanMiguel.pdf; Confederación Sindical de Trabajadores/as de las Américas, Consejo del Pueblos de Occidente, Movimiento Sindical, Indígena y Campesino Guatemalteco / International Trade Union Confederation (CSA-TUCA), *El Derecho de Consulta de los Pueblos Indígenas en Guatemala: La Ruptura entre el Discurso y la Práctica, 1996–Marzo 2010*, 2010, ituc-csi.org/IMG/pdf/Informe_PCGIG.pdf; J. P. Laplante and Catherine Nolin, "Consultas and Socially Responsible Investing in Guatemala: A Case Study Examining Maya Perspectives on the Indigenous Right to Free, Prior, and Informed Consent," *Society and Natural Resources: An International Journal* 27, no. 3 (2014): 1-18; "Listado de Consultas realizadas: (2005—2010)," in Savia, *Realidad Ecológica de Guatemala*, 2nd ed., 2011, 34, landmatrix.org/media/uploads/ guatemalaatnavegation_linksarchivo1-201120savia20la20realidad20ecologica202011pdf. pdf; Ellen Moore, Guatemala Programs Coordinator, NISGUA, email correspondence with author, June 13, 2014.

14. Patrick Ball, Paul Kobrak, and Herbert F. Spirer, *State Violence in Guatemala, 1960-1996: A Quantitative Reflection* (Washington, DC: American Association for the

Advancement of Science, Science [AAAS] and the International Centre for Human Rights Investigations [CIIDH], 1999), aaas.org/programs/scientific-responsibility-human-rights-law/publications; Comisión para el Esclarecimiento Histórico (CEH), *Guatemala: Memoria del silencio—Informe de la Comisión para el Esclarecimiento Histórico*, vol. 6 of 12, *Casos Ilustrativos, Anexo I* (Guatemala: Comisión para el Esclarecimiento Histórico, 1999), ProQuest. Publicly accessible excerpts from the report in English and Spanish can be found in links in Doc M. Billingsley's blog post "Informe de la comisión de esclarecimiento histórico: Memoria del silencio (full document)," March 11, 2014, blog.anthropo.org/category/guatemala; North American Congress on Latin America (NACLA), *Special Issue: Guatemala*, ed. S. Jonas and D. Tobis, 1974; Procurador de los Derechos Humanos (PDH), *La Minería*; Luís Solano, *Guatemala: petróleo y minería en las entrañas del poder* (Guatemala City: Inforpress Centroamérica, 2005).

15. Catherine Nolin and Jacqui Stephens, "'We Have to Protect the Investors': 'Development' and Canadian Mining Companies in Guatemala," *Journal of Rural and Community Development* 5, no. 3 (2010): 37–70.

16. J. P. Laplante, "'La Voz del Pueblo': Maya Consultas and the Challenge of Self-Determination for Socially Responsible Investment in the Mining Sector" (master's thesis, University of Northern British Columbia, 2014), 70, arcabc.ca/islandora/object/unbc%3A16965/datastream/PDF/view.

17. United Nations (UN), *Agreement on the Identity and Rights of Indigenous Peoples*, UN reference no. A/49/882-S/1995/256, 1995, peacemaker.un.org/sites/peacemaker.un.org/files/GT_950331_AgreementIdentityAndRightsOfIndigenousPeoples.pdf.

18. Michael L. Dougherty, "The Global Gold Mining Industry, Junior Firms, and Civil Society Resistance in Guatemala," *Bulletin of Latin American Research* 30, no. 4 (2011): 403–18; Laplante, "'La Voz del Pueblo'"; Procurador de los Derechos Humanos (PDH), *La Minería*; Solano, *Guatemala: petróleo y minería*.

19. United Nations (UN), *United Nations Declaration on the Rights of Indigenous Peoples*, UN reference no. A/RES/61/295, 2007, un.org/esa/socdev/unpfii/documents/DRIPS_en.pdf.

20. Laplante, "'La Voz del Pueblo,'" 90.

21. International Labour Organization (ILO), *Convention 169 Concerning Indigenous and Tribal Peoples*, 1989, ilo.org/dyn/normlex/en/f?p=NORMLEXPUB:12100:0::NO:12100:P12100_ILO_CODE:C169.

22. United Nations (UN), *United Nations Declaration*.

23. International Crisis Group (ICG), *Guatemala: Squeezed*; Comisión Internacional contra la Impunidad en Guatemala (CICIG), *Noveno Informe*; United States Department of State, *Guatemala 2016*.

24. Marco Chown Oved, "Canadian Company Tried to Stop Referendum on Mine in Guatemala," *Toronto Star*, August 11, 2016, thestar.com/news/world/2016/08/11/canadian-company-tried-to-stop-referendum-on-mine-in-guatemala.html; Imai et al., "Breaching Indigenous Law."

25. Goldcorp, "News Release: New Voluntary Royalty Agreement to Benefit Stakeholders of Goldcorp's Marlin Mine," January 27, 2012, newswire.

ca/news-releases/new-voluntary-royalty-agreement-to-benefit-stakeholders-of-g
oldcorps-marlin-mine-509501381.html.

26. Nathan Einbinder and Catherine Nolin, "Voices from the Edge: A Mayan
Community Shares Stories of its Struggle to Avoid Forced Eviction by a Nickel Mine,"
Cultural Survival Quarterly 34, no. 3 (2010): 28–33; Jeff Gray, "Not Responsible for
Killing at Guatemalan Mine, Hudbay Says," *Globe and Mail*, March 5, 2013, updated
May 11, 2018, theglobeandmail.com/globe-investor/not-responsible-for-killing-
at-guatemalan-mine-hudbay-says/article9318696; Marina Jimenez, "Mayan Families'
Quest for Justice against Canadian Mining Company Hudbay, Part 1 of 2," *Toronto
Star*, June 20, 2016, thestar.com/news/world/2016/06/20/the-mayans-vs-the-mine.html;
Klippensteins Barristers & Solicitors, "Our Cases—Lawsuit against Canadian Mining
Corporation over Brutal Shootings and Rapes in Guatemala," 2014, klippensteins.ca/
our-cases; Nina Lakhani, "The Canadian Company Mining Hills of Silver—and the People
Dying to Stop It," *The Guardian*, July 13, 2017, theguardian.com/environment/2017/jul/13/
the-canadian-company-mining-hills-of-silver-and-the-people-dying-to-stop-it.

27. Henry Lazenby, "Guatemala Court Clarifies Consultation Area, Denies Action
on Export Permit," *Mining Weekly*, September 27, 2017, miningweekly.com/print-version/
guatemala-court-clarifies-consultation-area-denies-action-on-export-permit-2017-09-27;
Redacción, "CSJ ordena consulta a pueblo Xinca y permite operar a Minera San Rafael,"
Prensa Libre, September 8, 2017, prensalibre.com/guatemala/justicia/csj-ordena-consulta-
a-pueblo-xinca-y-permite-operar-a-mina-san-rafael.

28. J. P. Laplante and Catherine Nolin, "Snake Oil and the Myth of Corporate Social
Responsibility," in "Bad Neighbours: A Focus on Canadian Mining Abroad," special
issue, *Canadian Dimension* 45, no. 1 (January 2011): 24–27, canadiandimension.com/
articles/3613/.

29. Laplante, "'La Voz del Pueblo,'" 116.

30. Francisco Osmundo Oxlaj Ordoñez, speaker at Fourth Assembly of the Consejo de
los Pueblos del Quiché / Council of the Peoples of the Quiché gathered on August 28, 2010,
CN fieldnotes.

31. Natural Resources Canada (NRCan), "Canadian Mining Assets."

32. Natural Resources Canada (NRCan), "Canadian Mining Assets," paras. 1–2.

33. Mining Association of Canada, *Facts and Figures*, 2017, 6, mining.ca/documents/
facts-and-figures-2017.

34. Shin Imai, Leah Gardner, and Sarah Weinberger, "The 'Canada Brand': Violence
and Canadian Mining Companies in Latin America," Osgoode Legal Studies Research
Paper 17/2017, December 1, 2017, ssrn.com/abstract=2886584.

35. John Ruggie, *Protect, Respect and Remedy: A Framework for Business and Human
Rights*, Report of the Special Representative of the Secretary-General on the Issue of
Human Rights and Transnational Corporations and other Business Enterprises, UNHRC,
8th Sess., UN Doc A/HRC/8/5.7 (Geneva, Switzerland: Human Rights Council, 2008),
para. 3.

36. Hudbay Minerals Inc., *Realizing Potential, Corporate Social Responsibility*

NOTES / CHAPTER 6

Report 08, 2008, 1 & 9, s23.q4cdn.com/405985100/files/doc_financials/annual_reports/csr/HudBay_SustainReport_2008.pdf.

37. Hudbay, *Realizing*.

38. See, for example, Cameroon FIPA, *Agreement between Canada and the Republic of Cameroon for the Promotion and Protection of Investments (FIPA)*, December 16, 2016, international.gc.ca/trade-commerce/trade-agreements-accords-commerciaux/agr-acc/cameroon-cameroun/fipa-apie/index.aspx.

39. Cameroon FIPA, *Agreement* art. 15.2.

40. Government of Canada, "News Release: The Government of Canada Brings Leadership to Responsible Business Conduct Abroad," January 17, 2018, canada.ca/en/global-affairs/news/2018/01/the_government_ofcanadabringsleadershiptoresponsiblebusinesscond.html.

41. Canadian Network on Corporate Accountability (CNCA), "News Release: Government of Canada Turns Back on Communities Harmed by Canadian Mining Overseas, Loses Trust of Canadian Civil Society," July 11, 2019, cnca-rcrce.ca/recent-works/news-release-government-of-canada-turns-back-on-communities-harmed-by-canadian-mining-overseas-loses-trust-of-canadian-civil-society/.

42. *Choc v. HudBay Minerals Inc.*, ONSC 1414 (CanLII), 2013, canlii.ca/t/glron; Suzanne Daley, "Guatemalan Women's Claims Put Focus on Canadian Firms' Conduct Abroad," *New York Times*, April 2, 2016, nytimes.com/2016/04/03/world/americas/guatemalan-womens-claims-put-focus-on-canadian-firms-conduct-abroad.html; Klippensteins Barristers & Solicitors, *Case Website: Choc v. HudBay Minerals Inc.*, 2019, chocversushudbay.com.

43. *Araya v. Nevsun Resources Ltd.*, BCCA 402 (CanLII), 2017, canlii.ca/t/hnspr; Business & Human Rights Resource Centre, *Nevsun Lawsuit* (re: Bisha mine, Eritrea), 2019, business-humanrights.org/en/nevsun-lawsuit-re-bisha-mine-eritrea; Ashifa Kassam, "Canadian Firm to Face Historic Legal Case over Alleged Labour Abuses in Eritrea," *The Guardian*, November 23, 2017, theguardian.com/global-development/2017/nov/23/canadian-mining-firm-historic-legal-case-alleged-labour-abuses-eritrea-nevsun-resources.

44. *García v. Tahoe Resources Inc.*, BCCA 39 (CanLII) 2017, canlii.ca/t/gx49k; Business & Human Rights Resource Centre, *Tahoe Resources Lawsuit* (re: Guatemala), 2019, business-humanrights.org/en/tahoe-resources-lawsuit-re-guatemala.

45. Pan American Silver Corp., "Press Release: Pan American Silver Announces Resolution of *Garcia v. Tahoe* Case," July 30, 2019, prnewswire.com/news-releases/pan-american-silver-announces-resolution-of-garcia-v-tahoe-case-300893365.html.

46. Barrick Gold, Barrick Gold Corporation, *Annual Report 2017*, 2017, para. 22, barrick.com/English/investors/annual-report/default.aspx.

47. Barrick Gold, Barrick Gold Corporation, *Annual Information Form 2017*, March 23, 2018, barrick.com/English/sustainability/reports-and-policies/default.aspx.

Conclusion: Visions of a Way Foreward

1. José Luis Granados Ceja and Urooba Jamal, "Canada's Broken Pledge to Human Rights Defenders," *NACLA Report on the Americas* (July 30, 2019), nacla.org/news/2019/08/01/canada%E2%80%99s-broken-pledge-human-rights-defenders.

2. Granados Ceja and Jamal, "Canada's Broken Pledge," para. 3.

3. Charlotte Connolly, *Exporting Canada's Extractives Approach to Development: The Nexus of Law, Violence and Development in the Case of Tahoe Resources Inc. in Guatemala* (master's thesis, University of Northern British Columbia, 2019), 56, 89, 98.

4. Connolly, *Exporting*, 99; Jared Ferrie, "Mining Gold, and Outrage, in Guatemala," *The Tyee*, December 21, 2005, para. 40, thetyee.ca/News/2005/12/21/GuatamalaOutrage/.

5. James Lambert, "Minería en Canadá: Como Guatemala, Canadá es reconocido en el mundo entero por la riqueza de sus recursos naturales / Mining in Canada: Like Guatemala, Canada Is Recognized Worldwide for Its Wealth of Natural Resources," *Prensa Libre*, November 4, 2004; Catherine Nolin and Jacqui Stephens, "'We Have to Protect the Investors': 'Development' and Canadian Mining Companies in Guatemala," *Journal of Rural and Community Development* 5, no. 3 (2010): 49.

6. Grahame Russell, "More Tahoe Resources Repression in Guatemala: Canadian and U.S. Governments Continue Covering-up Mining Violence and Harms," *Rights Action*, July 21, 2017; Grahame Russell, "Canadian Companies Mining with the Genocidal Generals in Guatemala," *Rights Action*, 2020, rightsaction.org/articles/canadian-companies-mining-with-the-genocidal-generals-in-guatemala.

7. Jen Moore and Manuel Perez Rocha, *Extraction Casino: Mining Companies Gambling with Latin American Lives and Sovereignty through Supranational Arbitration*, MiningWatch Canada Report (Ottawa, ON: MiningWatch Canada, 2019), miningwatch.ca/publications/2019/5/2/extraction-casino-mining-companies-gambling-latin-american-lives-and.

8. Moore and Perez Rocha, *Extraction Casino*.

9. Charlotte Connolly, *Lobbying by Mining Industry on the Proposed Canadian Ombudsperson for Responsible Enterprise (CORE)*, Justice and Corporate Accountability Project (JCAP) Report (July 24, 2019), t.co/Xb9tHaepU3.

10. Justin Ling, "The Sovereignty of States and Multinational Corporate Accountability," *CBA National Magazine*, January 11, 2019, nationalmagazine.ca/en-ca/articles/law/hot-topics-in-law/2019/the-sovereignty-of-states-and-multinational-corpor; Grahame Russell, "Is Justice Possible in Canada or Guatemala for HudBay Minerals Mining Repression in Guatemala?" *Rights Action*, October 29, 2018, mailchi.mp/rightsaction/is-justice-possible-in-canada-or-guatemala-for-hudbay-minerals-mining-repression-in-guatemala.

11. Kalowatie Deonandan and Michael Dougherty, *Mining in Latin America: Critical Approaches to the New Extraction* (Oxon: Routledge, 2016), 250.

12. *Chevron Corp. v. Yaiguaje*, Supreme Court of Canada, *Factum of the Joint Intervener*, 2014, 7, ihrp.law.utoronto.ca/utfl_file/count/PUBLICATIONS/KLIPPENSTEINSChevronFactum%2O-OTT_LAW-4722211-v1.pdf.

13. World Bank, *Understanding Poverty: Extractive Industries* (New York: World Bank, 2019), worldbank.org/en/topic/extractiveindustries; World Bank, *Extractives Global Programmatic Support (EGPS) Multi-Donor Trust Fund* (New York: World Bank, 2019), worldbank.org/en/programs/egps.

14. "Ottawa Should Make Mining Companies More Accountable," editorial, *Toronto Star*, August 21, 2016, thestar.com/opinion/editorials/2016/08/21/ottawa-should-make-mining-companies-more-accountable-editorial.html.

15. J. P. Laplante and Catherine Nolin, "Snake Oil and the Myth of Corporate Social Responsibility," in "Bad Neighbours: A Focus on Canadian Mining Abroad," special issue, *Canadian Dimension* 45, no. 1 (January 2011): 24–27, canadiandimension.com/articles/3613/.

16. Irma Alicia Velásquez Nimatuj, "CACIF Is Not More Important than the Communities," *El Periódico*, May 16, 2016, elperiodico.com.gt/opinion/opiniones-de-hoy/2016/05/14/el-cacif-no-esta-por-sobre-las-comunidades.

17. Velásquez Nimatuj, "CACIF."

18. Howard Zinn, *You Can't Be Neutral on a Moving Train* (Boston, MA: Beacon Press, 2002 [updated in 2018]).

Contributors

Jeff Abbott is an independent journalist based in Guatemala, where he has lived for the past five years. He reports on human rights, immigration and forced migration, politics, community defence struggles, and environmental issues. Twitter: @palabrasdeabajo

Miguel Ángel Bámaca is a Maya Mam farmer and member of FREDEMI (San Miguel Ixtahuacán Defense Front), resisting and denouncing harms and violations caused by Goldcorp Inc.'s Marlin mine. He has suffered attacks, criminalizations, and threats for his community defence work.

Angélica Choc is a Maya Q'eqchi' community / human rights / territorial defender and widow of Adolfo Ich, killed September 27, 2009, by security guards working in Guatemala for the Canadian mining company Hudbay Minerals. Angélica is a plaintiff in the Hudbay Minerals lawsuits and co-prosecutor in a criminal trial in Guatemala against Mynor Padilla, Hudbay's former head of security.

José Choc Ich is the son of Angélica Choc and Adolfo Ich. José is a witness to the attack against his father that resulted in his death. José is a witness in the Hudbay Minerals lawsuits and Mynor Padilla criminal trial.

German Chub is a Maya Q'eqchi' farmer who was shot and left paralyzed on September 27, 2009, by security guards working in Guatemala for the Canadian mining company Hudbay Minerals. German is a plaintiff in the Hudbay Minerals lawsuits and a victim-witness in a criminal trial in Guatemala against Mynor Padilla, Hudbay's former head of security.

María Magdalena Cuc Choc is the sister of Angélica Choc, and also a courageous Maya Q'eqchi' woman who, in early 2018, was criminalized and jailed on trumped up charges for her community, human rights, and territorial defence work.

Sandra Cuffe is a freelance journalist based in Central America, where she has lived for ten of the past fifteen years. She reports on human rights, social movements, politics, and environmental issues, primarily in Guatemala and Honduras. Twitter: @Sandra_Cuffe

Nathan Einbinder recently completed his doctoral studies at the *Colegio de la Frontera Sur* in Chiapas, Mexico. His present research focuses on agroecology and development in the Maya-Achí territory in Guatemala. Email: nathaneinbinder@gmail.com

Patricia Flores is a Toronto-based human rights activist, artist, and data analyst who does solidarity work in relation to Honduras and Latin America. She uses her art to support human rights work. She holds an International Comparative Studies degree from Huron University–UWO and is currently pursuing Data and Predictive Analytics at Ryerson University. Twitter: @patfloTO

Heather Gies is the Managing Editor of *NACLA Report on the Americas* and a freelance journalist who writes about politics, human rights, inequality, and resource conflicts in Central America. Her work has appeared in *Al Jazeera, The Guardian, In These Times,* and other outlets. Twitter: @HeatherGies

Simon Granovsky-Larsen is an Associate Professor of Politics and International Studies at the University of Regina. He is author of *Dealing with Peace: The Guatemalan Campesino Movement and the Post-Conflict Neoliberal State* (University of Toronto Press, 2019) and co-editor, with Dawn Paley, of *Organized Violence* (University of Regina Press, 2019). Twitter: @simon_gl

Annie Hylton is an international human rights lawyer and investigative journalist from Saskatchewan, based in New York. Twitter: @HyltonAnne

Sebastian Iboy Osorio is a Maya Achí farmer, and survivor of and eyewitness to the World Bank / Chixoy dam massacres that killed over 440 people from Río Negro, Baja Verapaz.

J. P. Laplante has worked for over a decade for Indigenous communities in Canada, focused on the protection of traditional lands and waters, environmental assessment for mining projects, and advancing the Indigenous right to free, prior, and informed consent for projects affecting Indigenous communities. In 2010, he lived in Guatemala and volunteered as a Commissioner for International Observers at the *Consulta Comunitaria de Buena Fe* held in Santa Cruz del Quiché, and was an International Observer at two other *consultas* that affirmed communities' lack of consent for mineral development. Email: jlaplante@tsilhqotin.ca

Aniseto López Díaz is a Maya Mam farmer and leader of community movements resisting and denouncing harms and violations caused by Goldcorp Inc.'s Marlin mine in western Guatemala. He has suffered attacks, criminalizations, and threats for his community defence work.

W. George Lovell is Professor Emeritus in the Department of Geography at Queen's University in Kingston, Ontario, Canada. He is the author of, among other books, *A Beauty That Hurts: Life and Death in Guatemala*.

Jackie McVicar has accompanied human rights social movements and land protectors in Central America for more than fifteen years. She has worked in communications, advocacy, and adult education with the Guatemala Human Rights Commission (GHRC), United for Mining Justice (UMJ), and the Maritimes-Guatemala Breaking the Silence Network (BTS), in addition to her work as a freelance writer for publications such as *America Magazine, NACLA Report on the Americas,* and *GHRC.* Twitter: @pajarolindo

Yuri Melini (Dr. Yuri Giovanni Melini) is a professor in the Escuela de Ciencias Políticas de la Universidad de San Carlos de Guatemala (USAC). In 2000, Yuri founded CALAS (Centro de Acción Legal, Ambiental y Social de Guatemala) and worked there until 2016. He has suffered attacks and threats, including one attack when he was struck by seven bullets, for his work with CALAS. Email: yurimelini@gmail.com; Twitter: @yuri_melini

Cyril Mychalejko is a writer who covers human rights, international trade and development, and US foreign policy. He was an editor at *UpsideDownWorld*, an online magazine covering activism and politics in Latin America, for over a decade. Twitter: @cmychalejko

Alexandra Pedersen received her PhD in Geography from Queen's University, Kingston in 2018. Her dissertation focused on geographies of violence related to Canadian mining operations in Guatemala. She co-instructs a yearly seminar course in the Queen's Faculty of Law on mining law, policies, and communities. Email: a.pedersen@queensu.ca; Twitter: @Alex_Pedersen0

Alfredo Pérez is a Maya Sipakapan farmer and leader of community movements resisting and denouncing harms and violations caused by Goldcorp Inc.'s Marlin mine in western Guatemala. He has suffered attacks, criminalizations, and threats for his community defence work.

James Rodríguez is a documentary photographer based in Guatemala since 2006. James's work focuses on social issues in Latin America, but primarily post-war Guatemala: transitional justice processes, land tenure conflicts due to extractive industries, human rights abuses, and the effects of the internal war in its daily life. James is currently represented by Panos Pictures. Internet: mimundo.org; Twitter: @mimundo_org

Alvaro Sandoval and **Ana Sandoval** are father and daughter, Guatemalan community members at the forefront of the "La Puya" community movement resisting harms and violations caused by the KCA mining company. They both have suffered attacks, criminalizations, and threats for their community defence work.

Rachel Schmidt is an award-winning Canadian documentary film producer and director. Rachel has travelled the globe to work with organizations like the Nobel Women's Initiative, African Women's Millennium Initiative, and Rights Action to document important women's rights and community defence stories. Email: rschmidtfilms@shaw.ca

Emilie Smith is an Argentine-born, Canadian Anglican priest and theologian. Since 1984 she has walked with the peoples of Guatemala. Emilie is the co-president of SICSAL (Servicio Internacional Cristiano de Solidaridad con los Pueblos de América Latina—Óscar Romero / the Oscar

Romero liberation theology network), a Christian solidarity network with the people of Latin America founded in the months after St. Romero's death. Email: emilietsmith@gmail.com

Cory Wanless and **Murray Klippenstein** are Toronto-based lawyers who represent thirteen Maya Q'eqchi' in precedent-setting lawsuits against Canadian company Hudbay Minerals (chocversushudbay.com) regarding human rights abuse in Guatemala. Emails: cory@waddellphillips.ca, murray.klippenstein@klippensteins.ca

Caren Weisbart is a PhD candidate in Environmental Studies at York University and a research associate at the Centre for Research on Latin America and the Caribbean. She has been an active member of the Maritimes–Guatemala Breaking the Silence Network (BTS) since 2001 and organizes with the Mining Injustice Solidarity Network (MISN). Twitter: @carenweisbart

Index

Catherine Nolin is a Professor of Geography and Chair of the Department of Geography, Earth and Environmental Sciences at the University of Northern British Columbia (UNBC) in Prince George, British Columbia, Canada. In 2020, Catherine was elected Chair of the Conference of Latin American Geography (CLAG) for a two-year term. CLAG is the premier geographic organization for geographers engaging in research in Latin America and the Caribbean and works to foster research, education, and service related to Latin American geographical studies. Catherine is a long-time insurgent researcher and social justice advocate who has been grappling with the afterlives of the Guatemalan genocides for more than twenty-five years. Twitter: @cnolin

Grahame Russell is a non-practising Canadian lawyer and adjunct professor in the Geography Program at UNBC and, since 1995, Director of Rights Action which works in Honduras and Guatemala in support of community / environmental / human rights / territory defenders resisting widespread harms and (often deadly) violence caused by different sectors of the global economy, including mining, hydroelectric dams, African palm, sugar cane, bananas, coffee, tourism, and the garment industry. Rights Action carries out education and activism work in the US and Canada focusing on how our governments and companies (and the US military) often contribute directly to and benefit from human rights violations (including repression), environmental harms, exploitation, corruption, and impunity in these countries. Twitter: @RightsAction